"An Asian scholar with a passionate love of Christ presents a pointed critique of pluralism and focuses on the incomparable resurrection of the Nazarene."

—CARL F.H. HENRY
Evangelical Theologian and Author

"Ajith Fernando is a distinguished scholar and a keenly sensitive cross-cultural communicator. Here he tackles the grandest theme for the Christian and the most controversial one for the antagonist. With studied brilliance, clear reasoning, and compelling scriptural support he presents the supremacy of Christ. Both friend and foe will have to reckon with his argument."

—RAVI ZACHARIAS
President of Ravi Zacharias International Ministries

"The curious thing about this precious book is not its title but the fact that it was written from a strikingly global perspective—very unusual, very valuable. It treats familiar truths with fresh, fascinating perspective. It bristles with vitality, brilliant insights and illustrations that lift the reader completely out of the usual Western setting."

—RALPH D. WINTER
General Director
U.S. Center for World Mission

"In defense of the Gospel, Ajith Fernando follows in the tradition of Paul the Apostle, presenting profound biblical theology in practical, understandable terms. Here is a book ples with the best of contemporary East as well as in the West, yet is bas book for layperson and theologian, f *Supremacy of Christ* is full of insights to ... more effective sharing of it."

—ROBERTSON McQUILKIN
President Emeritus, Columbia International University;
Author; Conference Speaker

"Offers rare wisdom for Christians relating to people with alternative religious influences. I highly recommend this timely, readable gem for witnessing to 'religious' relatives, small group studies, a series of sermons, and courses in Christian schools."

—GORDON R. LEWIS
Senior Professor of Theology and Philosophy
Denver Seminary

"As a very capable Bible scholar, an effective evangelist, and a leading theologian with many years of experience in Buddhist and Hindu contexts, Ajith Fernando is especially qualified to address one of the most controversial issues of our day—the uniqueness of Jesus Christ in a pluralistic world. His sensitive, informed, and thoroughly biblical treatment of the subject should be read carefully by all interested in the current debate."

—HAROLD NETLAND
Assistant Professor of Philosophy of Religion and Mission
Trinity Evangelical Divinity School

THE
SUPREMACY
OF CHRIST

Ajith Fernando

CROSSWAY BOOKS • WHEATON, ILLINOIS
A DIVISION OF GOOD NEWS PUBLISHERS

The Supremacy of Christ

Copyright © 1995 by Ajith Fernando

Published by Crossway Books
        a division of Good News Publishers
        1300 Crescent Street
        Wheaton, Illinois 60187

Editing: Leonard G. Goss and Jan M. Ortiz

Cover design: Dennis Hill

Art Direction/Design: Mark Schramm

First printing 1995

Printed in the United States of America

Royalties from the sale of this book will be used for the promotion of Christian literature and education in Sri Lanka.

Library of Congress Cataloging-in-Publication Data
Fernando, Ajith.
    The supremacy of Christ / Ajith Fernando.
       p.   cm.
    1. Apologetics. 2. Jesus Christ—Person and offices.
3. Bible. N.T. Gospels—Evidences, authority, etc. I. Title.
BT1102.F43 1995   239—dc20   95-15316
ISBN 0-89107-855-X

02		01		00		99		98		97		96		95
15	14	13	12	11	10	9	8	7	6	5	4	3	2	1

To my seminary teachers

Robert E. Coleman
now at Trinity Evangelical Divinity School
Donald E. Demaray
Harold B. Kuhn
John N. Oswalt
John T. Seamands
Robert A. Traina and
Joseph S. Wang
from Asbury Theological Seminary
and
Daniel P. Fuller
and Arthur F. Glasser
from Fuller Theological Seminary

In this book is evidence of your
investment in my life.

CONTENTS

Part Three: **Jesus Is the Life**

ACKNOWLEDGMENTS

T HOSE WHO HAVE HELPED ME in writing this book are too many to be named. I will attempt to pay tribute to but a few of them. The reader will soon realize that I have learned much from the writings of four great missionaries to my neighbor nation, India: my seminary teacher John T. Seamands, E. Stanley Jones, Stephen Neill, and Lesslie Newbigin. It is difficult for me to avoid the conclusion that life in Asia helped them to develop the style of integration needed, in this era of overspecialization, that will effectively penetrate our cultures through relevant ministries of the Gospel.

I was delighted to see how many times I have referred to Dr. Leon Morris in this book. Reading through his *Tyndale Commentary* on 1 Corinthians[1] as a youth introduced me to the thrill of Bible study that has not left me these many years. I have also referred often to the writings of John Stott. I will never forget the thrill I felt when, as a young university student, I read his book *The Preacher's Portrait*[2] and his Bible expositions given at the Urbana student missionary conferences of the 1960s. He became a model of how the Bible should be used in thinking Christianly. I feel his book *The Cross of Christ*[3] is the most enriching theological book I have ever read, and the insights that I received from it have often found their way into this book.

---

[1]Leon Morris, "The First Epistle of Paul to the Corinthians," *Tyndale New Testament Commentaries* (London: Tyndale; Grand Rapids: Eerdmans, 1985).
[2]John R. W. Stott, *The Preacher's Portrait* (London: Tyndale, 1961).
[3]John R. W. Stott, *The Cross of Christ* (Leicester and Downers Grove, Ill.: InterVarsity Press, 1986).

As I was writing this book, I often felt a deep sense of gratitude to my teachers whose lives and ministries have impacted me greatly and have influenced the shape of this book so markedly. I think especially of my pastor in my teen-age years, George Good, my YFC leader Sam Sherrard, and my teachers in theological seminary. It is a pleasure, therefore, to dedicate this book to some of my seminary teachers.

I am grateful to many friends abroad, especially Dr. Brian Stiller, Mr. and Mrs. Loran Grant, Dr. Ramesh Richard, Rev. Robert Crumbley and the Evangelical Literature Trust, through its scholar's grant program, who supplied me with many of the books that I needed for writing this book.

In terms of the struggle for time to write in the midst of a busy ministry, I think this has been the hardest of my books to write. The one who suffered most from this struggle was my beloved wife Nelun. To her I give thanks for believing in this book and for paying the price of that belief. To Nirmali and Asiri go thanks for bringing boundless joy to their father.

To my colleagues in YFC go thanks for releasing me for and encouraging me in the writing ministry. I am particularly grateful to my secretary, Helen Selliah, and my assistant, Timothy Godwin, for helping with this book in numerous ways. The YFC staff were the first to hear much of the material of this book. The animated discussions that took place during my sessions with them always resulted in my making extensive revisions of the material. The same thing happened as a result of my teaching this material at Colombo Theological Seminary and other seminaries in the USA.

The above partial list of people who have impacted my thinking shows that I cannot claim the credit for the things that I write. Every book is the product of segments of the body of Christ who have, in turn, been influenced by other segments of the body. And what may be good in it is the result of God's merciful enlightening of the writer's feeble mind through the influence of many of his servants.

INTRODUCTION

T HE SUPREMACY OF CHRIST: the title itself seems completely out of step with the way many people are thinking today. Do intelligent people still hold such so-called outmoded attitudes that they can still speak of the supremacy of Christ? Many think that the sooner what they call the vestiges of the imperialistic mentality are removed from the church the better. This shows that each era in history brings with it fresh challenges that call for relevant apologetics and theological formulation in the church. In this era, pluralism has become a dominant philosophy, Eastern religions have adopted a strong missionary stance, New Age thinking is making huge inroads into different spheres of western society, and the evangelical movement, especially in the West, seems to have lost its cutting-edge commitment to the radical truth of the Gospel. In the social sphere, race, class, ethnic, and religious strife is rampant, and often Christians are seen as the villains.

This book is an attempt at apologetics and theological formulation to meet the challenges of today. During the past eighteen years of ministry with Youth for Christ and fourteen years of involvement in a church that is reaching out primarily to Buddhists, I have spoken to hundreds of Buddhists and Hindus about the Gospel of Christ. I have listened to their questions and objections to this message, and I have taught the essentials of the faith to many who converted to Christianity. I have also spoken to scores of Christians who have had questions about the Christian claim to uniqueness. Many of them have strongly disagreed with me. In this book I will seek to demonstrate the supremacy of Jesus by appealing to the content of his Gospel. I will attempt to show

xii THE SUPREMACY OF CHRIST

that who Jesus is and what he has done, and continues to do today in our lives, leaves us with no choice but to affirm that he is indeed supreme.

We will focus primarily on the claims Jesus made, and secondarily on the claims that the writers of the New Testament made about Jesus and His work and explore some of the implications of those claims. We will look at whether the Gospels are a reliable source of information of what Jesus said, as that is a key question in the debate surrounding religious pluralism. We will show that if Jesus really said and did the things the Gospels claim He said and did, He must really be supreme. We will study the claims of Christ in respect to other competing ideologies and consider the objections their adherents make to the Christian Gospel. We cannot with validity say something is supreme unless we give its "competition" due consideration.

In this book we are dealing with the uniqueness of the Christian religion out of the conviction that it is the answer to the fallen creation provided by the Creator of all of life. Christianity thus encompasses all of life. Therefore, this book will deal with a wide variety of topics and move in a lot of spheres that are usually dealt with separately in different books. Here you will find biblical exegesis, New Testament criticism, theology, apologetics, biography, inspiration, and challenge. I make no apology for such integration of different disciplines of study in a single book even though in the West, with its high specialization, this type of integration is not very common and is sometimes viewed with disdain.

The Bible is a very integrated book. The most theological book in the Bible, the book of Romans, has a sublime doxology to conclude its most theological section (Rom. 9–11). Then it moves into a very practical section (Rom. 12–15). Just before the highly theological section is one of the most inspirational chapters of the whole Bible (Rom. 8). So I make no apology for attempting an integrated approach to the supremacy of Christ.

There are some excellent books on this topic written in a more technical style. I have written in a style that is accessible to a layperson. Therefore, I have tried to avoid using technical language. I believe that the uniqueness of Christianity is an issue that the Christian layperson also faces. But a theological student or professional Christian worker will also find this book helpful, as it deals with issues they face and as it has come from years of reflection on and study of the topic. In fact, portions of this material have been taught at Gordon-Conwell Theological Seminary, Denver Seminary, and Trinity Evangelical Divinity School in USA as well as at Colombo Theological Seminary in Sri Lanka.

As I am using the content of the Gospel as the base for describing the supremacy of Christ, this book will be helpful to evangelists and all those who seek to witness about Christ to non-Christians and pluralists. My teacher Dr. Daniel Fuller used to say that all our theology must result in evangelism. I hope that this will be the case with this book. A lot of the points in this book have been used in evangelistic settings, though it has been presented in a style more understandable to non-Christians. In fact, I have written an evangelistic booklet published in the Sinhala and Tamil languages called *The Jesus Way to Life*, using some of the points in this book. Part Two, "Jesus Is the Way," began as a lecture given to about seventy Buddhist monks on the Christian doctrine of forgiveness. My hope is that this will be a theology book that preachers will often consult not only for doctrinal points but also for practical applications and illustrations of those points.

Occasionally I have, for the sake of completeness, included some material though it is not immediately essential to the argument of this book. This is because my hope is that this book will be used as a fairly comprehensive treatment of apologetics and of the person and work of Christ.

It is not possible for me, living in Sri Lanka, to be conversant with all the literature on this topic written in the West. But I believe the books I did get to read have given me a fair understanding of the debate on pluralism that is raging in the West. I trust that my lack of reading all the books will be compensated for by the stimulation received from conversations with hundreds of people who hold views different from mine.

I need to point out that this book is different from my earlier book, *The Christian's Attitude Toward World Religions.*[1] This supplements what

---

[1] Ajith Fernando, *The Christian's Attitude Toward World Religions* (Wheaton, Ill.: Tyndale House, 1987; Bombay: GLS, 1988). British ed., *Jesus and the World Religions* (Bromley: STL, 1988)

was written there. That book did not tackle pluralism, which has become a key issue since I wrote it. But many important topics related to pluralism that are discussed in that book are not discussed in detail here. Examples are the question of truth in other religions, the fate of those who haven't heard the Gospel, the relationship between persuasion and tolerance, the difference between conversion and proselytism (in the modern derogatory sense of that term), and the charge that those who believe in the uniqueness of Christ are guilty of arrogance.

Part One

JESUS IS THE TRUTH

CHAPTER ONE

THE SUPREME CHRIST AND THE CHALLENGE OF PLURALISM

O N A RECENT TRIP to a neighboring Asian country, I stayed at the home of a missionary family from the United States. I had gone for a walk with the husband, and when we returned home we found the missionary wife in an angry and deeply troubled mood. She had just read an article in *Time* magazine about three new books on Jesus Christ.[1] All three books had been written by "respected scholars,"[2] but they presented a very different Christ than the one who has been worshiped by Christians for twenty centuries. They were able to do this by denying that the Gospels are a reliable source of accurate information on who the real Jesus was. There has been a spate of simi-

---

[1] Richard N. Ostling, "Jesus Christ, Plain and Simple," *Time*, January 10, 1994, 34-35.
[2] John Dominic Crossan, *Jesus: A Revolutionary Biography* (San Francisco: Harper San Francisco, 1993); Burton Mack, *The Lost Gospel* (San Francisco: Harper San Francisco, 1994); The Jesus Seminar, *The Five Gospels: The Search for the Authentic Words of Jesus* (New York: Macmillan, 1993).

lar books emerging in the past few years.[3] Most of them have received wide publicity. The front cover of one of these books, *Jesus the Man: A New Interpretation of the Dead Sea Scrolls* by Sydney University professor Barbara Thiering, describes the book as "the controversial bestseller that will change forever your view of Christianity."

What we are seeing recently is the climax of a trend that has been evident for about a century. In 1901 an influential German theologian, Ernst Troeltsch, wrote a book on the theme of the uniqueness of Christianity called *The Absolute Validity of Christianity.*[4] There he argued for the absolute uniqueness of Christianity. Over twenty years later he wrote a paper to be delivered at Oxford University, but he died before delivering it. In the paper, he argued that Christianity is absolute for Christians, while the other faiths are absolute for their adherents.[5] With such major shifts occurring in the minds of many within the church, relativism has become a key to understanding religious truth in many circles.

Of course, not every one who has changed their minds about Jesus has moved in the direction of rejecting His uniqueness and supremacy. One of Asia's great evangelists was John Sung (1901-44), a brilliant Chinese man. The son of a Chinese pastor, he went to the United States of America for studies in 1920. He did brilliantly and received his Ph.D. in chemistry from Ohio State University. Then, though he had been losing his faith in the Christian way of salvation through faith in Christ alone, he enrolled at Union Theological Seminary in New York. There, without the faith that had once sustained him, he turned to Buddhist

[3]E.g., Barbara Thiering, *Jesus the Man: A New Interpretation of the Dead Sea Scrolls* (London: Corgi, 1993), originally published as *Jesus and the Riddle of the Dead Sea Scrolls* (Garden City, N.Y.: Doubleday, 1992); A. N. Wilson, *Jesus: A Life* (New York: Ballantine, 1992); John Shelby Spong, *Born of a Woman: A Bishop Rethinks the Birth of Jesus* (San Francisco: Harper San Francisco, 1992); Ian Wilson, *Jesus: The Evidence* (London: Weidenfeld & Nicolson, 1984). N. T. Wright, a New Testament lecturer at Oxford University, has written a response to the first three books mentioned above, entitled *Who Was Jesus?* (London: SPCK; Grand Rapids: Eerdmans, 1992).
[4]Reissued under the title, *The Absoluteness of Christianity* (Atlanta: John Knox, 1971; London: SCM Press, 1972).
[5]Reprinted as "The Place of Christianity Among the World Religions," in *Christianity and Other Religions*, eds. John Hick and Brian Hebblethwaite (Edinburgh: Collins, 1980), 11-31.

and Taoist mysticism in an attempt to find peace of mind. During this time he went with some friends to the Calvary Baptist Church in New York for an evangelistic meeting expecting to hear an eloquent and learned preacher, but instead the speaker was a fifteen-year-old girl![6] Although his friends scoffed at what happened there, Sung was so impressed that he went back for four consecutive evenings. This led him to return to his former faith in the absolute uniqueness of Jesus Christ.

The change in John Sung's life was so marked and his desire to share his faith so intense that he was pronounced insane and hospitalized in a psychopathic ward. After six months he was released, following the intervention of friends on his behalf, on the condition that he would return immediately to China. He did go back in 1927 and lived only until 1944. But during that time he was a flaming evangelist and an agent of revival in many parts of East Asia.

I have seen this type of thing happening with ministers who rejected the orthodox beliefs about Christ in theological seminary. After some years of ministry they return to the views they held as youths, possibly as a result of realizing the inability of their new ideas to effect a transformation in the lives of those they minister to as well as in their own lives. Yet the new view of Christ that denies His supremacy is gaining followers all over the world. In this book I consider the life and work of Jesus and show that there are very reasonable grounds for believing that Jesus is indeed supreme.

REJECTING THE MESSAGE OF
TIME-HONORED PROOF TEXTS

During the first eighteen centuries, often when Christians have wanted to express the uniqueness of their faith, they quoted statements in the Bible like John 14:6: "I am the way and the truth and the life. No one comes to the Father except through me"; and Acts 4:12: "Salvation is found in no one else, for there is no other name under heaven given to men by which we must be saved." Yet many are saying today that we cannot build our conviction on so key a topic on isolated verses like that. Those who are saying this do not believe in the verbal authority of

---

[6]Leslie T. Lyall, *A Biography of John Sung* (London: CIM, 1961), 31. The story related here is taken from that book.

Scripture either. An influential Indian theologian, Stanley Samartha, objects to the use of biblical proof texts like this to build a case for the absolute uniqueness of Christianity. He complains that "very often, claims for the 'normativeness' of Christ are based on the authority of the Bible. Exclusive texts are hurled back and forth as if just by uttering texts from the Scriptures the problem is settled."[7] He thinks that this method is insufficient and inappropriate.

This shift from thinking of Christianity in absolute terms is evidenced in the West also, where there is a great deal of skepticism today about the possibility of knowing truth. A poll by George Barna in 1991 yielded the statistic that 67 percent of the American people believe there is no such thing as absolute truth. What is more surprising is that 53 percent of those claiming to be Bible-believing conservative Christians said there is no such thing as absolute truth.[8] A student in a secular campus encounters over and over again the belief that no one has the right to claim they can know for sure that theirs is the only correct answer to a given issue.

It is our belief that texts like John 14:6 are not the only case we have for the absolute uniqueness of the Christian Gospel revealed in the Scriptures. These texts explicitly articulate a truth that shines through the Scriptures with unmistakable clarity. In this book I hope to show that what John 14:6 claims is true. I will show that the general picture we get from the Bible is that its writers believed that the Christian Gospel is absolutely true in a sense that no other gospel is. I will show that we must conclude that Christ also believed this. Then I will try to convince the reader that we must accept as valid what Christ believed about Himself. In other words, I seek to convince even those who do not accept that the Bible is the infallible authority of faith. If our case for the supremacy of Christ rests only on a few texts, only those who believe in the infallibility of Scripture will be convinced. I want to show

---

[7]Stanley Samartha, "The Cross and the Rainbow," in *The Myth of Christian Uniqueness*, eds. John Hick and Paul F. Knitter (London: SCM Press; Maryknoll, N.Y.: Orbis, 1987), 78. See also Wesley Ariarajah, *The Bible and People of Other Faiths* (Geneva: World Council of Churches, 1985), 21.

[8]George Barna, *What Americans Believe* (Ventura, Calif.: Regal, 1991), quoted in Charles Colson, *The Body* (Dallas: Word, 1992), 171, 184.

others also that the evidence is such that they will be driven to the inescapable conclusion of Christ's supremacy.

Many reasons can be given for the erosion in our confidence about Jesus being absolute truth. Here we will look at a major reason, which is the philosophy of the pluralism that seems to dominate the thinking of many people when it comes to the issue of religious truth.

THE PHILOSOPHY OF PLURALISM

The philosophy of *pluralism* lies at the heart of the thinking of the New Age movement and also of some so-called Christian theologies.[9] It fits in with well Buddhist and Hindu thought too. We are not talking here of the pluralism that allows for the existence of political, ethnic, and cultural differences in a society or a church. I think that type of pluralism is healthy for both church and society. Rather, we are referring here to "a philosophical stance"[10] that recognizes more than one ultimate principle and that therefore claims it is not possible for us to say that any one system of thought is absolute truth. Donald Carson describes this as a "stance which insists that tolerance is mandated on the ground that no current in the sea of diversity has the right to take precedence over other currents." He says that "in the religious sphere, no religion has the right to pronounce itself true and others false. The only absolute creed is the creed of pluralism."[11]

Perhaps the best-known modern pluralist is the British Presbyterian theologian John Hick, who is now at Claremont Graduate School in California. In the 1970s he called for a Copernican revolution in our theology of religions. He says, "Copernicus realized that it is the sun, and not the earth, that is at the center, and that all heavenly bodies, including our own earth, revolve around it." He applies this analogy to our approach to religions. He says that Christians have kept Christ or Christianity in the center and viewed the other faiths in relation to Christianity. Instead, says Hick, "We have

---

[9] For a comprehensive study of the issue of pluralism, see Ken Gnanakan, *The Pluralistic Predicament* (Bangalore: Theological Book Trust, 1992).

[10] D. A. Carson, "Christian Witness in an Age of Pluralism," in *God and Culture*, eds. D. A. Carson and John D. Woodbridge (Grand Rapids, Mich.: Eerdmans; Carlisle: Paternoster, 1993), 33.

[11] Ibid., 33.

to realize that the universe of Faiths centers upon God, and not upon Christianity or upon any other religion. He is the sun, the originative source of light and life, whom all the religions reflect in their own different ways."[12] In his later writing Hick has modified this position somewhat. Now he does not place God in the center, but what he calls "the Real." This allows him to include into his "solar system" of faiths the Theravada Buddhists[13] who do not take the divine into account in their religious system. According to this idea, the Muslim would apprehend the Real as personal, while the Hindu would apprehend it as impersonal.[14]

In contrast to this type of pluralism is *inclusivism*. This view, which has been advocated by Roman Catholic theologians like Karl Rahner,[15] Hans Küng,[16] and Raimundo Panikkar,[17] is gaining popularity in Protestant circles too. Here salvation is viewed as being only through Christ. However, Christ could use other means to save than those that require the hearing of the Gospel. Examples of such means are what in typical Roman Catholic language are called the sacraments of other religions.[18] Rahner described the saved people of other religions as "anonymous Christians." Küng refers to the non-Christian religions as the "ordinary" way to salvation, whereas Christianity is a "very special and extraordinary" way to salvation. Evangelical thinkers like Sir

---

[12]John Hick, "Whatever Path Men Choose Is Mine," in *Christianity and Other Religions* eds. John Hick and Brian Hebblethwaite (Philadelphia: Fortress; Glasgow: Collins, 1980), 182. For a fuller study of this view, see Hick's *God and the Universe of Faiths* (London: Macmillan, 1973).

[13]Theravada Buddhism is the orthodox form of Buddhism found in countries like Sri Lanka, Thailand, Burma, and Laos. Theravada means "the way of the elders."

[14]See John Hick, *An Interpretation of Religion* (New Haven, Conn.: Yale University Press, 1988).

[15]See Karl Rahner, "Christianity and the Non-Christian Religions," in *Christianity and Other Religions*, 52-79 and *Theological Investigations*, vol. 5 of *Later Writings* (London: Darton, Longman and Todd, 1966), 115-34.

[16]See Hans Küng, in *Christian Revelation and World Religions*, ed. Joseph Neuner (London: Burns and Oats, 1967), 52-53.

[17]See Raimundo Panikkar, *The Unknown Christ of Hinduism*, rev. ed. (Maryknoll, N.Y.: Orbis, 1981).

[18]See Nihal Abeysingha, *A Theological Evaluation of Non-Christian Rites* (Bangalore: Theological Publications, 1979).

Norman Anderson[19] and, more radically, Clark Pinnock[20] and John Sanders[21] also see the possibility of salvation apart from explicit knowledge of the Gospel of Christ. They see one's attitude of repentance and faith as a means that mediates salvation through the grace of God in Christ.

The traditional Christian view about the world religions is called *exclusivism.* Here the Christian Gospel is held to be the only ultimate truth, and acceptance of this Gospel is the only way by which people may be saved.[22]

PLURALISM AND REVELATION

Religious pluralism espouses a new idea of revelation. Over the years Christians have understood revelation as God's disclosure of truth to humanity. He did this generally in ways accessible to all people, for example through nature and conscience, and specifically in the Scriptures and supremely in Jesus Christ. According to the new idea, truth is *not disclosed* to us but is *discovered* by us through our experience. The writings of the different religions, whether Hindu, New Age, Muslim, or Christian, are said to reflect different discoveries (through experience) of the one God. The different religions are different expressions of the Absolute. Each contains facets of truth.

A Hindu parable is often used to describe this idea. A few people are blindfolded and taken to an elephant and asked to describe what is

[19]See Sir Norman Anderson, *Christianity and World Religions* (Leicester and Downers Grove, Ill.: InterVarsity Press, 1984), 137-61.
[20]See Clark Pinnock, "The Finality of Christ in a World of Religions," *Christian Faith and Practice in the Modern World*, eds. Mark A. Noll and David F. Wells (Grand Rapids, Mich.: Eerdmans, 1988), 152-68 and "Toward an Evangelical Theology of Religions," *Journal of the Evangelical Theological Society* 33 (Sept. 1990): 359-68.
[21]John Sanders, *No Other Name: An Investigation into the Destiny of the Unevangelized* (Grand Rapids, Mich.: Eerdmans, 1992).
[22]Dr. Ramesh P. Richard has presented a comprehensive critique of the evangelical inclusivist position in *The Population of Heaven* (Chicago: Moody Press, 1994). See also my book *The Christian's Attitude Toward World Religions* (Wheaton, Ill.: Tyndale House, 1987); Robertson McQuilkin, "The Narrow Way," in *Perspectives on the World Christian Movement: A Reader*, eds. Ralph D. Winter and Steven C. Hawthorne (Pasadena, Calif.: William Carey Library, 1981), 127-34; Dick Dowsett, *God, That's Not Fair!* (Sevenoaks: OMF; Bromley: STL, 1982); and J. Oswald Sanders, *How Lost Are the Heathen?* (Chicago: Moody Press, 1972).

there by touching the object before them. One feels the trunk and says that it is like a tree. The other feels a leg and says it is like a pillar and so on. These are the gropings of those who have felt different parts of the huge elephant. Our different religious ideas are likened to this. Such truth, of course, cannot be absolute. In fact, in Hinduism the Absolute deity is unknowable. And Hinduism is in many ways the mother of New Age thinking.

PLURALISM AND INTERRELIGIOUS ENCOUNTER

It would be clear from the above description that pluralists cannot accept the idea that one way is the only true way. They would therefore frown at the idea of working for the conversion of people from another faith. I spoke once at a conference in Sri Lanka, along with another speaker, on the topic of Christian mission in Sri Lanka. The other speaker said that when a Buddhist came to him expressing a desire to become a Christian, he told him, "You have such a great religion. Why do you want to become a Christian? Why don't you study your religion more carefully and be a better Buddhist?"

One of the keys to interreligious encounter is to learn from one another.[23] So dialogue has replaced apologetics in interreligious encounter. Such encounter is said to involve everyone's meeting as equals, refusing to insist that one's own way is the only correct way. The Sri Lankan Christian leader, Wesley Ariarajah, who is Deputy General Secretary of the World Council of Churches, wrote, "Anyone who approaches another with an *a priori* assumption that his story is 'the only true story' kills the dialogue before it begins."[24] Once a church leader speaking at the annual conference of my denomination said that we must take the word *only* out of the Christian vocabulary.

The new aim in mission is for the different religions to enrich each other through their distinctive contributions and to combine to battle the irreligious materialism that is attacking the soul of contemporary society.

---

[23]I have dealt with the issue of learning from other faiths in my book *The Christian's Attitude Toward World Religions* (pp. 110-13). There I have shown that because God's general revelation is available to all humanity, there are things that we can learn from people of other faiths.

[24]Wesley Ariarajah, "Toward a Theology of Dialogue," *The Ecumenical Review of Theology*, 19, no. 1 (Jan. 1977): 5.

This understanding of tolerance is built into the structure of Hindu and Buddhist thought. In practice, however, we are seeing much intolerance among their leaders when one of their adherents becomes a Christian. This is the principle of tolerance of all except those who reject pluralism. I think we see this in the West too.

In light of the developments outlined above it is not surprising that many Christians are asking whether Christian claims to a unique and absolute revelation still hold in this modern era. It is my hope to show that they do.

CHAPTER TWO

JESUS IS ABSOLUTE TRUTH

WE HAVE SEEN how the pluralistic mood makes people today skeptical about the idea of knowing absolute truth. Into this environment of uncertainty about truth, the biblical Christian comes with the claim that we can know Absolute Truth. We say that we have found it in Jesus; that Jesus is the truth as He Himself claimed in John 14:6. This means that He is the personification, the embodiment of truth. Jesus did not only say, "What I say is true;" which means, "I am true." He said, "I am the truth," the ultimate reality.

WE BELIEVE IN A DEFINITE REVELATION

This revelation is not something primarily discovered by experience. The pluralist says that what we call revelation is actually the record of the religious experiences of a given people. We say it is disclosed by God and not primarily discovered by humankind.

Dr. Wesley Ariarajah, Associate General Secretary of the World Council of Churches, expresses the pluralist position on revelation well. He says that "truth in the absolute sense is beyond anyone's grasp," that "the insistence on absolute and objective truth comes from certain cultural and philosophical traditions that are alien to the Bible." His view about the Bible is that what is written there "are not attempts to project objective truth, but a struggle to understand, to celebrate, to witness and to relate."[1] So, according to the typical pluralist, the Scriptures of the different religions record what their authors have discovered through their experience of the one God.

In contrast to this, we affirm that God has spoken in the Scriptures and supremely in the person of Christ. Hebrews 1:1-2 summarizes this view well. Verse 1 talks of the revelation in the Old Testament: "In the past God spoke to our forefathers through the prophets at many times and in various ways." Verse 2 presents the revelation in Jesus: "but in these last days he has spoken to us by his Son, whom he appointed heir of all things, and through whom he made the universe."

JESUS IS ABSOLUTE TRUTH

Jesus substantiates His claim to be the truth in the verses that follow John 14:6. He first expands on this by explaining what it means to claim that He is the truth. Verse 7 says, "If you really knew me, you would know my Father as well. From now on, you do know him and have seen him." To know Jesus is to know the Father. Because the disciples have not fully grasped the truth about Jesus, He says, "If you really knew me." But that situation will soon change. Jesus goes on to say, "From now on, you do know him." Leon Morris points out that when Jesus said we can know God, he "goes beyond anything that the holy people of old normally claimed. . . . Jesus brings to those who believe something new and outstanding in religious experience, the real knowledge of God."[2]

Jesus makes one more strong point in John 14:7. He says, "From now on, you do know him and have seen him." Jesus is saying that the disciples have seen God the Father. William Barclay says, "It may well be that to the ancient world this was the most staggering thing that Jesus ever said. To the Greeks, God was characteristically *The Invisible*. The Jews would count it as an article of faith that no man has seen God at

---

[1]Wesley Ariarajah, *The Bible and People of Other Faiths* (Geneva: World Council of Churches, 1985), 27.
[2]Leon Morris, *Reflections on the Gospel of John*, vol. 3 (Grand Rapids, Mich.: Baker, 1988), 495

any time."[3] Leon Morris concludes: "He is claiming something far, far greater than anyone else had claimed."[4]

But the disciples do not seem to have grasped this. So in John 14:8, Philip says, "Lord, show us the Father and that will be enough for us." Jesus responds, "Don't you know me, Philip, even after I have been among you such a long time? Anyone who has seen me has seen the Father. How can you say, 'Show us the Father'? Don't you believe that I am in the Father, and that the Father is in me?" (verses 9 and 10a).

It is interesting that though the opponents of Jesus understood that Jesus claimed to be equal with God, the disciples did not. Perhaps this is because the opponents were not averse to thinking bad thoughts about Christ. A claim to deity would confirm in their minds what they wanted to believe: that Jesus was not a good person. So when they heard Jesus make a statement about His deity, they tried to stone Him "for blasphemy, because," they said, "you, a mere man, claim to be God" (John 10:33). The disciples of Christ didn't want to think of Christ as a blasphemer; so they would have tried to understand Jesus' claims to divinity differently. They loved Him, and they did not want to attribute blasphemy to Him. The Resurrection changed all of that, for then they knew that Jesus was indeed divine, and that those statements were not blasphemous but gloriously true.

A similar thing is happening today. When non-Christians accuse us of arrogance and exclusivism because we say Christ is the only way, some Christians try to overcome the charge by rejecting the claims to exclusivism in the Gospels. They do this either by claiming that Jesus did not really say such things or by claiming that the exclusivistic interpretation of those statements is incorrect. We will respond to both these options in the course of this book.

So Jesus is claiming to be equal with God in John 14:7-10, and He is saying that because He is equal with God, when we see Jesus we see God. This claim was explained more clearly by John in the first chapter of his gospel. The first three verses of John use many statements that proclaim that the Word was the Absolute: "In the beginning was the Word, and the Word was with God, and the Word was God. He was with God in the

[3]William Barclay, *The Gospel of John*, vol. 2 (Philadelphia: Westminster, 1975), 159
[4]Morris, *Reflections*, 496.

beginning. Through him all things were made; without him nothing was made that has been made." These are statements about the Absolute God.

John 1:14 says that this Absolute has become concrete in the person of Jesus: "The Word became flesh and lived for a while among us." We have seen that *Word* here refers to the Absolute. *Flesh* on the other hand is an earthly, almost a crude word. John is saying then that the Absolute has become concrete by becoming fully human. F. F. Bruce summarized the teaching in John 1 like this: "God, who had revealed himself—'sent his word'—in a variety of ways from the beginning, made himself known at last in a real historical person: when 'the Word became flesh,' God became man."[5]

But John does not stop at that. Verse 14 of chapter 1 goes on to say: "We have seen his glory, the glory of the One and Only Son, who came from the Father, full of grace and truth." This whole verse is loaded with deep significance derived from the Old Testament understanding of the *shekinah* glory of God that came down when God visited the tabernacle. The language used by John directs us to this Old Testament imagery. This is especially true of the Greek verb *skenoō*, which is translated "made his dwelling" and literally means "pitched his tabernacle."[6] Don Carson says, "It is nothing less than God's glory that John and his friends witnessed in the word-made-flesh."[7] John says they saw this glory "full of grace and truth."

John explains this concept again in 1:18: "No one has ever seen God, but God the only Son, who is at the Father's side, has made him known." He is teaching that when we see Jesus, we see the Absolute God. So we conclude that *absolute truth can be known because the Absolute has become concrete in history in the person of Jesus.*

Paul makes this same claim in Colossians 2:9: "For in Christ all the fullness of the Deity lives in bodily form." Peter O'Brien points out that the word translated *Deity* here (*theotes*) is to be distinguished from *he theiotes*, which means "divine nature" or "divine quality" or "godlikeness." The word Paul used means "the divine essence." This is why several English versions translate it as "Godhead." O'Brien quotes an

---

[5]F. F. Bruce, *The Gospel of John* (England: Pickering and Inglis; Grand Rapids, Mich.: Eerdmans, 1983), 40.

[6]D. A. Carson, *The Gospel According to John* (Leicester: Inter-Varsity Press; Grand Rapids, Mich.: Eerdmans, 1991), 127.

[7]Ibid., 128.

earlier commentator, H. A. W. Meyer, as saying, "The essence of God, undivided and in its whole fullness, dwells in Christ."[8]

Hebrews 1:2-3a also presents this idea from the perspective of explaining the revelation that took place at the Incarnation: "in these last days [God] has spoken to us by his Son, whom he appointed heir of all things, and through whom he made the universe. The Son is the radiance of God's glory and the exact representation of his being."

Now the apostolic eyewitnesses saw and experienced Jesus and interpreted what they saw and experienced through what Jesus taught them under the direction of the Holy Spirit. Jesus Himself promised: "But when he, the Spirit of truth, comes, he will guide you into all truth. He will not speak on his own; he will speak only what he hears, and he will tell you what is yet to come" (John 16:13). The New Testament is the result of this activity of the Spirit. And through that we are able to get to know absolute truth.

The Hindus say the Absolute (*paramatman*) is unknowable. They call it *Nirguna Brahman. Nirguna* means "without attributes." New Age ideas follow this and speak of an impersonal world soul. We say the Absolute is a person, Jesus Christ.

Here then is our argument for the claim that we believe in absolute truth. We say Jesus is God. Therefore, to know Jesus is to know the Absolute. Our belief in the absoluteness of the Christian Gospel is an extension of our belief that Jesus is God incarnate. It is interesting that John Hick, who is this generation's most prominent pluralist, rejects the Christian doctrine of incarnation.[9] It was he who edited the controversial book, *The Myth of God Incarnate*.[10]

KNOWING THE ABSOLUTE THROUGH A RELATIONSHIP

Now we come to the question of how and in what sense we know absolute truth. If truth is a person, then we will know the truth in the

---

[8]Peter T. O'Brien, *Colossians and Philemon*, vol. 44, *Word Biblical Commentary* (Waco, Tex.: Word, 1982), 111.
[9]See John Hick, "Jesus and the World Religions," in *The Myth of God Incarnate*, ed. John Hick (London: SCM Press, 1977), 167-85.
[10]Ibid.

way we know persons; and that is through facts about them and through a relationship with them. So we know the Absolute through a relationship, because that is the way He has chosen to communicate truth. He did it personally.

Therefore, to enter into the knowledge of the Absolute we need to get to know God. John's gospel has a lot to say about belief as the way we get to know God. *Belief* appears ninety-eight times in that gospel. It essentially means "to trust." And in that gospel, believing is equivalent to receiving Christ (1:12), obeying Him (3:36), and abiding in Him (15:1-11). J. Carl Laney says, "'Believing' in Christ does not merely refer to intellectual assent to a proposition about Christ. Rather, the biblical concept of 'belief' involves a personal response and commitment to Christ's Person."[11] That opens the way to a knowledge of absolute truth.

E. Stanley Jones tells the story about a doctor who lay dying. A Christian doctor sat beside him and urged him to surrender and have faith in Christ. The dying doctor listened in amazement. Light dawned. He joyously said, "All my life I have been bothered with *what* to believe, and now I see it is *whom* to trust."[12] Belief is entrusting ourselves to Jesus.

We are not saying that the content of the Gospel is unimportant. It is the content that tells us who Jesus is and what He has done. Later I will show that revelation is given in propositions. It is the knowledge of the facts of the Gospel that opens the door to a relationship with God, and that relationship is the heart of Christian salvation. Jesus said, "Now this is eternal life: that they may know you, the only true God, and Jesus Christ, whom you have sent" (John 17:3). When the word *know* is used in the Bible with the object being a person, usually it refers to an intimate personal relationship.[13] So we love Him as our friend and follow Him as our Lord. This is why the basic call of Christ was not "Follow My teaching" but "Follow Me."

It is interesting that Jesus said, "But I tell you the truth: It is for your good that I am going away. Unless I go away, the Counselor will not

[11]Carl Laney, *Moody Gospel Commentary: John* (Chicago: Moody Press, 1992), 20.

[12]From E. Stanley Jones, *The Christ of the Indian Road* (1925), in *Selections from E. Stanley Jones* (Nashville: Abingdon, 1972), 224.

[13]R. C. H. Lenski, *The Interpretation of St. John's Gospel* (1942; reprint, Minneapolis: Augsburg, 1942), 1121.

come to you; but if I go, I will send him to you" (John 16:7). The time when Jesus was away from them would be better than the time they had Him with them physically on earth. This is because the Holy Spirit was going to mediate that intimate, personal relationship among them and God, which is the heart of Christian knowledge.

Of course, we do not know everything there is to know about Him. In fact, there is a lot more that we have to learn. But once we receive Him, we know the Absolute personally.

In 1983 we had a terrible riot in our land. The home of a young Hindu who was converted through the Youth for Christ ministry was burned in that riot. He and his Hindu mother came to live in our home for six months. His brother and sister lived in other homes. In a beautiful way the sister was also converted to Christ, and she and her brother were ready for baptism in the church I attend. (The second brother was baptized a few years later.)

The day before the baptism service we had a retreat in our home for those who were to be baptized. Their mother attended our sessions, as she was living in our home. She heard her two children give eloquent testimony to their faith in Christ. After they had spoken, the mother said, "I cannot speak like my children, as I am not educated like them. I do not understand all the things about Christianity as they do. But I want you to know that their God is my God, and he is the One I follow." I called the pastor and told him what she had said, and I told him that I believed she was a genuine Christian. I asked him whether we could make an exception and baptize her along with her children even though she had not attended the necessary classes. He agreed, and she was baptized. And today, ten years later, she continues to be a devoted follower of Jesus. There was much that she did not know about the Absolute. But she knew the Absolute personally as her Savior, Lord, and Friend.

An elderly woman in Scotland was being tested by her minister as to her fitness to become a full member of the church. She cried out, "Sir, I cannot answer all your hard questions. All I know is that I would gladly die for Him."[14] She knew the Absolute, and this knowledge meant so much to her that she was willing to die for it.

---

[14]Stephen Neill, *The Supremacy of Jesus* (London: Hodder and Stoughton, 1984), 69.

Paul described the imperfection of our knowledge when he said, "Now we see but a poor reflection; then we shall see face to face. Now I know in part; then I shall know fully, even as I am fully known" (1 Cor 13:12). But because we know the Absolute personally, we can say that we know absolute truth.

This knowledge is not only something subjective. The Gospel of Jesus is about certain things that happened in history. As Lesslie Newbigin says, "What has happened has happened, and nothing can change it."[15] But while truth doesn't change, our interpretation of it may vary because of our human shortcomings. In fact, I believe that God, who gave us minds to think and be creative, intended for us to grapple with truth. Newbigin points out that this is why Jesus never wrote a book. Instead we have four gospels that look at Jesus from different perspectives. Newbigin says this is a scandal to the Muslims, who believe that the Koran was given directly by God to the Prophet in a dictation-type style of inspiration.

So throughout the history of the church, we have seen groups of Christians who have differed on the way portions of the Bible must be interpreted. And that is one reason why we have so many denominations. That is why there are equally sincere Christians who are Calvinists and Arminians; paedobaptists and adult Baptists; pre-, post- and amillennialists and pre-, mid- and post-tribulationists.

This was the price God paid for giving us a truth with which we can grapple. When He made us human, He gave us creativity. When He gave us a revelation, He did it in such a way that this revelation will give ample opportunity to use our creativity. We grapple with truth, and through that grappling we experience depth and maturity.

This should make us humble about our convictions. We are dogmatic about the truth of the Bible. I believe in the inerrancy of Scripture, but I do not believe in the inerrancy of my interpretation of Scripture. Therefore, I am willing to stand corrected about my convictions if those corrections are shown to be a more accurate interpretation of the revelation of God in the Bible. We must also remember that the Bible does not give us clear-cut answers to every question faced by a given generation. It gives us principles out of which we can derive a

---

[15]Lesslie Newbigin, *Truth To Tell* (Grand Rapids, Mich.: Eerdmans, 1991), 6-7.

basis for living in every age and culture, but it does not give direct and specific answers to all the earthly questions we face.

I believe that one reason for the loss of confidence about absolute truth is that some who accept the absolute inspiration and authority of the Scriptures have proclaimed things that do not belong to the Gospel with the same authority that they proclaimed the truth of the Gospel. No earthly idea or interpretation can take the place of authority contained in the Bible. But sometimes we have presented our opinions and interpretations as if they were the gospel truth. Even though we know that every political system, whether capitalist, socialist, or communist, is flawed, at different times one particular system has been presented as the totally Christian alternative. And when these systems fail and people give them up, they also give up the belief that Christianity is the truth. A similar thing has happened when people presented their interpretations regarding the timing and the events preceding the return of Christ as the only acceptable alternative for true Christians. This has also happened with ethical issues about which the Bible has no definite guidelines, like going to the movies. When people rejected the interpretation, they also rejected the Bible from which these interpretations were supposed to have been derived. The interpretation had been presented with an authority and dogmatism that can only be given to the Scriptures.

REVELATION IS PROPOSITIONAL AND PERSONAL

Before we continue, we will look at a statement that Christ made in John 14:11. Jesus commands His disciples, "Believe me when I say that I am in the Father and the Father is in me." Earlier we said that our knowledge of absolute truth is the knowledge of Jesus and is expressed in a relationship. We also said there is much to learn that we do not know and that there is a diversity of interpretations on certain issues within the church. This does not mean that the facts about Jesus are not important. There are propositions in revelation about which there can be no compromise; and the truth about Jesus' relationship with God is one of them. So He commands them, "Believe me when I say that I am in the Father and the Father is in me." This is a proposition to believe.

Some modern theologians tell us that revelation is not in propositions but is a revelation of the person of God. Therefore, they say that propositions are not important. In response to this Leon Morris rightly asks: "How can we know God unless we know something about him?"[16] And how can we express what we know about Him without a proposition, such as "God is loving" or "God is holy"? Morris says, "The more I can know about him the more I can know him."[17]

Of course, there is a dynamic interplay between the propositions and our personal experience of the truth. But that subject is beyond the scope of this book. For the moment we will affirm the point we have argued for thus far in our case of the supremacy of Jesus: Jesus is Absolute Truth because He is equal with God.

---

[16]Leon Morris, *I Believe in Revelation* (Grand Rapids, Mich.: Eerdmans, 1976), 115.
[17]Ibid., 115.

CHAPTER THREE

HIS WORDS AFFIRM HIS ABSOLUTENESS

THUS FAR we have said that, according to the Gospel of John, Jesus is equal to God and is therefore absolute truth. But is this all make-believe? How do we know that what John recorded as Jesus' statement about Himself and His relationship with God is true? That question will occupy us in the next few chapters. John 14:10b-11 points to an answer to it.

WHY WE BELIEVE THAT JESUS IS THE ABSOLUTE

In John 14:10b-11, Jesus substantiates His claim to be equal with God. He says, "The words I say to you are not just my own. Rather, it is the Father, living in me, who is doing his work. Believe me when I say that I am in the Father and the Father is in me; or at least believe on the evidence of the miracles themselves." He gives two evidences to back His claim that He is equal with God. The first is His words (verse 10b). The second is His works (verse 11).

NOTE: THE RELATIONSHIP BETWEEN JESUS AND THE FATHER

Before we go into these two reasons we need to look at an implication that could be made from verse 10b, which says, "The words I say to you are not just my own. Rather, it is the Father, living in me, who is doing his work." Some might think that this and similar verses suggest that Jesus is not divine, as it presents Jesus as distinct from, though intimately related to, the Father. Groups that deny the deity of Christ, like the Jehovah's Witnesses and Muslims, often use this type of statement to buttress their case.

When we look at John as a whole, we see a dual nature of Jesus presented often without much speculation on the way these two natures coexist. Jesus is presented as fully human and thus distinct from the Father. But he is also fully divine and thus a unity with the Father. John 5:17-19 is a good example of this: "Jesus said to them, 'My Father is always at his work to this very day, and I, too, am working'" (verse 17). The next verse shows that his listeners sense the implications of this statement: "For this reason the Jews tried all the harder to kill him; not only was he breaking the Sabbath, but he was even calling God his own Father, making himself equal with God." So Jesus further explains what he means: "Jesus gave them this answer: 'I tell you the truth, the Son can do nothing by himself; he can do only what he sees his Father doing, because whatever the Father does the Son also does'" (verse 19).

Leon Morris says that verse 19 contains "the thought of subordination, for the Son is pictured as completely obedient to the Father." Along with this "there is also a mighty claim, for the Son does 'what things soever' the Father does." Morris says, "Neither the lowly obedience, nor the implication of deity should be overlooked."[1]

G. E. Ladd has a helpful summary about the way John handles the dual truth of the humanity and the deity of Jesus.

> We may conclude that John portrays Jesus in a twofold light without reflection or speculation. He is equal to God; he is indeed God in the flesh; yet he is fully human. John provides some of the most important biblical materials for the later doctrine of the dual nature of Jesus, but John is not interested in such speculations. He reports a sound memory of the impact Jesus made without indulging in speculative questions.[2]

---

[1]Leon Morris, "The Gospel According to St. John," in *The New International Commentary on the New Testament* (Grand Rapids, Mich.: Eerdmans, 1971), 313.
[2]George Eldon Ladd, *A Theology of the New Testament*, rev. ed., ed. Donald A. Hagner (Grand Rapids, Mich.: Eerdmans, 1993), 252.

Having said this, we must add that there are places in the New Testament where Jesus is explicitly presented as being God in essence. This will be discussed in the next chapter.

Regarding the evidence that Jesus is equal with God, John 14:10b says, "The words I say to you are not just my own. Rather, it is the Father, living in me, who is doing his work." When Jesus speaks, it is the Father who is working through him. We would have expected Jesus to say, "the Father speaks through me." Instead He says, "the Father who dwells in me does his works." This is because, as Archbishop William Temple put it, "The *words* of Jesus are *works* of God."[3]

What Jesus is saying here is that we must take His words seriously because when He speaks, God speaks. His words authenticate His claims to deity. The authenticating value of the words of Jesus lies in two areas. First, their relevance and penetrating insight suggest that this is no ordinary person who is speaking, that in them is God's answer to life's problems. There is an amazing attractiveness to His teaching. Second, His claims about Himself leave us with the inescapable conclusion that He viewed Himself as equal to God.

THE ATTRACTIVENESS OF JESUS' TEACHING

Jesus says that His words ought to show people that what He claims for Himself is true. In the twenty centuries since Jesus lived, people have come to this conclusion as a result of reading the Gospels. I heard a story about a young non-Christian man who was studying English and was using one of the Gospels for reading. He suddenly got up in the middle of a lesson and paced up and down the room and said, "These are not the words of a man, these are the words of God."

Francis Cornford was an English poetess and the granddaughter of Charles Darwin. She had been brought up to believe that religion was good for some people but not for the Darwins. When her children began to ask awkward questions about religion, she thought she should get some information, and she turned to the New Testament. A short time

---

[3]William Temple, *Readings in John's Gospel* (1939, 1940; reprint, Wilton: Moorehouse Barlow, 1985), 225 (italics his).

after that she remarked to a friend, "Mr. Angus, I have been reading the Gospels, and I find that the things Jesus said about God are true."[4]

His teaching was profound, yet simple. As Bishop Stephen Neill has said, "The quality of ordinariness runs through much of the teaching of Jesus. It is this perhaps which has given to his words their extraordinary power to move the hearts of men and women through almost twenty centuries."[5] "The large crowd [that is, the common people] listened to him with delight" (Mark 12:37). The "tax collectors and 'sinners'" gathered "around to hear him" (Luke 15:1). The temple guards who were sent to arrest Jesus returned without him. And when they were asked, "Why didn't you bring him in?" they responded, "No one ever spoke the way this man does" (John 7:46). W. Griffith Thomas points out that it is remarkable that nothing of the teachings of Jesus has had to be dropped after so many centuries of discoveries.[6]

Neill contrasts Jesus' teaching to that of Gautama, the Buddha, who "came from a princely lineage; [and] through all the records marches as a most superior person." The intricacies of Buddhist metaphysics are for the intellectual elite and beyond the reach of ordinary people. This is why Buddhism has been kept alive through the religious order of monks and nuns, which Neill calls "a particular aristocracy." Similarly Plato was an aristocrat. His "later thinking leads us into a difficult world of thought in which the soldier, sailor, tinker, tailor cannot readily find themselves at home."[7]

Prior to His public ministry, Jesus had lived as an ordinary person, a carpenter. During His ministry He moved with all kinds of people. He knew what ordinary people went through. I was talking about Christ to a Buddhist whom I had sat next to at a wedding reception. This person made a statement that startled me. He said, "Christ is superior to the Buddha because he knew what poverty was. He did not grow up in a palace and then renounce that life, like the Buddha did." I could not fully understand what he meant. He had studied in a Roman Catholic school, so he knew many things about Jesus. Then I

---

[4]Stephen Neill, *The Supremacy of Jesus* (London: Hodder and Stoughton, 1984), 68.
[5]Ibid., 67.
[6]W. Griffith Thomas in *Christianity Is Christ* (1948; reprint, New Canaan, Conn.: Keats Publishing, 1981), 34.
[7]Neill, *Supremacy of Jesus*, 67.

thought that perhaps what he meant was that Jesus was superior because He lived and taught as one who identified with ordinary people.

His teaching abounds with stories that were true to life:

- A rich man whose two sons displayed a whole complex of human emotions.

- A poor woman who lost a precious coin and was desperate to find it.

- A home where a visitor has come and there is no food to give him.

- A man waylaid by robbers and people who avoided helping him.

- A poor widow and an uncaring judge.

- A rich man living in splendor and a beggar living off the crumbs of his table.

- A dinner where people want to sit at the prominent seats.

- Invitees who send apologies for absence from a reception.

- A shrewd manager who wins the support of people who could help him when he's out of a job.

- A rich farmer who saves enough for a comfortable retirement.

R. T. France says, "One of the secrets of the appeal of the teaching of Jesus over so many centuries is its firm earthing in ordinary everyday life and in the unchanging features of human character."[8]

So the greatest saint, the most powerful biblical Christian, can be a person with minimal education. Being minimally educated does not make one unable to understand the teaching of Jesus. I like to think of myself as a Bible teacher. I have studied the Bible under professional scholars and have read and taught much about the Bible. But I consider my mother to be the most influential Bible teacher in my life. What I have learned has been built on the foundation she laid. She had no formal Bible training. In fact, she was a convert from Buddhism who was introduced to Christ in her late teens. But the Bible was accessible to her and she became an effective Bible teacher.

---

[8]R. T. France, *Jesus the Radical* (Leicester: InterVarsity Press, 1989), 46.

Let me say that for those of us in ministry, *the cost of ordinariness is involvement in the affairs of people.* And that is very difficult in this age of specialists. We can regard ourselves as specialists in a certain discipline and then resent having to do things that we think do not relate to our specialization. This is particularly difficult for a minister who has just come out of theological school with a lot of expectations. Take the person with a call to preach or teach. How we would like to have hours of uninterrupted study. But a preacher or teacher is a servant of the people, as Paul said (2 Cor. 4:5). The needs of people can take hours from the time we have set apart for uninterrupted study. Yet, ministering to people provides the context out of which we preach and teach. Without this we may produce a lot of excellent material, but the material will lack the penetrating insight that is needed to effect change for good in the lives and thinking of people.

Much of the great thinking in the history of the church has come from people who, though they were active in ministry, gave time for study and writing. One thinks of the apostle Paul, Augustine, Martin Luther, John Calvin, Jonathan Edwards, and John Wesley. These were greatly influential thinkers who theologized from within the context of active ministry.

The story of Augustine is particularly interesting. He had a little community in a place called Tagaste, where he taught the Bible and was able to give himself to a contemplative life. He feared the pastorate because he knew that it would deprive him of the time for reflection that he desired. He was a good preacher, and he was often invited to preach; but he would not accept appointments at churches where there was no pastor. He feared they might ask him to come as pastor there!

Once Augustine was invited to Hippo to counsel someone. He was not afraid to go there as there was a pastor, Bishop Valerius, in Hippo. He went to church to hear the bishop preach; and the bishop seeing him, told the people that there was an urgent need for a second ordained man there. "At once the congregation laid hands on Augustine and brought him to the front amid general acclamation. There was no escape. . . . He was ordained on the spot." He began to weep. Some thought that he was weeping because he had not been made bishop right away. "But the real reason was that he knew ordination meant the end of his dream of a tranquil Christian life, withdrawn from the pressures and strife of the world."[9]

He served in Hippo until his death almost forty years later. What an influence this one man had! He has been called "the greatest Christian theologian since the apostle Paul."[10] Some of his books took a long time to write because of the pressures of ministry. One, *The Trinity,* took seventeen years to finish. He had to drop this project each time a challenge came his way that needed to be addressed.[11] The solitude Augustine desired, he got only during the last ten days of his life when, confined to his bed, he asked not to be disturbed.[12]

I often complain about how my grand plans to study are "ruined" by challenges in the ministry. On one of these occasions a colleague reminded me of a statement he had read: "I used to complain about the interruptions to my work, until God told me that these interruptions were my work." Hard as they are on me, I can testify to the truth of that statement and also say that few things have helped my ministry more than the "interruptions" that at the time seemed only to be annoying nuisances.

So, the teaching of Jesus was relevant because He moved among people and knew what was in them. Yet, *there is a depth to Christ's teaching the extent of which we can never plumb.* However much you learn, there is more to learn. So there is for us an exciting pilgrimage—one that will last until we get to heaven. I received a letter from one of America's great preachers of a previous generation, Paul S. Rees. He had helped me get a scholarship to go to the United States to study, and we had corresponded since that time. In a letter he wrote to me shortly before he died, he said, "I'm ninety years old and still a learner in the school of Christ!" Paul said, "Oh, the depth of the riches of the wisdom and knowledge of God! How unsearchable his judgments, and his paths beyond tracing out! "(Rom 11:33).

I commend to you this quest for more of the truth. It is one of the most thrilling experiences in life, for we are dealing with that which

---

[9]David Bentley-Taylor, *Augustine: Wayward Genius* (London: Hodder and Stoughton; Grand Rapids, Mich.: Baker, 1980 and 1981), 58.

[10]Tony Lane, *The Lion Concise Book of Christian Thought* (Herts: Lion Publishing, 1984), 40.

[11]Bentley-Taylor, *Augustine,* 189.

[12]Ibid., 238.

holds the key to the meaning of life, that which opens the door to the greatest of all experiences, the knowledge of God.

So the teaching of Jesus was unique because it was profoundly simple and relevant to our experience. It presents itself as the answer given by the Creator of life to human need. And that attests His divinity.

JESUS' CLAIMS ABOUT HIMSELF

But there is another side to His teaching. What Jesus said, no ordinary human being in his or her right senses would dare to say.

He spoke with great authority. Shortly before His ascension, Jesus told His disciples, "All authority in heaven and on earth has been given to me" (Matt. 28:18). The way He spoke befitted one who could make such a claim. About His teaching He said, "Heaven and earth will pass away, but my words will never pass away" (Matt. 24:35). After the Sermon on the Mount "the crowds were amazed at his teaching, because he taught as one who had authority, and not as their teachers of the law" (Matt. 7:28-29). R. T. France says, "Any other Jewish teacher made very sure that his teaching was documented with extensive quotations from scripture and with the names of his teachers added to give weight to his opinion; his authority must always be second-hand. But not Jesus. He simply laid down the law."[13] He did not say, "Scripture says" or "Rabbi X says," as the teachers at that time would do. Instead He said, "I say."

Six times in the Sermon on the Mount we find a sequence that went something like this: Jesus says, "You have heard that it was said . . ." and a quotation from the Old Testament follows. Then He says, "But I tell you . . ." and a modification of the Old Testament principle follows.[14]

He would introduce His particularly weighty utterances with the words, "Truly, truly . . ." ("I tell you the truth . . ." in the NIV). The original (Greek) Gospels record this by transliterating the Aramaic words: *"Amēn, amēn."* This expression appears seventy-eight times in the Gospels (which reduces to fifty-nine occurrences when parallels in more than one gospel are subtracted). German New Testament scholar Joachim Jeremias says that this use of *amēn, amēn* "to strengthen a person's own words . . . is without parallel in the whole Jewish literature and

---

[13]France, *Jesus the Radical,* 204.
[14]See Matthew 5:21-22, 27-28, 31-32, 33-34, 38-39, 43-44.

the rest of the New Testament."[15] He says that "the only substantial analogy to [this] that can be produced is the messenger formula, 'Thus says the Lord,' which is used by the prophets to show that their words are not their own wisdom, but a divine message."[16] Jeremias says that what we have here is a consciousness of majesty expressed in a claim to divine omnipotence.[17]

He claimed to have the authority to forgive sin. When He forgave the sins of a paralytic and the people questioned His right to do that, He proved it by performing a miracle. He said He was doing it "that [they] may know that the Son of Man has authority on earth to forgive sins" (Mark 2:10). The man was healed, and "this amazed everyone and they praised God, saying, 'We have never seen anything like this!'" (verse 12).

He did not only say to people, "Follow My teaching"—he said, "Follow Me" and demanded total allegiance. He said, "Anyone who loves his father or mother more than me is not worthy of me; anyone who loves his son or daughter more than me is not worthy of me; and anyone who does not take his cross and follow me is not worthy of me" (Matt. 10:37-38; see also Luke 14:26).

He took on titles that were given to God in the Old Testament. Psalm 27:1 says, "The Lord is my light and my salvation" (see also Isa. 60:20). Jesus said, "I am the light of the world" (John 8:12). Psalm 23:1 says, "The Lord is my shepherd" (see also Ezek. 34:15). Jesus said, "I am the good shepherd" (John 10:11).

He considered Himself worthy of receiving the honor that was due to God. Isaiah 42:8 says, "I am the Lord; that is my name! I will not give my glory to another or my praise to idols" (see also Isa. 48:11). Jesus prayed, "Father, the time has come. Glorify your Son, that your Son may glorify you.... And now, Father, glorify me in your presence with the glory I had with you before the world began" (John 17:1, 5). He said, "Moreover, the Father judges no one, but has entrusted all judgment to the Son, that all may honor the Son just as they honor the Father. He

---

[15]Joachim Jeremias, *New Testament Theology: The Proclamation of Jesus*, trans. John Bowden (New York: Scribner's, 1971), 35.

[16]Ibid., 36.

[17]Joachim Jeremias, *The Prayers of Jesus* (Naperville, Ill.: Allenson,1967), 108-15; quoted in I. Howard Marshall, *The Origins of New Testament Christology* (Leicester and Downers Grove, Ill.: InterVarsity Press, 1976), 45.

who does not honor the Son does not honor the Father, who sent him" (John 5:22-23).

He claimed to have a unique Father-Son relationship with God. He called Himself God's Son, and He called God "my Father." "My Father" is not the way Jews usually referred to God. They did speak of "our Father," and while they might use "my Father" in prayer they usually qualified it with something like "in heaven" "to remove the suggestion of familiarity. Jesus did no such thing here or elsewhere."[18] The various references to this relationship in the Gospels show that He intended to convey that His was a relationship that no other human being could have with God. When Jesus stilled the storm and the disciples knew He was more than a ordinary human being, they "worshiped him." At that time their conclusion was, "Truly you are the Son of God" (Matt. 14:33).

He claimed to be the judge of humankind, as the statement quoted above (John 5:23) implies. He once said, "When the Son of Man comes in his glory, and all the angels with him, he will sit on his throne in heavenly glory" (Matt. 25:31). Then He went on to describe how He will judge the nations (verses 32-46). Of Himself He says, "And [the Father] has given him authority to judge because he is the Son of Man" (John 5:27). Leon Morris points out that "If Jesus was anything less than God [this] is a claim entirely without foundation." Morris says, "No creature can determine the eternal destiny of his fellow-creatures."[19]

He said that people's eternal destiny depended on their relationship with him. After His basic call to deny oneself, take up the cross, and follow him, He said, "For whoever wants to save his life will lose it, but whoever loses his life for me and for the gospel will save it. What good is it for a man to gain the whole world, yet forfeit his soul? Or what can a man give in exchange for his soul?" (Mark 8:35-37).

He said that He will give us things that only God can give. He said, "For just as the Father raises the dead and gives them life, even so the Son gives life to whom he is pleased to give it" (John 5:21; see also John 11:25). He said He will give "water welling up to eternal life" (John 4:14). He spoke of giving "my peace" (John 14:27) and "my joy" (John

---

[18]Morris, "John," 309.
[19]Leon Morris, *The Lord from Heaven* (Leicester and Downers Grove, Ill.: InterVarsity Press, 1974), 36.

15:11). Among the "I am" statements in John, we find Jesus saying that He will give the bread of life (John 6:35), the light of life (John 8:12), and the sustenance needed to bear fruit (John 15:1-8). He says He is the gate to salvation (John 10:7-9) and the way to salvation (John 14:6) and to life that conquers death (John 11:25-26).

NOTE: JOHN'S USE OF THE EMPHATIC PRONOUN FOR JESUS

John uses the expression *ego eimi* in Greek ("I am") thirty times when recording the statements of Jesus. As the significance of this is in John's Greek translation of Jesus' words, we cannot include it in this section about Jesus' claims. But it is relevant to our study. In the Greek language the way the verb ends varies according to the subject. This happens rarely in English, and *am* is one of those times. When you see the word *am*, you know the subject is *I*. This happens all the time in Greek. Therefore, it is not necessary in Greek to use the subject in a sentence if it is a pronoun like *I* or *he* or *we*. So in a statement like, "I am the bread," it would be sufficient to say, "Am the bread" in Greek. But if you want to emphasize the subject, then you would use the pronoun. John does this thirty times in the "I am" statements of Jesus. We can say it was used because John wanted to give it a special emphasis.

In the Greek translation of the Old Testament (the Septuagint), which was very popular with the Christians in the first century, when the translators came to the words for God, "they apparently thought that they should be translated differently from the words for [humans]." So "they tended to use the emphatic form with the pronoun '*I*.'"[20] We used to do something like this when we quoted one of the Ten Commandments. We would begin with the words, "Thou shalt not..."[21] Similarly, they would have thought it was appropriate to use the emphatic pronoun when quoting the words of God. God named himself to Moses in Exodus 3:14 ("I am who I am"), and these are the words that are used in the Septuagint. So when John rendered statements of

---

[20]Leon Morris, *Reflections on the Gospel of John*, vol. 2 (Grand Rapids, Mich.: Baker, 1987), 217.

[21]Leon Morris, *Jesus Is the Christ: Studies in the Theology of John* (Grand Rapids, Mich.: Eerdmans; Leicester: InterVarsity Press, 1989), 107.

Jesus with the emphatic pronoun he was using "the style of deity."[22] This was one of John's ways to show that Jesus was more than a human being. He was implying that the words for deity were appropriate for Jesus.

Often, in different ways, He claimed to be equal with God, as we have already seen.

- Above we said that the style of deity is found in the "I am" statements of John. There is one such statement, however, where there is a more definite implication of deity. In John 8:58 Jesus says, "I tell you the truth [*amēn, amēn*], before Abraham was born, I am!" He said, "I am" rather than "I was." This expression indicates "eternity of being and not simply being which lasted through several centuries."[23] Following a discussion of the biblical background that illuminates the meaning of this statement of Jesus, Donald Guthrie says, "There seems to be little doubt . . . that [it] is intended to convey in an extraordinary way such divine qualities as changelessness and pre-existence."[24] Jesus' hearers understood that this was a claim to divinity, and John says that "at this, they picked up stones to stone him" (John 8:59).

- He asked the disciples to baptize people "in the name of the Father and of the Son and of the Holy Spirit" (Matt. 28:19), indicating the equality of the three persons of the Trinity. Significantly, *the name* is in the singular. This underlines "the unity of the three Persons."[25]

- When Thomas saw Jesus after His resurrection he exclaimed, "My Lord and my God!" (John 20:28). He used two divine ascriptions, "Lord" and "God."[26] Jesus should have protested this if He was not God. Instead He addresses Thomas with a word of

[22]Ibid., 107.

[23]Morris, "John," 474.

[24]Donald Guthrie, *New Testament Theology* (Leicester and Downers Grove, Ill.: InterVarsity Press, 1981), 332.

[25]R. T. France, "The Gospel According to Matthew," in *The Tyndale New Testament Commentaries* (Leicester: InterVarsity Press; Grand Rapids, Mich.: Eerdmans, 1985), 415.

[26]F. F. Bruce, *The Gospel of John* (London: Pickering and Inglis; Grand Rapids, Mich.: Eerdmans, 1983), 394.

approval and commends those who will come to the same conclusion without even seeing Jesus.

- Jesus said that when we see Jesus, we see God, as the following
statements show: "When he looks at me, he sees the one who sent
me" (John 12:45); "Don't you know me, Philip, even after I have
been among you such a long time? Anyone who has seen me
has seen the Father. How can you say, 'Show us the Father'?"
(John 14:9).

- He said, "I and the Father are one" (John 10:30).

NOTE: OBJECTIONS TO THE USE OF JOHN 10:30

There are some who feel that this verse speaks of a harmony that is less
than oneness in essence. Those who don't accept the deity of Christ say
that John 10:30 is speaking of a unity like that mentioned in John 17:22:
"that they may be one as we are one." Their argument is that the unity
of the Father and the Son is of the same quality as the unity of
Christians within the body—that is, a unity of purpose and action. In
answer to this, Don Carson says, "In 17:22, the order of the comparison
is not reciprocal. The unity of the Father and the Son is the reality
against which the unity of believers is to be measured, not the
reverse.... And like any analogy that generates a comparison, the analogy cannot be pushed to exhaustion."[27]

John 10:30 may not be an unmistakably precise statement of total
identity between the Father and the Son. But when you look at this
statement from the perspective of the rest of the book, which talks about
the Word being God and about Thomas calling Jesus "God," then it is
not difficult to conclude that something more than simple unity of purpose is intended here. This is substantiated by the fact that the Jews
tried to stone him after he made this statement. If Jesus was saying that
his words and actions were regulated according to the will of God, then
the Jews would not have regarded this statement as blasphemy.[28]

---

[27]D. A. Carson, *The Gospel According to John* (Leicester: InterVarsity Press; Grand
Rapids, Mich.: Eerdmans, 1991), 395.
[28]This point is made by Sir Edwyn Hoskyns in *The Fourth Gospel*, ed. F. N. Davey
(London: Faber and Faber, 1954); quoted in Morris, "John," 523.

Achieving the will of God was an aim of the Jewish religion. The Jews here, however, accused Jesus of "claim[ing] to be God" (John 10:33).

In response to the anger of the Jews, Jesus quoted from the Psalms and said, "Is it not written in your Law, 'I have said you are gods'?" (John 10:34). This is used by groups like the Jehovah's Witnesses and the Muslims to deny the deity of Christ. They say that when John says Jesus is God he means it in a different sense to what Trinitarian Christians claim. We must remember that Jesus was in an argument here. Jesus goes on to say, "If he called them 'gods,' to whom the word of God came—and the Scripture cannot be broken—what about the one whom the Father set apart as his very own and sent into the world? Why then do you accuse me of blasphemy because I said, 'I am God's Son'?" (John 10:35-36).

As Don Carson shows, Jesus is saying that "this Scripture proves that the word 'god' is legitimately used to refer to others other than God himself. If there are others whom God (the author of Scripture) can address as 'god' and 'sons of the Most High' (i.e. sons of God), on what biblical basis should anyone object when Jesus says, 'I am God's Son.'"[29] Jesus' point is that "divine commissioning permits individuals to bear the divine title."[30] New Testament scholars tell us that Jesus is using "a typically rabbinical argument to answer his accusers."[31] As William Barclay explains, "This is one of those biblical arguments the force of which it is difficult for us to feel; but which to a Jewish Rabbi would have been entirely convincing."[32]

His opponents, the Jewish leaders, understood the implications of His claims. In a discussion about the Sabbath, Jesus made the statement, "My Father is always at his work to this very day, and I, too, am working." The next verse says, "For this reason the Jews tried all the harder to kill him; not only was he breaking the Sabbath, but he was even calling God his own Father, making himself equal with God" (John

---

[29]Carson, *The Gospel According to John*, 397.
[30]W. Gary Phillips, "An Apologetic Study of John 10.34-36," *Bibliotheca Sacra* 146 (October-December, 1989): 409, quoted in J. Carl Laney, *Moody Gospel Commentary: John* (Chicago: Moody Press, 1992), 197.
[31]Laney, *Moody Gospel Commentary: John*, 196.
[32]William Barclay, "The Gospel of John," *The Daily Study Bible Series*, rev. ed., vol. 2 (Philadelphia: Westminster, 1975), 78.

5.17-18). When Jesus said, "'I tell you the truth, before Abraham was born, I am!' ... they picked up stones to stone him" (John 8:58-59). Another time when "the Jews picked up stones to stone him" (John 10:31), they explained their action saying, "We are not stoning you for any of these, but for blasphemy, because you, a mere man, claim to be God" (John 10:33).

The above discussion shows that there are many different ways in which Jesus' statements imply His deity. Some explicitly proclaim His deity. In other cases it is implicit. But the implication is a necessary one, especially in the fourth gospel where these cases must be taken alongside the explicit statements about His deity.

Someone said of the words of Christ, "If it is not superhuman authority that speaks to us here, it is surely superhuman arrogance."[33] A person named Bronson Alcott once told the Scottish writer Thomas Carlyle that he could honestly use the words of Jesus, "I and the Father are one." Carlyle responded saying, "Yes, but Jesus got the world to believe him."[34]

There can be no doubt that Jesus viewed Himself as the Absolute. There are some who reject these claims saying they appear in John, which is a highly theological document and therefore should not be taken as an objective account of what Jesus said. I will refute this claim in chapter 6. But here I will say that this picture of uniqueness does not come only from John's gospel. I have shown in my book *The Christian's Attitude Toward World Religions* that the first three gospels also clearly proclaim this truth.[35]

The special feature about the teaching of Jesus is how closely it is associated with Himself. Griffith Thomas said, "There is no word in his teaching that he does not in some way make to depend on himself."[36] Many, like Mahatma Gandhi, who esteem highly the life and teaching of Christ, nevertheless reject His claims. They say that the principle has priority over the person. What is important is the teaching, not so much

---

[33]Quoted in Thomas, *Christianity Is Christ*, 26.

[34]Ibid., 25.

[35]Ajith Fernando, *The Christian's Attitude Toward World Religions* (Wheaton, Ill.: Tyndale House, 1987), 84-85.

[36]Thomas, *Christianity Is Christ*, 38.

the one who communicated it.[37] But that approach is not possible with the teaching of Christ. Here *the principle is the person.* As Griffith Thomas points out, "There is scarcely a passage in the Gospels without a self-assertion of Jesus coming out in connection with his teaching. His message and his claims are really inextricable."[38] If you remove His claims, you will have to remove His life and teachings also. These three are so closely linked that you cannot remove one and keep the other.

THE MUSLIM RESPONSE TO CHRIST'S CLAIMS

The Muslims view Christ's claims to equality with God in much the same way as Christ's Jewish contemporaries did. But unlike those Jews, they treat Jesus as a prophet.[39] The Qur'an accepts His virgin birth and His miracles, and Jesus is the only one described in the Qur'an as being sinless. It calls Him "the Messiah," "the Word of God," "the sure saying," "a spirit sent from God," "the Servant of God," and "the Prophet of God." The *Traditions,* which is the next most important source of authority in Islam, describe Christ as an intercessor in heaven and as a judge.

But Islam rejects some key claims of Christ about His person. The major stumbling block is the deity of Christ. In Islam there is only one sin that God cannot forgive, and that is the association of partners with God. God is viewed as being so transcendent and indescribably great and a unity that to associate a human with God is the unforgivable sin that they call *shirk.* This is applied in the Qur'an to the concept of the Trinity. It talks with horror about the idea of God's having a son.

It may be that the prophet Muhammad had been exposed to a sub-Christian view of the Trinity. He may indeed have rejected the idea that the Trinity consisted of the Father, Jesus, and Mary and the idea that the relationship between the Father and the Son was a purely physical relationship, that God married and had a son. Islamics scholar Kenneth Cragg thinks that what the Qur'an "repeatedly . . . disavows . . . is not

---

[37]On Gandhi's view, see M. M. Thomas, *The Acknowledged Christ of the Indian Renaissance* (London: SCM Press, 1969), 200, 236.

[38]Thomas, *Christianity Is Christ,* 41.

[39]For a summary of the Islamic view of Christ, see Colin Chapman, *Christianity on Trial* (Wheaton, Ill.: Tyndale House, 1974), 406-11.

the Christian doctrine of incarnation, but the Christian heresy of adoptionism." This is the idea that Jesus was essentially a human and then was elevated to the status of son of God; that is, that He climbed up to be God. Cragg thinks that by presenting a biblical picture of Christ's person we could overcome many of the repudiations in the Qur'an.[40]

In spite of all this, we must remember that the Qur'an has Jesus in a very unique position. I have been told that there are Muslims who have come to faith in Christ by reading the Qur'an. They became curious about all that is said about Christ and were led to make inquiries about him, which resulted in their conversion to Christ. There is a small group of excommunicated Muslims in Nigeria called Isawa (literally "Jesus-ists") who have concluded, by reading the Qur'an, that Jesus is superior to Muhammad. They deny the death and resurrection of Christ in keeping with the teaching of the Qur'an; but their existence is evidence of the power of the testimony of the Qur'an to Christ.[41]

Colin Chapman says that this is a good place to begin when talking with Muslims. He suggests asking the Muslim, "If you accept the Qur'an as a reliable source of evidence about Jesus but are not satisfied with the incompleteness of this picture, are you willing to supplement it with the fuller picture of Jesus in the Gospels?"[42] Stephen Neill points out that it may be difficult to persuade a Muslim to do this. For one thing the typical devout Muslim would say that there is no need to supplement what the Qur'an says about Jesus, for the Qur'an is the very Word of God. Then he would say that if the New Testament picture of Christ contradicts the description of Christ in the Qur'an, the New Testament must be wrong because the Qur'an is God's Word.[43] In spite of these hazards, the endeavor to get a Muslim to read the Gospels is well worth attempting.

Chapman points out that the original disciples were as firmly con-

---

[40]Kenneth Cragg, "Islam and Incarnation," in *Truth and Dialogue*, ed. John Hick (London: Sheldon Press, 1974), 138-39; quoted in Neill, *Supremacy of Jesus*, 116-17.

[41]Reported by Stan Guthrie, "Muslim Mission Breakthrough," *Christianity Today*, 13 December 1993, 26.

[42]Chapman, *Christianity on Trial*, 409.

[43]Stephen Neill, *Crises of Belief* (London: Hodder and Stoughton, 1984), 82 (North American edition, *Christian Faith and Other Faiths* [Downers Grove, Ill.: InterVarsity Press]).

vinced as any Muslim that God is one. "It was their basic creed, their basic assumption." At first they could not believe that Jesus was claiming to be God, as the Gospel records show (e.g., John 14:7-9). However, says Chapman, "through their contact with Jesus over a period of three years they were gradually forced by what they saw and heard and experienced to *revise* their understanding of the oneness of God. They did not *reject it;* they simply revised their idea of oneness in the light of the inescapable evidence which confronted them."[44] In this way we are able to confront the Muslim with the uniqueness of Christ without some of the misunderstandings of Christianity that horrify the Muslim.

CONCLUSION

We have shown that in Christianity the teaching of the founder is inextricably linked with His claims about Himself. Griffith Thomas named his classic book on Jesus, *Christianity Is Christ* and opened the book with the words, "Christianity is the only religion in the world which rests on the person of its founder."[45] Following the Christian practice of naming a religion after its founder, westerners sometimes call Islam "Mohammedanism" and Muslims "Mohammedans." But the Muslims do not approve of this. Muhammad is only a prophet, a passive recipient of revelation, not the basis of their faith. Muslims place the emphasis on God when they refer to their religion (*Islam* means "submission to God," and *Muslim* means "one who lives his life according to God's will"). The followers of Jesus, however, had no qualms about accepting the name *Christian* that was given to them in Antioch (Acts 11:26).

At the time of the death of the Buddha, his followers asked him how it would be best to remember him. But "he simply urged them not to trouble themselves about such a question. It did not matter much whether they remembered him or not. The essential thing was the teaching."[46] Jesus, on the other hand, shortly before His death, institut-

---

[44]Chapman, *Christianity on Trial*, 410 (italics his).

[45]Thomas, *Christianity Is Christ*, 1.

[46]This point is made by H. D. Lewis in *World Religions* (London, 1966), 174, and quoted by Sir Norman Anderson in *Christianity and the World Religions* (Leicester and Downers Grove, Ill.: InterVarsity Press, 1984), 80.

ing the Lord's Supper, said, "This is my body given for you; do this in remembrance of me" (Luke 22:19).

Clearly, the way that Jesus taught depended on His person. We will see in the next chapter that His words were backed by His life and that this adds to the inescapable nature of the claims of Christ. I will close this chapter with the memorable words of C. S. Lewis in his book *Mere Christianity*. He was trying to explain that it is a really foolish thing to say about Christ, "I am ready to accept Jesus as a great moral teacher, but I don't accept his claim to be God." Lewis says:

> That is one thing we must not say. A man who was merely a man and said the sort of things Jesus said would not be a great moral teacher. He would either be a lunatic—on a level with the man who says he is a poached egg—or else he would be the devil of hell. You can shut him up for a fool, you can spit at him and kill him as a demon; or you can fall at his feet and call him Lord and God. But let us not come with any patronizing nonsense about His being a great human teacher. He has not left that open to us. He did not intend to.[47]

---

[47]C. S. Lewis, *Mere Christianity* (New York: Macmillan, 1952), 56.

CHAPTER FOUR

HIS WORKS
AUTHENTICATE
HIS WORDS

WE HAVE LOOKED at the sayings of Jesus and said that they clearly imply that He is the absolute, divine Lord. But could Jesus have been mistaken in making the claims He made for Himself? In this chapter we will show that the way He lived and the things He did make such a conclusion impossible. We showed how in John 14 Jesus says He is one with God (John 14:7-10a) and how as evidence of that He appeals to His words: "The words I say to you are not just my own. Rather, it is the Father, living in me, who is doing his work" (verse 10b). Then to those who may find it difficult to accept His words, He presents His works as authenticating His words (John 14:11).

BELIEVING BECAUSE OF THE WORKS OF JESUS

Jesus says, "Believe me when I say that I am in the Father and the Father is in me; or at least believe on the evidence of the miracles themselves" (John 14:11). Jesus makes some very bold claims in the Gospels, but He recognizes that some will find it difficult to believe these, and He gives them His works as aids to belief.

The NIV translates the word for these aids as *miracles*. The word used here, *ergon*, "refers especially to his miracles, but the expression is general enough to include all the good deeds that Jesus did, miraculous or not."[1] "Works" is a more literal translation. So, we believe that all the works of Jesus were meant by this statement. We will study the works of Christ by looking first at His matchless life, which demonstrates that He is suited to be the perfect mediator between God and humankind, and then by looking at His miracles.

SUITED TO BE THE PERFECT MEDIATOR

HIS BIRTH AND EARLY LIFE

Right from the incidents surrounding His birth, Jesus' experience presented a unique mingling of transcendent divinity and sheer humanity. His birth was the result of a virginal conception. (Some theologians today prefer to use the term *virginal conception* rather than *virgin birth* because the latter name could lead to misunderstandings not implied by the biblical records.) This has been rejected by those who reject the miraculous elements in the Bible. But their arguments have been brilliantly countered, even by scholars of an earlier generation like J. Gresham Machen[2] and James Orr.[3] There has been debate in the church as to whether the virginal conception was necessary for the divinity and the sinlessness of Christ. The Bible does not seem to clearly affirm that. But it does affirm that He was "conceived by the Holy Spirit [and] born of the Virgin Mary," as the creeds put it (see Matt. 1:18-25; Luke 1:26-38). It was a sign that Jesus had a very special divine mission that was going to prove Him more than an ordinary human being.[4]

Yet the circumstances of His birth present Him as facing limitations typical of ordinary human beings. Luke puts it succinctly when he says, "and she gave birth to her firstborn, a son. She wrapped him in strips of cloth and placed him in a manger, because there was no room for them in the inn" (Luke 2:7). R. T. France and others have shown that the

---

[1]Leon Morris, *New Testament Theology* (Grand Rapids, Mich.: Zondervan, 1986), 244.
[2]J. Gresham Machen, *The Virgin Birth of Christ* (1930; reprint, Grand Rapids, Mich.: Baker, 1974).
[3]James Orr, *The Virgin Birth of Christ* (New York: Scribner's, 1907).
[4]For a discussion of the significance of the Virgin Birth, see Millard J. Erickson, *Christian Theology* (Grand Rapids, Mich.: Baker, 1985), 739-58.

manger in those days was not as smelly and dirty a place as our mod-ern-day representations indicate.[5] But the fact remains that He was born outside the comfort of His own home. Two groups are recorded to have visited the infant Jesus: shepherds, who were considered ordinary peo-ple in society, and wise men, who were considered extraordinary peo-ple. Both were informed of this birth in unusual ways. Then when Mary and Joseph presented Jesus at the temple, the offering they gave was two turtle-doves (Luke 2:24) rather than the usual lamb. This was a conces-sion made for those who could not afford to give a lamb (Lev. 12:8). Soon afterwards the family had to flee to Egypt to escape the wrath of Herod. Certainly, in His early years Jesus' family identified with suf-fering humanity.

We can guess that the suggestion that Jesus was an illegitimate child may have been the subject of gossip in Nazareth where Jesus grew up. The story that Jesus' father was a Roman soldier billeted in Nazareth was common in Jewish polemic against Christianity from at least the middle of the second century.[6] The one glimpse we have of Jesus' boy-hood was His conversation at the age of twelve with the teachers at the temple. There we see that His mother, unable to understand Him, rebukes Him for the way He has treated them (Luke 2:48). This, of course, has been a common experience of young people throughout history. But in the temple the people realized He was a special person: "Everyone who heard him was amazed at his understanding and his answers" (Luke 2:47).

From the observations that Joseph does not appear alongside Mary in the gospel narratives and that Jesus was known as "Mary's son" (Mark 6:3), R. T. France concludes that it is probable that Joseph died when Jesus was young . Because of this, Jesus, as the eldest son, would have had to manage the family carpentry business. France says, "With at least four younger brothers and an unknown number of sisters to be brought up [Mark 6:3], the hope of formal education beyond the normal level must have been remote." Therefore, "to the superior eyes of Jerusalem he was uneducated" (John 7:15).[7] He had experienced a handicap all too

---

[5] R. T. France, *Jesus the Radical* (Leicester: InterVarsity Press, 1989), 41-43.
[6] Ibid., 43. France quotes Origen, *Contra Celsum* i. 32.
[7] France, *Jesus the Radical*, 45.

common in poorer homes today. But His poverty would have given Him a superb education about life. So, His childhood and youth certainly prepared Him to be the one Mediator between God and humankind (1 Tim. 2:5).

HUMAN BUT SINLESS

The Bible presents Jesus as one who had feelings just like ours and who was thus capable of being tempted. But it also presents Him as being sinless. Hebrews 4:15 says, "For we do not have a high priest who is unable to sympathize with our weaknesses, but we have one who has been tempted in every way, just as we are—yet was without sin." There is great appeal here, for He was not a superhuman being above human struggle, which would make it impossible for us to identify with Him. This is the case with the Avatars (or incarnations of the gods) of Hinduism, who are described as superhuman beings.

Jesus moved like a normal person, and this was a problem, especially in His hometown, Nazareth. After He spoke at the synagogue, we are told, "All spoke well of him and were amazed at the gracious words that came from his lips. 'Isn't this Joseph's son?' they asked" (Luke 4:22). This prompted Jesus to speak about prophets not being accepted in their hometown. After that, "All the people in the synagogue were furious when they heard this. They got up, drove him out of the town, and took him to the brow of the hill on which the town was built, in order to throw him down the cliff" (Luke 4:28-29). They saw Him as Joseph's son, not as a special person.

Some of the apocryphal writings tried to make Him into a supernatural wonder-worker with sometimes bizarre stories of superhuman feats. But the Gospels have none of that. In the East, the typical gurus have an aura that separates them from normal people. People treat them with reverence and awe. Even some Christian leaders have developed this "distance of sacredness" from the people. And some of the consequences of this have been very dishonoring to God, especially when these gurus who were put on a pedestal and were accountable to no one fell into sin, showing that they were fallible human beings like anyone else. The picture we have of Jesus is not that of a distant guru but of a servant of the people who identified with them. In His presence even the worst sinners felt loved and important.

His humanness is well expressed in His vulnerability to tiredness and physical weakness. We find Him asleep in a boat while a storm raged around Him (Matt. 8:24). The earlier part of the chapter in which this incident appears gives a key to the reason for His incredibly sound sleep. Leon Morris explains, "Jesus had had a very heavy day with healing and teaching, and dealing with potential disciples. Wearied as He was with all his labor, He fell asleep and remained asleep despite the magnitude of the storm."[8] In Samaria, after a long walk, while His disciples go into the town to find food, we find Jesus seated by Jacob's well because He was "tired ... from the journey" (John 4:6). He does not have an implement to draw water from the well; so He has to ask the woman who comes there for some water. Also, most commentators are agreed that in contrast to the usual practice of the condemned one's carrying his own cross to the site of the crucifixion, Simon of Cyrene was compelled to carry Christ's cross because Christ was too weak to carry it beyond a certain point on the way to Golgotha.

We see Jesus expressing His divine and human natures beautifully at the tomb of Lazarus. As a human, He wept as He identified with His sorrowing friends (John 11:35). John says that Jesus wept after He "saw [Mary] weeping, and the Jews who had come along with her also weeping, [and] he was deeply moved in spirit and troubled" (John 11:33). But He knew that as divine Lord, He was going to raise Lazarus from the dead, and He made a statement that confirmed His divinity: "I am the resurrection and the life. He who believes in me will live, even though he dies; and whoever lives and believes in me will never die. Do you believe this?" (John 11:25-26).

When Jesus took on humanity, He did not make Himself immune from the frustrations common to humans. It amazes me that Jesus had as His treasurer Judas who "as keeper of the money bag ... used to help himself to what was put into it" (John 12:6). Most of us know the anger of having been taken for a ride by a fraud. Jesus allowed Himself to be defrauded by His own treasurer.

While at the beginning of His ministry we find Jesus overcoming the temptation of Satan with what seems like relative ease, at the end

---

[8]Leon Morris, *The Gospel According to Matthew* (Grand Rapids, Mich.: Eerdmans; Leicester: InterVarsity Press, 1992), 205.

of His ministry we find Him struggling in the garden. As Hebrews 2:18 says, "he himself suffered when he was tempted." Yet the writer goes on to say that because of this "he is able to help those who are being tempted." The previous verse says, "For this reason he had to be made like his brothers in every way, in order that he might become a merciful and faithful high priest in service to God, and that he might make atonement for the sins of the people" (Heb. 2:17). His full humanity certainly qualified Him to be our mediator and leader.

His sinlessness also qualified Him to be this. First Peter 2:22 says, "'He committed no sin, and no deceit was found in his mouth.'" First John 3:5 says, "But you know that he appeared so that he might take away our sins. And in him is no sin." Second Corinthians 5:21 says, "God made him who had no sin to be sin for us, so that in him we might become the righteousness of God." Jesus Himself claimed to be without sin. He said, "Can any of you prove me guilty of sin? If I am telling the truth, why don't you believe me?" (John 8:46).

Yet Jesus said so much about the importance of admitting *our* sinfulness. He began His kingdom manifesto, the Sermon on the Mount, with four surprising statements: "Blessed are the poor in spirit"; "Blessed are those who mourn"; "Blessed are the meek"; "Blessed are those who hunger and thirst for righteousness" (Matt. 5:3-6). These are people who accept their sinfulness and weaknesses.

He told the story of a Pharisee who, proud of his righteousness, went away without God's righteousness, while a sinner who confessed his sinfulness was accepted by God (Luke 18:9-14). He taught His disciples to ask to be forgiven whenever they prayed. Yet He Himself never gave a hint that He had sinned. The best reason we have for believing in the sinlessness of Jesus is the fact that He allowed His dearest friends to think that He was sinless. As C. E. Jefferson points out "There is in all his talk, no trace of regret or hint of compunction, or suggestion of sorrow or shortcoming, or slightest vestige of remorse."[9]

This fact is all the more powerful because the Gospels, frank accounts of His life, do not hide embarrassing facts. Few events are recorded in all four gospels. But all four record Peter's denial of Christ

---

[9]Quoted in Sir Norman Anderson, *Jesus Christ: The Witness of History* (Leicester and Downers Grove, Ill.: InterVarsity Press, 1985), 62.

(Matt. 26:69-75; Mark 14:66-72; Luke 22:56-62; John 18:15-18, 25-27), even though he was a revered leader in the church at the time the Gospels were written. James and John were also revered figures, but we find silly statements by them about fire falling on Samaria because the people there did not accept Christ's teaching (Luke 9.54) and about their ambition to be above the rest of the apostles (Mark 10:35-45). We have records of the disciples quarreling on the eve of the Crucifixion (Luke 22:24-30).

I would like to add to this an observation that the famed New Testament scholar Leon Morris makes that "the Gospels never praise Jesus." He says, "I do not think there is any word of praise for the Master in any one of the four gospels from start to finish. The evangelists simply record what happened, and let it go at that." Morris confesses that he does not know how the evangelists were able to do this. He says, "I think it would be very difficult for any Christian today, or for that matter in any age, to compose a writing about Jesus the length of a gospel and never for one moment slip into praise. Yet this the four evangelists did."[10] Occasionally we have a report of people praising Him, but there is no praise coming from the evangelists themselves.

GOOD AND CAPABLE

This is an age when young people are disillusioned with their leaders. There is a cynicism in people's minds when they think about leadership. Capable leaders are usually unscrupulous people who get to the top by using many unjust methods and continue to do this after becoming leaders. Good people are usually nice people who are quite ineffective and thus achieve very little in life. The expression "goody-goody" is used of people today in a derogatory sense.

Often in movies and on TV, a Christian minister is portrayed either as a fraud or as a nice fellow whose thinking is up in the clouds, one who is totally out of touch with reality. He is a person clumsy with His hands and quite out of place in a situation where practical skill is required. All He can do is to pray when He should be acting to avert a crisis. John P. Meier, in a recent book on Jesus, refers to "the airy weakling often

---

[10]Leon Morris, *The Lord from Heaven* (Downers Grove, Ill.: InterVarsity Press, 1974), 21.

presented to us in pious paintings and Hollywood movies." He says that such a person "would hardly have survived the rigors of being Nazareth's *tekton* [woodworker], from his youth to his early thirties."[11] Meier says that as the village woodworker Jesus must have possessed a fair level of technical skill and must have been physically strong.

So, Jesus was a good person, the perfect person. But He was also an achiever. In fact, He achieved more than any person has in the history of the world. Carl Henry observes that "the three years of Jesus' public ministry have stimulated more comment and literature across nineteen centuries than any other comparable segment of human history."[12] The words of H. G. Wells in his book *Outline of History* gives us a clue as to how historians view His influence. Wells was not an orthodox Christian, but he has several pages in this book on the impact of Jesus. Here are some of the things he says:

> He was like some terrible moral huntsman digging mankind out of the snug burrows in which they had lived hitherto.... Is it any wonder that men were dazzled and blinded and cried out against him? ... Is it any wonder that to this day this Galilean is too much for our small hearts?[13]

Jesus inaugurated a movement that within three centuries won the allegiance of the mighty Roman Empire. This is all the more impressive because Jesus was a Jew. R. T. France points out that "the Jews among whom Jesus lived and died, were a strange, remote people, little understood and little liked by most Europeans of the time, more often the butt of Roman humor than of serious interest."[14] Therefore, predictably Jesus received almost no attention in the Roman history

---

[11]John P. Meier, *A Marginal Jew: Rethinking the Historical Jesus* (Garden City, N.Y.: Doubleday, 1991), quoted in N. T. Wright, "The New Unimproved Jesus," *Christianity Today*, September 13, 1993, 24.

[12]Carl F. H. Henry, *A Plea for Evangelical Demonstration* (Grand Rapids, Mich.: Baker, 1971), 55.

[13]H. G. Wells, *The Outline of History*, 4th ed. (New York: The Review of Reviews Co., 1992), quoted in John Young, *The Case against Christ* (London: Hodder and Stoughton, 1986), 142.

[14]R. T. France, *The Evidence for Jesus* (Downers Grove, Ill.: InterVarsity Press; London: Hodder and Stoughton, 1986), 20.

books of the time. Yet, within three centuries Rome had bowed its knee to Him.

So, His matchless life attests His deity. And His experience of the frustrations and pain of humanity attests His humanity.

HIS MIRACLES

The second way of looking at the works of Jesus is through His miracles, which may have been what Jesus primarily meant when He asked the disciples to believe Him because of His works.

The Gospels give three motives for the miracles of Jesus. The first motive is *compassion*. On the way to Jericho when two men told Jesus, "Lord, we want our sight," the text says, "Jesus had compassion on them and touched their eyes" (Matt. 20:29-34). When He fed the four thousand, we are told that Jesus had compassion on the people because they had been three days with nothing to eat (Mark 8:1-13).

Second, the miracles were *a means of glorifying God.* When the disciples asked why a man had been born blind, Jesus said, "this happened so that the work of God might be displayed in his life" (John 9:3).

Third, the miracles were presented as *evidence to support the claims of Christ.* When the people murmured about Jesus' statement to the paralytic that His sins were forgiven, He healed the man, saying He did it so "that you may know that the Son of Man has authority on earth to forgive sins" (Mark 2:8-11). When the Jews accused Him of blasphemy saying, "you, a mere man, claim to be God" (John 10:33), Jesus said in His response, "Do not believe me unless I do what my Father does. But if I do it, even though you do not believe me, believe the miracles, that you may learn and understand that the Father is in me, and I in the Father" (John 10:37-38). Similarly, when John the Baptist had doubts about whether Jesus was the Messiah, Jesus told John's disciples to go and report about the miracles and that the Gospel was preached to the poor (Matt. 11:2-5). The miracles, then, were an aid to the inquiring mind, aimed at pointing people to a deeper truth about Jesus.

Now, it is said that others have also done miracles as claims to their divinity. Today the Indian guru Sathya Sai Baba, who claims to be an incarnation of the god Shiva, is credited with performing many miracles. But this should not surprise us. Jesus Himself and the book of Revelation predicted that in the last days false messiahs would come performing many miracles, so that many would be deceived. The Bible accepts that demonic forces have some, though limited, miraculous power. We must not think that demonic forces always manifest themselves in gross and ugly ways. If that were so, many would not be deceived. Sometimes they can come in sophisticated and godly looking ways. Paul said, "Satan himself masquerades as an angel of light" (2 Cor. 11:14).

Yet, we must remember that the miracles are not the only proof of the claims of Christ. They are only one of the witnesses. It is the whole message, and primarily His death and resurrection, that makes the case for the uniqueness of Christ. The Resurrection, of course, is the final and decisive proof, as we shall show in chapter 15. Craig Blomberg says, "No religion stands or falls with a claim about the resurrection of its founder in the way that Christianity does."[15]

REMOVING THE MIRACLES FROM THE STORY

There are some who try to remove the miracles from the story of Jesus as recorded in the Gospels. But the connection between the works and words of Jesus is so close that you cannot separate one from the other. As a writer from an earlier generation said, "The narratives of miracles are woven into the very texture of the evangelical record. How many of the sayings of Jesus are closely linked with works of healing? How many of the most beautiful and attractive traits in the portrait of Jesus are drawn from his dealing with sufferers who came to him for relief?"[16]

If we remove the miracles, we are left with no story at all. Sir Norman Anderson says that the attempt of the older liberal theologians to remove the miraculous from the life of Jesus "was doomed to failure, for they found that the miracles were so intertwined with the teaching,

---

[15]Craig Blomberg, *The Historical Reliability of the Gospels* (Leicester and Downers Grove, Ill.: InterVarsity Press, 1987), 77.

[16]A. F. Garvie, *Studies in the Inner Life of Jesus* (London: Hodder and Stoughton, 1907), 51, quoted in W Griffith Thomas, *Christianity Is Christ* (1948; reprint, New Canaan, Conn.: Keats Publishing, 1981), 48.

and the supernatural with the natural, that they could not discard the one and retain the other."[17]

ARE MIRACLES SCIENTIFICALLY IMPOSSIBLE?

There are those who reject the miraculous elements of the Gospels on the grounds that the miracles could not have happened. Others have ably responded to this challenge, and the reader is directed to several good books on this topic.[18] In chapter 6 we will see that the miracle stories cannot be easily dismissed from the viewpoint of historical studies. Here I will make a brief comment about the challenge from science.

Some people say that miracles are scientifically impossible, that they are a violation of the laws of nature. We do not agree. Craig Blomberg points out that "despite all the marvelous advances of physics, no one has yet proved, if God ... exists, why he might not occasionally suspend or transcend the otherwise fixed regularities of nature."[19] His point is that if you introduce a new causal agent, the force of whose activity supersedes that of the so-called forces of nature, then no physical principles are violated. We say that such a causal agent did indeed exist, and that this agent is God, the Creator of nature, who is above nature and can act upon nature.

We do not believe that this is a closed universe, as the deists and the atheists do. We believe that there is a Creator God who can intervene in the affairs of this world. This makes it theoretically possible, if God is more powerful than the so-called forces of nature, for Him to supersede the forces of nature and act in ways we call miraculous. We say that God does indeed do this occasionally.

Blomberg brings an analogy from the behavior of human beings. Despite our finite powers, by freely choosing to start and end various actions, we regularly bring about events that would not have occurred

---

[17]Anderson, *Jesus Christ: The Witness of History*, 26-27.

[18]Colin Brown, *Miracles and the Critical Mind* (Exeter: Paternoster Press; Grand Rapids, Mich.: Eerdmans, 1984); Colin Brown, *That You May Believe: Miracles and Faith Then and Now* (Exeter: Paternoster; Grand Rapids, Mich.: Eerdmans, 1985); Norman L. Geisler, *Miracles and Modern Thought* (Grand Rapids, Mich.: Zondervan; Exeter: Paternoster, 1982); and C. S. Lewis, *Miracles* (London: Geoffrey Bles; New York: Macmillan, 1947).

[19]Blomberg, *Historical Reliability of the Gospels*, 75.

by natural forces alone. A good example is the damming of a river to form a reservoir. Blomberg says, "If persons can change the physical world, how much more ought God to be able to do so!"[20] Norman Geisler explains this as follows: "Belief in miracles does not destroy the *integrity* of scientific methodology, only its *sovereignty.* It says in effect that science does not have a sovereign claim to explain all events as natural, but only those that are regular, repeatable and/or predictable."[21] P. Medawer recently wrote a book called *The Limits of Science,* where he shows that the notion that science has proved the supernatural impossible must be abandoned.[22]

I have used the expression "so-called forces of nature" above. This is because the miracles are not supernatural events if we were to look at them biblically. As Steve Bishop points out, "God is the God of the laws of nature: he does not violate his own principles to work a miracle. Miracles are natural events." Bishop describes them as "part of the created order."[23] This is the Christian approach to the relationship between science, nature, and miracles.[24]

So, we say that the objection to miracles on the grounds that they are contrary to science does not stand. In fact, if we believe that there is a supreme God who is Creator of the universe, the case against miracles fades away even more.

Coming to the accounts of the miracles in the Gospels, if these accounts are shown to be historically reliable, then we have no legitimate grounds for rejecting their authenticity. And this is what we hope to show in chapter 6.

---

[20]Ibid., 75.

[21]Geisler, *Miracles and Modern Thought,* 58, quoted in Blomberg, *Historical Reliability of the Gospels,* 75.

[22]P. Medawer, *The Limits of Science* (San Francisco: Harper & Row, 1984; Oxford: Oxford University Press, 1985), quoted in Blomberg, *Historical Reliability of the Gospels,* 76. Medawer, incidentally, denies God's existence due to the problem of evil.

[23]Steve Bishop, "Science and Faith: Boa Constrictors and Warthogs?" *Themelios* 19, no. 1 (October 1993): 8.

[24]For more on this see J. H. Deimer, *Nature and Miracle* (Toronto: Wedge Publishing Foundation, 1977) and John Polkinghorne, *Science and Providence: God's Interaction with the World* (London: SPCK, 1989).

THE CLAIMS ARE BACKED
BY THE WORKS

This, then, is the evidence to support our claim that Jesus is absolute Lord and thus the communicator of absolute truth: He made this claim for Himself through His words. Those words were divine in that they were amazingly attractive and made claims that were outrageously audacious. He backed these claims by His works, which consisted of His spotless life and His miracles, the supreme one of which was His resurrection from the dead. The point I am trying to make is this: if one were to really consider the life of Christ, that person would have to come to grips with His claims, for His life authenticates His words.

I have a friend in Sri Lanka who was a devout Buddhist and a voracious reader. One day he went to his city's public library and checked out a book on the life of Christ. After reading it he realized that Jesus' life was unparalleled in human history. He knew he had to do something about the claims Jesus made. He went in search of someone who could tell him more about Christ. This contact with Christians led to his becoming a fervent follower of Jesus Christ.

DOES THE NEW TESTAMENT TEACH
THE DEITY OF CHRIST?

A book of this nature would be incomplete without at least a brief note on whether the New Testament really teaches that Jesus is God. We have already implied that it does when we looked at evidence for the supremacy of Christ. But I have encountered some sincere Christians who, possibly through the influence of the arguments put forth by cultists and others, think that the deity of Christ is not taught in the Scriptures but was deduced by the church after the New Testament era. There is ample evidence, however, that the New Testament writers also believed in Christ's deity. This chapter and chapter 3 has already given some of this evidence. I give below a comprehensive list of New Testament evidences for the deity of Christ. This list is from a brilliant book on the use of the word *God* (*theos* in Greek) in reference to Jesus in the New Testament, called *Jesus as God* and written by New Testament scholar Murray Harris.[25] Some of the points in this list have appeared already in my treatment of the words and works of Jesus.

A. Implicit Christology
   1. Divine functions performed by Jesus.
      a. In relation to the universe
         (1) Creator (John 1:3; Col. 1:16; Heb. 1:2)
         (2) Sustainer (1 Cor. 8:6; Col. 1:17; Heb. 1:3)
         (3) Author of Life (John 1:4; Acts 3:15)
         (4) Ruler (Matt. 28:18; Rom. 14:9; Rev. 1:5)
      b. In relation to human beings
         (1) Healing the sick (Mark 1:32-34; Acts 3:6; 10:38)
         (2) Teaching authoritatively (Mark 1:21-22; 13:31)
         (3) Forgiving sins (Mark 2:1-12; Luke 24:47; Acts 5:31; Col. 3:13)
         (4) Granting salvation or imparting eternal life (Acts 4:12; Rom. 10:12-13)
         (5) Dispensing the Spirit (Matt. 3:11; Acts 2:17, 33)
         (6) Raising the dead (Luke 7:11-17; John 5:21; 6:40)
         (7) Exercising judgment (Matt. 25:31-46; John 5:19-30; Acts 10:42; 1 Cor. 4:4-5)
   2. Divine status claimed by or accorded to Jesus.
      a. In relation to his Father
         (1) Possessor of divine attributes (John 1:4; 10:30; 21:17; Eph. 4:10; Col. 1:19; 2:9)
         (2) Eternally existent (John 1:1; 8:58; 12:41; 17:5; 1 Cor. 10:4; Phil. 2:6; Heb. 11:26; 13:8; Jude 5)
         (3) Equal in dignity (Matt. 28:19; John 5:23; 2 Cor. 13:14; Rev. 22:13; cf. 21:6)
         (4) Perfect revealer (John 1:18; 14:9; Col. 1:15; Heb. 1:1-3)
         (5) Embodiment of truth (John 1:9, 14; 6:32; 14:6; Rev. 3:7, 14)
         (6) Joint possessor of the kingdom (Eph. 5:5; Rev. 11:15), churches (Rom. 16:16), Spirit (Rom. 8:9; Phil 1:19), temple (Rev. 21:22), divine name (Matt. 28:19; cf. Rev. 14:1), and throne (Rev. 22:1, 3)
      b. In relation to human beings

---

[25]Murray J. Harris, *Jesus as God* (Grand Rapids, Mich.: Baker, 1992), 315-17. Harris expands on these points in his more recent book, *3 Crucial Questions About Jesus* (Grand Rapids, Mich.: Baker, 1994), 65-103.

(1) Recipient of praise (Matt. 21:15-16; Eph. 5:20; 1 Tim. 1:12; Rev. 5:8-14)

(2) Recipient of prayer (Acts 1:24; 7:59-60; 9:10-17, 21; 22:16, 19; 1 Cor. 1:2; 16:22; 2 Cor. 12:8)

(3) Object of saving faith (John 14:1; Acts 10:43; 16:31; Rom. 10:8-13)

(4) Object of worship (Matt. 14:33; 28:9, 17; John 5:23; 20:28; Phil. 2:10-11; Heb. 1:6; Rev. 5:8-12)

(5) Joint source of blessing (1 Cor. 1:3; 2 Cor. 1:2; Gal. 1:3; 1 Thess. 3:11; 2 Thess. 2:16)

(6) Object of doxologies (2 Tim. 4:18; 2 Pet. 3:18; Rev. 1:5b-6; 5:13)

B. Explicit Christology

   1. Old Testament passages referring to Yahweh applied to Jesus

      a. Character of Yahweh (Exod. 3:14 and Isa. 43:11 alluded to in John 8:58; Ps. 101:27-28 LXX[26] [MT[27] 102:28-29] quoted in Heb. 1:11-12; Isa. 44:6 alluded to in Rev. 1:17)

      b. Holiness of Yahweh (Isa. 8:12-13 [cf. 29:23] quoted in 1 Pet. 3:14-15)

      c. Descriptions of Yahweh (Ezek. 43:2 and Dan. 10:5-6 alluded to in Rev. 1:13-16)

      d. Worship of Yahweh (Isa. 45:23 alluded to in Phil. 2:10-11; Deut. 32:43 LXX and Ps. 96:7 LXX [MT 97:7] quoted in Heb. 1:6)

      e. Work of Yahweh in creation (Ps. 101:26 LXX [MT 102:27] quoted in Heb. 1:10)

      f. Salvation of Yahweh (Joel 2:32 [MT 3:5] quoted in Rom. 10:13; cf. Acts 2:21; Isa. 40:3 quoted in Matt. 3:3)

      g. Trustworthiness of Yahweh (Isa. 28:16 quoted in Rom. 9:33; 10:11; 1 Pet. 2:6)

      h. Judgment of Yahweh (Isa. 6:10 alluded to in John 12:41; Isa. 8:14 quoted in Rom. 9:33 and 1 Pet. 2:6)

      i. Triumph of Yahweh (Ps. 68:18 [MT v. 19] quoted in Eph. 4:8)

   2. Divine titles claimed by or applied to Jesus

      a. Son of Man (Matt. 16:28; 24:30; Mark 8:38; 14:62-64; Acts 7:56)

      b. Son of God (Matt. 11:27; Mark 15:39; John 1:18; Rom. 1:4; Gal. 4:4; Heb. 1:2)

      c. Messiah (Matt. 16:16; Mark 14:61; John 20:31)

---

[26]LXX refers to the Septuagint, which is the Greek version of the Old Testament, translated around 250 B.C.

[27]MT refers to the Masoretic Text, which is a text of the Hebrew Bible, prepared around A.D. 700.

    d. Lord (Mark 12:35-37; John 20:28; Rom. 10:9; 1 Cor. 8:5-6; 12:3; 16:22; Phil. 2:11; 1 Pet. 2:3; 3:15)

    e. Alpha and Omega (Rev. 22:13; cf. 1:8; 21:6)

    f. God (John 1:1, 18; 20:28; Rom. 9:5; Tit. 2:13; Heb. 1:8; 2 Pet. 1:1)

The bulk of Harris's book is a careful study of the texts given last in the above list: those that use the title *God* for Jesus. He shows that the application of the title *God* (*theos* in Greek) is not a late development, as is widely held, but was something used as early as a few days after the Resurrection (by Thomas in John 20:28 in A.D. 30 or 33). It was also used in Romans 9:5, which was written around A.D. 57. Harris's study challenges the view held by many that the Christology of the New Testament is entirely functional. By functional Christology is meant the idea that "the person of Christ (i.e., his unique relation to God) can be known only in his work."[28] Oscar Cullmann claimed that you cannot speak of the person of Christ apart from the work of Christ.

Harris concedes, "That the New Testament is primarily functional cannot be denied." But he points out that the "presupposition of functional Christology is ontological Christology."[29] By ontological Christology is meant "a Christology which identifies the ego of Jesus with an aspect of the Being of God." In other words the New Testament not only presents Jesus as God-in-action and God-in-revelation but also as God-by-nature.[30] Harris says, "Christ *performs* divine functions because he is divine. His ability to act 'divinely' rests on his being divine. . . . Temporally, being precedes doing. Logically, doing presupposes being."[31]

The above discussion would have shown that belief in Christ's deity is much more pronounced in the New Testament than is assumed by many people today.

The fact that the deity of Christ was proclaimed so early in the

---

[28]This is a quotation from O. Cullmann, *The Christology of the New Testament* (London: SCM, 1959). Cullmann advocates the view that "functional Christology is the only kind that exists" in the New Testament (p. 326).

[29]Harris, *Jesus as God*, 289.

[30]Ibid., 291.

[31]Ibid., 289 (italics his).

history of the church is significant. John Hick has said that the deifying of Christ by the church was similar to the deifying of the Buddha by his disciples.[32] But as James Orr has pointed out, "It was long centuries after his death, and within limited circles, that Buddha was regarded as Divine." It was very different with the deity of Christ. Orr says, "One short step takes us from the days when Christ himself lived and taught on earth, into the midst of a Church, founded by his apostles, which in all its branches worshipped and adored him as the veritable Son of God."[33]

---

[32]John Hick, "Jesus and the World Religions," in *The Myth of God Incarnate*, ed. John Hick (London: SCM Press, 1977), 168-70.

[33]James Orr, *The Christian View of God and the World* (1897; reprint, Grand Rapids, Mich.: Kregel, 1989), 217.

CHAPTER FIVE

JESUS, MIRACLES, AND MINISTRY TODAY

S TRANGE AS IT MAY SEEM, the life of Christ has had a very controversial history in the church from about the mid-nineteenth century. Two of the key questions that have occupied Christian thinkers during this century and a half has been what place the life of Christ should have in the evangelistic ministry of the church and what aspects of the record of that life in the Gospels should receive emphasis.

THE LIBERAL LIVES OF CHRIST

A theological movement that was given the name *liberalism* became very prominent in the church in the West in the nineteenth century. It sought "to adapt religious ideas to modern culture and modes of thinking."[1] The life of Jesus received much attention in this movement, and books were written on the topic by prominent scholars like the German David F. Strauss (1808-74), the Frenchman J. Ernst Renan (1823-92), the Englishman John Robert Seeley (1834-95), and climaxing in the work of the German church historian and theologian Adolf Harnack (1851-

---

[1] R. V. Pierard, "Theological Liberalism," in *Evangelical Dictionary of Theology*, ed. Walter A. Elwell (Grand Rapids, Mich.: Baker, 1984), 631.

1930) in his *What Is Christianity?* But the liberals studied the life of Jesus "with the intent of stripping off the dogmatic formulations of the church and getting back to the concrete historical personage." They felt that it was "necessary to get behind the 'Christ of the creeds' to the 'Jesus of history.'"[2] In doing this they stripped the life of Jesus of miracles and supernatural features.

The aim of the liberals was to present Jesus as the ideal man. This was coupled with the liberal emphasis on human potential; and the result was an emphasis on Jesus as the supreme example. He became our Savior in the sense that He is the ideal man whose example we follow. When they considered the death of Christ, their emphasis was on its inspiration. Thus, the focus was on the Gospels, especially the Synoptic Gospels (Matthew, Mark, and Luke), as John was considered too theological. Paul was viewed as one who reinterpreted the message of Christ. Therefore, his writings were not given much importance.

THE EVANGELICAL REACTION TO LIBERALISM

Reacting to the liberal emphasis on Jesus' being our Savior through His example, those in the evangelical movement rightly focused on His atoning work on the cross, the salvation achieved for us by Christ's taking on the punishment due to us. Naturally they placed much emphasis on Paul's explanation of this work of Christ, and Paul's statements figured heavily in their evangelistic proclamation. The idea of Christ as a model was downplayed, and the Gospels, especially the Synoptic Gospels, were not used very much in evangelism. So much emphasis was placed on the fact that we do nothing to merit salvation that the message of the Lordship of Jesus was left out of evangelistic preaching. Evangelicals feared that if they preached the Lordship of Jesus, they might fall into the trap of salvation by works and the liberal error of salvation through the example of Christ rather than through His atoning work.

In some circles, saving faith was defined as intellectual assent to the fact of the atoning death of Christ. The message of Lordship was left for later instruction and, in some instances, left out altogether. I heard about a preacher who was opposed by leaders of his church as being a

---

[2]Ibid., 633.

liberal because he had preached a series of messages on Christ's Sermon on the Mount. Conversion was defined as a change in legal status from being condemned to being justified, without much emphasis being given to the change in life that accompanies conversion.

In reacting to the clearly unscriptural liberal emphasis, the evangelical movement brought back to focus the basics of the Gospel—of which the church was in desperate need of recovering. But many in this movement may have missed some important biblical emphases that God intended to be included in the Gospel. Providentially this situation seems to have changed in recent years.

USING THE LIFE OF CHRIST IN EVANGELISM

There is much evidence in the Scriptures to suggest that the life of Christ should be an integral part of our evangelistic message.

First, the evangelistic messages in the book of Acts include the life of Christ as part of their Gospel. At Pentecost, Peter presented the miracles as evidence of Christ's accreditation by God (Acts 2:22). Then, at the home of Cornelius, he summarized the life of Christ "beginning in Galilee after the baptism that John preached" and ending with His post-resurrection appearances (Acts 10:37-42). After that, he presented what we would call the typical gospel presentation: "All the prophets testify about him that everyone who believes in him receives forgiveness of sins through his name" (Acts 10:43).

Second, though some may not use the four Gospels much in evangelism today, they were originally written as evangelistic tracts. John says that he wrote his gospel with an evangelistic aim in mind: "But these are written that you may believe that Jesus is the Christ, the Son of God, and that by believing you may have life in his name" (John 20:31). The second-century church father Irenaeus wrote concerning the second gospel, "Mark, the disciple and interpreter of Peter, also transmitted to us in writing the things preached by Peter."[3] The Gospel was a record of what Peter used to preach. John Stott says that "the gospel writers are therefore correctly called 'evangelists' and their

---

[3]Irenaeus, *Against Heresies*, III. i. 2, quoted in William L. Lane, "The Gospel According to Mark" *The New International Commentary on the New Testament* (Grand Rapids, Mich.: Eerdmans, 1974), 9.

literary compositions are rightly called 'gospels.'" This is because "they were setting forth the good news of Jesus Christ with a view to inducing their readers to believe in him."[4]

Third, there is great evangelistic appeal in the life of Christ. This would have become evident from the previous two chapters. Many people who have been converted to Christ from other faiths have been first attracted to Christianity by the life of Christ. In our ministry we have used the *Jesus* film with Buddhist and Hindu audiences. Despite the length of the film (over three hours with the time taken to change reels) and the fact that it is usually screened in the open-air, large crowds have stayed on to the end and have left deeply impressed. I can think of at least one leader in our ministry whose conversion resulted from a process that began with his seeing this film.

There was a brilliant Hindu scholar named Pandita Ramabhai (1858-1922) who was very committed to the uplifting of women in India. She began a movement to help in this endeavor and often gave lectures on the topic. She established a friendship with a Christian Englishwoman who was principal of a teacher training school and who agreed to teach her English. Through the Englishwoman, Ramabhai was introduced to the New Testament. She was deeply impressed by Christ's loving and courteous attitude toward women. Soon, though she was a Hindu, she began to quote almost exclusively from the Gospels in her lectures. She later went to England, and her contact with a community of Anglican sisters resulted in her being baptized as a Christian. But she had not yet grasped the meaning of salvation by grace through faith. Her change of religion was because she had become in a general way a follower of Jesus. It was many years later that she experienced the joy of a personal relationship with the Savior, Jesus, which made her one of God's great agents of revival in India.[5]

A. V. M. Rajan, a famous Tamil film actor in India, was a Hindu and saw a commercial film on the life of Christ. He was so impressed that it

---

[4]John Stott, *The Authentic Jesus* (Basingstoke, Hants: Marshalls, 1985), 20.
[5]Taken from John T. Seamands, *Pioneers of the Younger Churches* (Nashville: Abingdon, 1967), 103-7.

led him to seek more about Jesus until he finally became a Christian. He was an effective evangelist in India for many years.[6]

Pandita Ramabhai's pilgrimage is typical of that of many converts from non-Christian backgrounds. The message of the Cross may not make much sense to them at the start. In fact, the message of sacrifice for sin can make Christianity into an abhorrent "bloody religion" to Buddhists who are "taught to reverence all kinds of life."[7] But they find the life of Jesus very attractive. This opens them to the Christian message. And that openness ultimately leads to their accepting the Gospel and their responding in faith to the message of the Cross. My wife worked with a Buddhist lady who was a follower of Christ for many years before she experienced the freedom of salvation by grace through faith.

Bishop Stephen Neill tells about how an experienced missionary, who had spent many years in Christian work among Muslims, was asked what it was in the Christian faith that drew Muslims toward it. He answered without hesitation, "The person of Jesus." We must remember that the Muslims deny that Christ died by crucifixion, as that is considered too ignoble a death for a prophet. Neill makes an interesting observation about the many books about the prophet Muhammad that have been written recently for western and Christian consumption. He claims that in "all of these the less agreeable features of the character of Muhammed have been softened down and christianized, so that the rugged Prophet of Arabia has been transformed into a kindly and beneficent reformer."

Neill imagines a situation where an "enquiring Muslim student is prepared to turn from this composite picture of Muhammed as he is actually portrayed in the Koran and the traditions, and to Jesus of Nazareth as he is actually portrayed in the Gospels." He says that this student "may discover, perhaps with dismay, that his understanding of

---

[6]Rajan related his story shortly before his death to my colleague Nadarajah Satchithanandakumar, who is himself a convert from Hinduism.

[7]Tissa Weerasingha, *The Cross and the Bo Tree* (Taichung: Asia Theological Association, 1989), 72.

religion is undergoing a subtle change, and that the attractive power of Jesus is a force which he is finding increasingly difficult to resist."[8]

Of course, we need to bear in mind the growing phenomenon of Muslim fundamentalism that is seen to be in harmony with the rugged image of Muhammad. Yet there are many sensitive Muslims who are opposed to this phenomenon. In fact, Muslim fundamentalism may help give birth to a significant reaction against its harshness, which will make the person of Jesus increasingly attractive.

Fourth, when we preach the Gospel we are asking people to receive Christ's salvation and to follow Christ as their Lord. We should tell them who this Savior is who is staking a claim to be Lord of their life. And what better way is there to introduce Christ than showing them how He lived when He was on earth?

So the life of Christ is a key aspect of our evangelistic ministry. We should pray for the day that people will be enraptured by the person of Jesus. And toward that end we should use our creative energies to get that message across through the arts, through literature, and through personal witness.

MINISTERING THROUGH SIGNS AND WONDERS[9]

In the previous chapter we presented Jesus as one who performed miracles. We said that there were three reasons why He did this. They were (1) to show compassion, (2) to glorify God, and (3) to give evidence to support His claims. For the same three reasons He can act miraculously through our ministries also. The demonstration of the power of God over demonic and physical forces is particularly significant in winning a hearing for the Gospel. Prayer is a key ingredient in this strategy. Fear is a dominant emotion in the experience of many people. When we show the power of God over demons and sickness and the like, we create in people a desire to follow our God. And this opens the door to pro-

---

[8]Stephen Neill, *Crisis of Belief* (London: Hodder and Stoughton, 1984), 90 (North American edition, *Christian Faith and Other Faiths* [Downers Grove, Ill.: InterVarsity Press]).

[9]Many of the points in this section were presented in a paper, *Evangelizing Sri Lanka: Issues facing the Church*, published by the Navodaya Committee in Sri Lanka in 1992. It was the product of a subgroup of this committee, and I served as the writer for the group. I am grateful to my colleagues for permission to use this material here.

claiming the Gospel of the saving grace of Christ. It tells people who would otherwise not be interested in our message that this is a Gospel worthy of a hearing.

This ministry was certainly prominent in the book of Acts. In fact, when the first Christians faced the crisis of having evangelism outlawed, they had two petitions in their prayer. One was that they would "speak your word with great boldness" (Acts 4:29) The other was, "Stretch out your hand to heal and perform miraculous signs and wonders through the name of your holy servant Jesus" (Acts 4:30). Paul said regarding his ministry: "Christ has accomplished through me [the] leading [of] the Gentiles to obey God by what I have said and done—by the power of signs and miracles, through the power of the Spirit" (Rom. 15:18b-19a; see also 1 Thess. 1:5). This is part of the evidence regarding the Gospel that contributes to persuading people of its reality.

In the church that our family attends, a majority of the members are converts from Buddhism and Hinduism. About half of them were first led to seek the God of the Bible through a need in their life that friends told them would be answered by God. The day that I write these words we will baptize four converts from Buddhism. One is a person who has struggled with addiction to drugs. His wife brought him to church a few weeks after he had been released from prison. On the first Sunday he came, we took him to the Communion rails and knelt with him and asked God to help him overcome this terrible bondage to which he was subjected. For a few months after that he came for worship somewhat irregularly. I met him fairly regularly and finally explained the Gospel to him and asked him whether he would come to Christ for salvation. He answered in the affirmative, and it has been a joy to see him grow in grace in the months that have followed.

The second person had been subject to numerous demonic influences and had been taken to a church where she was prayed over and experienced healing. Some months later she came to work as a domestic helper in the home next to our church building. Her mistress encouraged her to attend church, and within eight months she is to be baptized.

The third person is the wife of the former custodian of our church. He was a Buddhist, but he came to Christ mainly through the friendship and concern of the church members. He subsequently fell ill and died. But the relationship we developed with his family resulted in his wife's coming for worship regularly and finally accepting Christ as her Savior. Here is the case of a person who did not see miraculous signs, who in fact saw what could be considered the opposite. But other aspects of the Gospel led her to accept Christ.

The fourth person is a neighbor of the third person. When she first came she had, and continues to have, many physical and family-life problems. She asked for prayer at the first worship service she attended. As far as I know, there were no spectacular positive answers to those prayers. But God became her refuge and strength, her ever-present help in trouble (Psa. 46:1). A few weeks after she started coming, I explained the Gospel to her and asked her if she would like to let Christ be her Savior. I told her what that meant in terms of her leaving behind her old religious practices. She was willing, and now, some months later, she is ready for baptism.

Each one saw the power of God in a different way. But as I think of it now, I believe each one learned much about God by participating in prayer with Christians.

This ministry of signs and wonders has, however, been abused so much in recent years that a few words of caution are in order.

First, as this ministry deals with power, it is possible for the evangelist to be corrupted by power and give in to pride. The taste of power may cause him or her to become authoritarian in his or her other dealings. We have seen this happen in Sri Lanka with a few people with such gifts. Thus, the prayer of all those involved in such "power ministries" should be for humility. They should seek to train themselves (1 Tim. 4:7) in humility.

An effective antidote to the abuse of power is accountability to a community. An active and loving biblical community would not let one of its members persist in pride without battling the pride. It is a source of grave concern to us that many who are engaged in power ministries have not submitted themselves to the discipline of accountability to a community. They are in danger of shipwrecking their ministries.

Second, we must remember that Satan attacks with particular vehemence those who challenge his hold on people. This makes those engaged in power ministry particularly susceptible to the wiles of Satan. Thus, they should become spiritually prepared for such ministry. We know of no better way to prepare for this than through corporate and private prayer (Mark 9:29; Eph. 6:18). Another source of strength for battling Satan is Christian community. Perhaps it is because Jesus knew these dangers that He sent out His disciples for power ministry two by two (Mark 6:7; Luke 10:1). When Paul gave his comprehensive teaching on spiritual warfare in Ephesians 6:10-20, he used the plural throughout, implying that he expects spiritual warfare to be done in teams rather than alone.

Third, the demonstration of power is very spectacular and effective in attracting crowds, but this could dethrone the Gospel from its place of supreme importance in evangelism. Power ministry must always be viewed as a servant of the Gospel and aimed at pointing people to the Gospel. Paul said that it is "the gospel" that is the power of God to salvation (Rom. 1:16). What follows that statement in Romans shows that by *"gospel"* Paul meant the work of God in justifying those who believe by the grace that flows from His cross (Rom. 1:16–5:21).

One who has not understood this basic Gospel stands on very shaky ground. In this present age Satan still has power, and the effects of the Fall are not completely rooted out from the earth. Therefore, Christians will have times when God will withhold His power and will not answer a prayer in the exact way in which we ask. At such a time those who have no grounding in the Gospel could get discouraged and fall away. Those who have a fuller understanding of God's nature are able to believe Him in the bleak times. They have the assurance that God will turn even the bleak experience into something good (Rom. 8:28).

Our goal in power ministry should be to elicit a response like that of Sergius Paulus to the power ministry of Paul in Paphos. When Sergius Paulus saw the power of God as God struck the false prophet Elymas with blindness, "he believed, for he was amazed at the teaching about the Lord" (Acts 13:12). Belief was his reaction to the miracle. The teaching about the Lord had been faithfully done. The miracle helped orient him in the direction of accepting this teaching. The Gospel facts always have the supreme place. They must figure prominently in our preaching and teaching.

The abuses of power ministry are many. But that should not deter us from engaging in it. It is a practice modeled for us by the apostles in the book of Acts. We should never fear to be biblical. It is when this is done in an unbiblical way that the abuses arise.

CHAPTER SIX

ARE THE GOSPELS HISTORICALLY ACCURATE ACCOUNTS?

T HE JESUS OF HISTORY and the Christ of faith are two separate beings, with very different stories. It is difficult enough to reconstruct the first, and in the attempt we are likely to do irreparable harm to the second." This how the British novelist A. N. Wilson begins his controversial book *Jesus.*[1] Toward the end of his book Wilson says, "We have reached the point in our narrative where we must abandon our efforts to pursue 'what really happened.' Subjectivity is the only criterion of Gospel truth."[2]

So far we have shown that if we take what the Gospels say about Christ seriously, then we must say that He is Absolute Truth. But people like A. N. Wilson say that what the Gospels present is not the Jesus of history, but the Christ of faith. That is, the Gospels are said to be a reflection of the faith of those who wrote them rather than an

---

[1]A. N. Wilson, *Jesus: A Life* (New York: Ballantine, 1992), vii.
[2]Ibid., 240-41.

accurate record of the life of Jesus. A recent work produced by seventy-four New Testament scholars, who call themselves the Jesus Seminar, claims that 82 percent of what the Gospels give as the words of Jesus are inauthentic, and that the other 18 percent is only doubtfully authentic.[3]

ACCEPTING HIS HEROISM WHILE REJECTING HIS LORDSHIP

By separating the Christ of faith from the Jesus of history many people are able to keep Jesus as a heroic figure while ignoring or rejecting His claims to absoluteness. They say that those claims were not made by Christ Himself but were attributed to Christ by the early Christians. This is how Mahatma Gandhi approached the person of Christ. He said that Jesus "came as near to perfection as possible."[4] Listen to what he says: "The gentle figure of Christ, so patient, so kind, so loving, so full of forgiveness that he taught his followers not to retaliate when abused or struck but to turn the other cheek—it was a beautiful example, I thought, of the perfect man."[5] He said, "The message of Jesus, as I understand it, is contained in his Sermon on the Mount." He said, "It is that Sermon which has endeared Jesus to me."[6] So he accepted some of the teachings of Jesus.

But Gandhi rejected the claims of Jesus. He said, "It was more than I could believe that Jesus was the only incarnate Son of God and that only he who believed in him would have everlasting life. If God could have sons, all of us were his sons. If Jesus was like God, or God himself, then all men were like God and could be God himself."[7]

Gandhi was able to do this by discarding the historical importance

---

[3]The Jesus Seminar, *The Five Gospels: The Search for the Authentic Words of Jesus* (New York: Macmillan, 1994); reported by D. A. Carson, "Five Gospels, No Christ," *Christianity Today*, April 25, 1994, 30.

[4]Quoted in M. M. Thomas, *The Acknowledged Christ of the Indian Renaissance* (London: SCM Press, 1969), 202.

[5]M. K. Gandhi, *The Message of Jesus Christ*, ed. A. T. Hingorani (Bombay: Bharatiya Vidya Bhauan, 1963), preface, quoted in Thomas, *The Acknowledged Christ*, 199.

[6]*The Message of Jesus Christ*, cover page, quoted in Thomas, *The Acknowledged Christ* 198.

[7]*The Message of Jesus Christ*, 12, 23, quoted in Thomas, *The Acknowledged Christ*, 201.

of the life of Jesus. He says, "I may say that I have never been interested in a historical Jesus. I could not care if it was proved by someone that the man called Jesus never lived, and that what was narrated in the Gospels was a figment of the writers imagination. For the Sermon on the Mount would still be true."[8] Gandhi says, "Do not preach the God of history, but show him as he lives today through you."[9]

THE GOSPELS VIEWED AS SUBJECTIVE AND NON-HISTORICAL

Gandhi is typical of the contemporary pluralist. As Indian theologian M. M. Thomas says, Gandhi affirms "the primacy of the Principle over the Person."[10] Gandhi is also a good example of the Hindu approach to religious history that is gaining in popularity all over the world. To the Hindu it is not very important whether the events of a religious story took place or not. What is important is what that story teaches. In fact, if you were to ask a person who is very devoted to Krishna whether Krishna lived or not, he would tell you that whether he lived or not is not of any significance. This is the general approach adopted by pluralists today.

To such people the idea that Christianity rests on certain events that took place in history is very strange. Events do not form the basis of religion, principles do, they would say. Lesslie Newbigin mentions a conversation that he had with a devout and learned teacher of the Hindu missionary movement, the Ramakrishna Mission. He says, "I have never forgotten the astonishment with which [the Hindu] regarded me when he discovered that I was prepared to rest my whole faith as a Christian upon the substantial historical record concerning Jesus in the New Testament." To this person "it seemed axiomatic that such vital matters of religious truth could not be allowed to depend upon the accidents of history."[11]

The pluralist would say that the New Testament gives a subjective account of what happened. Therefore, it is not historically accurate and

---

[8] *The Message of Jesus Christ*, 35, quoted in Thomas, *The Acknowledged Christ*, 199.
[9] *The Message of Jesus Christ*, 21, quoted in Thomas, *The Acknowledged Christ*, 200.
[10] Thomas, *The Acknowledged Christ*, 200.
[11] Lesslie Newbigin, *The Finality of Christ* (Richmond, Va.: John Knox, 1969), 50.

cannot be taken as absolute or objective. As truth is discovered by experience, it is said to be subjective. Truth therefore has to do with the
thinking subject—that is, the devotee—rather than to the object of
thought—that is, Jesus. The teachings of the Gospels are said to be the
ideas of the disciples based on their experiences of Christ, rather than
an objective account of what really happened.

This attitude to history is a modification of an approach to the
Gospels championed by the German theologian Rudolph Bultmann
(1884-1976). Bultmann distinguished between *historie*, which is a bare
account of what really happened, and *geschichte*, which is an account of
past events related from the perspective of the experience of the
Christians during the time the Gospels were written. So, what we have
in the Gospels is the Christ of faith. And this Christ of faith is not the
same as the historical Jesus. The Christians of the time during which the
Gospels were written were supposed to be uninterested in too much
study into what the historical Jesus did and said.

I am told that Bultmann used to preach inspiring messages on the
resurrection of Jesus. But if you were to ask him whether Jesus really
rose from the dead (the objective reality), he would say that is not
important. What is important is the subjective reality of experiencing
the resurrection life of Christ now.

So it was assumed that the Gospels do not give us a historically
reliable account of the life and ministry of Jesus. Because of this, the
pluralist can reject the claims of Christ, stating that they were not
uttered by Christ. This is particularly applied to John's gospel, which
is said to be the most theological and therefore the least historically
objective of the Gospels. I was participating in a small group at an
evangelism seminar in Sri Lanka, discussing what evangelism means to
us today in Sri Lanka. When we began to discuss the Great
Commission, a leading Roman Catholic scholar who was in our group
dismissed the topic by simply saying that the Great Commission was
not uttered by Jesus.

It has become evident that our case against pluralism depends on
the historicity of the Gospels. If Jesus did not claim the things the
Gospels say He claimed, then we cannot say that He is unique. I will
go so far as to say that the most important issue in the Christian
response to pluralism is the historical reliability of the Gospels.

THE GOSPELS PRESENT OBJECTIVE TRUTH

I will not try to give a detailed defense of the historicity of the Gospels. Several good books have been written on this.[12] Here I will only give some pointers to a response to the modern approach that rejects the objectivity of the Gospels.

EXPERIENCE DOES NOT NECESSARILY INVALIDATE ACCURACY

Lesslie Newbigin characterizes this approach to the Gospels as coming from "a false concept of objectivity—of a kind of knowledge from which the human subject has been removed."[13] Pluralists say the Gospels should not be viewed as an objective account of what really happened because the writers were so involved experientially in the story of Jesus. Rather the Gospels are said to give an account of the faith of the disciples. Passionate witnesses are assumed to "distort the evidence: they are likely to write down whatever they want you to believe, simply because they themselves believe it so strongly."[14] In response we say, in the words of Bishop Newbigin, that "what we have in the New Testament represents the faith of the disciples, namely their faith about 'what really happened.'"[15] They believed that the events really took place. The fact that they experienced the truth does not automatically take away the historical reliability of the events upon which that truth is supposed to be based.

Take the case of a statement I make that my wife is five feet tall. Just because I experience a love relationship with my wife does not make that observation inaccurate. That is an objective statement. What if I say that my wife is the most beautiful woman in the world? Most people

---

[12] I particularly recommend Craig Blomberg, *The Historical Reliability of the Gospels* (Leicester and Downers Grove, Ill.: InterVarsity Press, 1987); Colin Brown, ed., *History, Criticism and Faith* (Leicester and Downers Grove, Ill.: InterVarsity Press, 1976); F. F. Bruce, *The New Testament Documents: Are They Reliable?* (Leicester and Downers Grove, Ill.: InterVarsity Press, 1960); and Paul Barnett, *Is the New Testament History?* (London: Hodder and Stoughton, 1986).

[13] Lesslie Newbigin, *Truth to Tell* (Grand Rapids, Mich.: Eerdmans; Geneva: WCC Publications, 1991), 8.

[14] This is D. A. Carson's description of this view in "Five Gospels," 32.

[15] Newbigin, *Truth to Tell*, 8 (see p. 9 for further criticism of this method).

will not take that statement as an objective one. That is a subjective statement based on my individual tastes. For me that happens to be true, but not for most other people in the world. That is a subjective statement of praise from one who has grown to enjoy her beauty. The pluralist claims that the statements regarding the absoluteness of Christ in the Gospels belong to this category.[16]

We disagree. The evidence is strongly in favor of the fact that the gospel writers were writing a historically factual account. We have already cited Leon Morris's comment that there are no words of praise for Jesus from the writers of the Gospels.[17] They wrote books of the life of Christ that sought to objectively report what happened when He lived on earth. D. A. Carson has pointed out that the first survivors of the Holocaust were passionate in their witness, like the early Christians. "But by and large, their passion drove them toward great accuracy and carefulness, precisely because they wanted others to believe them."[18]

Let's look at some of the evidence for the historical reliability of the Gospels.

COMMITMENT TO WRITING AN ACCURATE ACCOUNT

First, we see that they took pains to write an accurate account. They wrote as if they were writing history. At the start of his gospel, Luke describes how he wrote his gospel. First, he says that his source of information is the word of eyewitnesses: "Many have undertaken to draw up an account of the things that have been fulfilled among us, just as they were handed down to us by *those who from the first were eyewitnesses* and servants of the word" (Luke 1:1-2). Then he describes his own qualification for writing the gospel: "Therefore, *since I myself have carefully investigated everything from the beginning,* it seemed good also to me to write an orderly account for you" (verse 3).

Where they can be checked about geographical, political, religious,

---

[16]See Wesley Ariarajah, *The Bible and People of Other Faiths* (Geneva: World Council of Churches, 1985), 25-26.

[17]Leon Morris, *The Lord from Heaven* (Downers Grove, Ill.: InterVarsity Press, 1974), 21.

[18]Carson, "Five Gospels," 32.

and social statements they make, the Gospels have been found to be accurate. This is particularly true of the book of John, which some consider to be the most subjective of the Gospels and therefore the least historically accurate. The fact is that John's gospel "reveals meticulous knowledge of Palestinian matters such as peoples' names, peoples' relationships, customs, geographical sites, numbers of things, precise movements of peoples, etc."[19] In terms of chronology and geography John supplies much more information than the other gospels.[20] In fact, New Testament scholars like the German Ethelbert Stauffer use the details that John has given to insist that he is the only evangelist who enables us to fix a chronology of Jesus.[21]

The treatment of John the Baptist in the fourth gospel is a highly theological one. We are not even told of John's baptizing Jesus. The author's aim (as John 1:7-8 shows) is to demonstrate that John bore witness to Jesus (a theological aim). So, according to the pluralist model, this would invariably not be reliable as history. But the teachings found in the Dead Sea Scrolls make points of contact with almost everything that the Baptist said in John. Biblical critics usually consider this to be a gauge of accuracy. Leon Morris comments, "If John can be accurate when he is demonstrably concerned to make a theological point, this creates a presumption that he is correct elsewhere." Morris asks, "If his portrait of John is a good one, why should we think anything else of his portrait of Jesus?"[22]

It is findings like these that caused a theologically radical scholar like John A. T. Robinson to vigorously defend the historical accuracy of John's gospel in his last book, *The Priority of John*, which was published posthumously.[23]

A specialist in Roman public law and administration at Oxford University, A. N. Sherwin-White, has written a book, *Roman Society and*

---

[19]Bernard Ramm, *An Evangelical Christology* (Nashville: Thomas Nelson, 1985), 143.

[20]Blomberg, *Historical Reliability*, 188.

[21]E. Stauffer, *Jesus and His Story* (London: SCM Press, 1960), 15-17, quoted in Leon Morris, "The Fourth Gospel and History," in *Jesus of Nazareth: Savior and Lord*, ed. Carl F. H. Henry (Grand Rapids, Mich.: Eerdmans, 1966), 126.

[22]Leon Morris, "Gospel According to John," in *The International Standard Bible Encyclopedia*, vol. 2, rev. ed. (Grand Rapids, Mich.: Eerdmans, 1982), 1106.

[23]J. A. T. Robinson, *The Priority of John* (London: SCM Press; Philadelphia: Westminster, 1986).

Roman Law in the New Testament, in which he shows that what the New Testament gives about the historical, social, and political background of the time attests its basic historicity. Toward the end of his book he mentions the way Graeco-Roman historians have been growing in confidence about the history of prominent people around the time of Jesus, such as Tiberias Caesar, Jesus' best-known contemporary. He says, "It is astonishing" that at the same time "the twentieth-century study of the Gospel narratives, starting with no less promising material, has taken so gloomy a turn."[24]

Lesslie Newbigin says, "Ancient writers show themselves perfectly capable of distinguishing between fact and fiction." He says that if we adopt the pluralist approach to truth that we have been critiquing, it "would wipe out our claim to know anything reliable about ancient history." He adds, "Many famous university departments would have to close."[25]

I think that what fuels this movement to negate the historical value of the Gospels is the implications of what the Gospels state. The Gospels go against the grain of the pluralistic thinking of our time. Pluralism says that absolute truth cannot be known, that Jesus is not unique, and that all religions are of equal value. The Gospels say that Jesus is unique. It is very convenient to dismiss these statements by claiming that they are not historical. This is a case of the biases of scholars influencing the way they handle the data before them.

One more thing needs to be mentioned under this discussion of the evangelists' intention to write an accurate account. The Gospel writers exhibited a real restraint in the way they reported the events. This stands in contrast to the apocryphal writings. We have already stated that the gospel writers do not praise Jesus in the Gospels. This again gives evidence of an attempt on the part of the writers to be historically accurate.

THE IMPROBABILITY OF JESUS' BEING INVENTED

Second, it is most unlikely that "unlettered Galilean fishermen, or even their immediate successors, invented a character which is so transcen-

---

[24]A. N. Sherwin-White, *Roman Society and Roman Law in the New Testament* (1963; reprint, Grand Rapids, Mich.: Baker, 1978), 187.
[25]Newbigin, *Truth to Tell*, 9.

dent as to cast into the shade the finest efforts of all the greatest writers of every age."[26] Theodore Parker said, "It takes a Newton to forge a Newton. What man could have fabricated a Jesus? No one but a Jesus."[27] W. Robertson Nicoll says, "The gospel has marks of truth so great, so striking, so perfectly inimitable, that the inventor of it would be more astonishing than the hero."[28]

Added to this is the fact that Jesus was a very public figure and that Christianity was a very controversial religion. As Paul told King Agrippa, "The king is familiar with these things, and I can speak freely to him. I am convinced that none of this has escaped his notice, because it was not done in a corner" (Acts 26:26). If Jesus had been a very private, shadowy figure, it would not be difficult to build untrue legends about Him. But you cannot do this with a very public figure, in a society that did not know privacy in the way we know it now.

Besides, as Christianity was such a controversial religion, there must have been a scrutiny of the facts of the Gospel. If these stories were untrue, they could easily have been contradicted by sincere followers of Christ and by the foes of Christianity. The controversy inside and outside the church was not about the facts of the story of Jesus but about the meaning of these facts. Actually, most of the twelve original apostles of Christ were martyred because of their commitment to these facts and their meaning. If they were untrue, at least one of them would have recanted rather than face death.

THE EARLY DATES OF THE GOSPELS

Third, we must remember that the Gospels were written within a few decades of the events. N. T. Wright points out that "In that oral culture, telling stories about ... a popular and controversial person could not be a secret process." This is evidenced in the remark of Cleopas on the road to Emmaus: "Are you the only one living in Jerusalem who doesn't

---

[26]W. Griffith Thomas, *Christianity Is Christ* (1948; reprint, New Canaan, Conn.: Keats Publishing, 1981), 89.

[27]From Theodore Parker, *The Life of Jesus*, 363, quoted in Thomas, *Christianity Is Christ*, 88.

[28]From W. Robertson Nicoll, *The Church's One Foundation* (New York: Armstrong; London: Hodder and Stoughton, 1902), 41, quoted in Griffith Thomas, *Christianity Is Christ*, 89.

know the things that have happened there in these days?" (Luke 24:18).[29] Even strangers should know what had happened in Jerusalem during those days.

Without an abundance of books and electronic media—there were none, we can imagine that the stories of Jesus were passed down with an accuracy we could never attain because of the influence of the media revolution on us. Of course, when there is a time lag between events and their recording it is possible for distortion to take place. But in the case of the Gospels there is a strong likelihood that this did not happen. Craig Blomberg's presentation of reasons for this likelihood is so concise and clear that I will quote him verbatim here.

1. Jesus was perceived by his followers as one who proclaimed God's Word in a way which demanded careful retelling.
2. Over ninety per cent of his teachings has poetic elements which would have made them easy to memorize.
3. The almost universal method of education in antiquity, and especially in Israel, was rote memorization, which enabled people accurately to recount quantities of material far greater than all of the Gospels put together.
4. Oral story-telling often permitted a wide range of freedom in selecting and describing details but required fixed points of a narrative to be preserved unchanged.
5. Written notes and a kind of shorthand were often privately kept by rabbis and their disciples, despite a publicly stated preference for oral tradition.
6. The lack of teachings ascribed to Jesus about later church controversies (e.g., circumcision, speaking in tongues) suggests that the disciples did not freely invent material and read it back onto the lips of Jesus.[30]

---

[29]N. T. Wright, "The New Unimproved Jesus," *Christianity Today*, September 13, 1993, 25-26.
[30]C. L. Blomberg, "Gospels (Historical Reliability)," in *Dictionary of Jesus and the Gospels*, eds. Joel B. Green, Scot McKnight, and I. Howard Marshall (Leicester and Downers Grove, Ill.: InterVarsity Press, 1992), 294.

THE CHRISTIAN COMMITMENT TO TRUTH

Fourth, we know that these early Christians were very committed to truth. The words *truth, true,* and related words appear 366 times in the New Testament. Ephesians 4:25 says, "Therefore each of you must put off falsehood and speak truthfully to his neighbor, for we are all members of one body." Colossians 3:9-10 says, "Do not lie to each other, since you have taken off your old self with its practices and have put on the new self." Peter accused Ananias of trying to lie to the Holy Spirit (Acts 5:3), and he and his wife Sapphira were killed as a judgment from God.

Again the Gospel of John is very significant here. Words related to truth (*alētheia, alēthēs,* and *alēthinos*) appear forty-eight times in John. Those related to witness or testify (*marturia* and *maturein*) appear forty-seven times. Leon Morris says, "Witness is a legal term. It signifies the kind of evidence that is allowed in a law court." Morris concedes that this is not the only way in which these words are used. But he adds, "Nevertheless the term is not without significance, and its constant use in this gospel shows that the author is confident of his facts. He is telling us that what he writes is well attested."[31] John said this about his source of information regarding the piercing of Jesus' side: "The man who saw it has given testimony, and his testimony is true. He knows that he tells the truth, and he testifies so that you also may believe" (John 19:35). He was probably talking about himself here.

Could we expect people who express such a commitment to truth to be untruthful about the basis of their faith?

"CULTURAL CHAUVINISM"

The problem with the attitude of the pluralist who rejects the historicity of the Gospels is, as we said, what Newbigin calls "a false concept of objectivity."[32] Pluralists seem to be saying that objective knowledge is a kind of knowledge from which the human subject has been removed. Because the writers of the Gospels were so involved in what they were writing, their writings are not considered objective. Because of this, pluralists reject the Gospels for what they feel is a more appropriate view of Jesus for today.

---

[31] Morris, "The Fourth Gospel and History," 130.
[32] Newbigin, *Truth to Tell,* 8.

This is a "case of importing twentieth-century rationalist ideals about the objectiveness of historians onto first-century texts."[33] Newbigin is forthright in his criticism of this view when he says, "It would be a remarkable example of cultural chauvinism if we supposed that our faith about what really happened, shaped as it is by our own cultural perspectives, must necessarily displace that of the immediate witnesses."[34] I trust that what we have said shows that this does not need to be the case.

Some of the other assumptions that influence this skeptical approach to the historicity of the Gospels are also very suspect. For example, it is assumed that if Jesus is reported to have said something that could have been said by His contemporaries, then we do not have to accept that those words came from Jesus. It is also assumed that if that saying is "demonstrably in line with later church teaching, it is best to suppose that the church created the saying."[35] In response to the first assumption Don Carson points out that "Jesus was, after all, a first-century Jewish man. To begin to argue that he must not sound like one is akin to arguing that Churchill must never sound like an Englishman." Carson also shows how illogical the second assumption is. It assumes that Jesus, who was "perhaps the most influential man in history," never said any of the things "that the church believed, cherished and passed on."[36] Especially in light of the reasons we have given above for believing that the story of Jesus was passed down accurately, is it not much more reasonable to accept that what the followers of Jesus said were the words of Jesus were really His words?

In light of all this, we reject the view that what the gospel writers presented as events did not really happen. The Gospels are presented as objective documents, and it is unreasonable, given the evidence, to think that they are anything else.

If the Gospels give an objective account of the life of Christ, then we cannot take the view of Gandhi and the modern-day pluralist. The absolute lordship of Christ does not emerge from a few proof texts in

---

[33]David Ball, "Some Recent Literature on John: A Review Article," *Themelios* 19, no. 1 (October 1993): 15.

[34]Newbigin, *Truth to Tell*, 8-9.

[35]This is D. A. Carson's explanation of this view in "Five Gospels," 32.

[36]Ibid., 32.

some isolated passages in the Gospels. They shine through all of it. If we were to take out those passages that contain teaching about the absolute lordship of Christ, we would be left with no life of Christ at all. In other words, the same material that gives evidence to His being a good man also gives evidence that He is Absolute Lord. You cannot say that He was good but not absolute. The view of the pluralist on this matter is untenable.

A SUMMARY OF WHAT WE HAVE ARGUED

Our arguments up to this point may be summarized as follows:

- Jesus claimed to be the Truth, the Ultimate Reality, the Absolute Truth (chapter 2).

- He could say that because He said that He is equal with God (chapter 2).

- His words are evidence for His being equal to God. There is great appeal in His teaching. There are also great claims that no other right-thinking human being ever made for himself or herself (chapter 3).

- His works authenticate His words. These works consist of a matchless life, of miraculous signs, and, supremely, of the sign of His death and resurrection (chapter 4).

- All of these arguments will be worthless unless the Gospels are historically objective documents. The evidence is that they are indeed such documents (chapter 6).

Different people are attracted to different aspects of this comprehensive case for Christ's absoluteness. Once they open their hearts through one aspect, the others soon fall into place. But the final appeal of the Gospel is the cumulative effect of all these points.

Others have taught the things that Jesus taught. Recently a leading Sri Lankan lawyer presented what many considered to be a convincing case against the uniqueness of Christianity by showing that the ethical teachings of Jesus are found in the other religions also. That is, to a certain extent, true. But the teachings of Jesus are not the sum of the

Gospel. Those ethical teachings are inextricably linked with His claims to absoluteness.

There are many religious leaders, especially Hindu gurus like Sathya Sai Baba, who perform miracles. Thus, some place him on par with Jesus as a manifestation of the one God. But the miracles of Jesus are only one aspect of the Gospel.

The feature in the Gospel that makes it exclusive is its completeness. Jesus was the perfect example of a holy and loving human being. He taught sublime truths, claimed to be equal with God, and performed miracles to substantiate those claims. Most importantly, He sacrificed His life, claiming to be dying to save the world. God gave proof of the validity of this scheme of salvation by raising Him from the dead. This last point is the clincher, and we have not come to that yet. The most unique thing about the Gospel of Jesus is His death and resurrection for the salvation of the whole world. It is this that ultimately separates the Gospel from the rest of the religions of the world.

CHAPTER SEVEN

MORE PRESSING QUESTIONS

I TRUST THAT I HAVE presented an adequate case for believing that in this pluralistic age we can still hold to the belief that Jesus is Absolute Truth. There are, however, a few more issues relating to this belief that we need to discuss. To these we will now turn.

DO ALL RELIGIONS TEACH ESSENTIALLY THE SAME THING?

How often we hear people saying that all religions teach essentially the same thing: they teach people to live good lives. This has been told to me both in Asia and in the West. If this is so, then we cannot claim that Christianity is either the ultimate reality or absolute.

Even a superficial look at the different religions will show that on certain key beliefs they are diametrically opposed to each other. At the very heart of the Christian Gospel is the belief that Jesus is God incarnate. To the Muslim that is blasphemy. Christianity is founded on the person and work of Jesus. Buddhism is based not on the person but on the teachings of the Buddha. Actually, as W. Griffith Thomas has said, "Christianity is the only religion in the world which rests on the Person of its founder."[1] Buddhism and Hinduism teach that salvation is attained through what one does. Christianity teaches that salvation is based on what Christ has done. Hindu and New Age pantheism say that we are all part of the divine. Christianity says that we are created by God who is transcendent and separate from us. Lesslie Newbigin points out that "the questions Hinduism asks and answers are not the questions with which the gospel is primarily concerned."[2] This points to the truth of the statement by German theologian Rudolph Otto (1869-1937) that the different religions turn on different axes.

Harold Netland points out that "two contradictory statements cannot be true."[3] One must be right and the other wrong. This is called the principle of noncontradiction and is the approach we take in the study of history, geography, science, and mathematics. Netland complains that although this rule is unquestioned in ordinary life, some consider it inappropriate in the field of religion.

It is true that in life we often come across situations where there are two or more acceptable ways to do a certain thing or to approach a certain problem. Different psychologists will use different methods to solve a disorder. In politics we find that equally devout Christians may take opposing sides on a given issue. Styles of leadership vary with the personalities of leaders. But the differences we are dealing with are fundamental and mutually exclusive. As we showed earlier, the Christian claim that Jesus is God incarnate is blasphemy to the Muslim. Buddhists say we must do certain things by our own efforts to be saved. Christianity says that we must not even try to do such things, for our salvation is a gift.

Now, some might object that such reasoning is influenced by the linear logical thinking of the Greeks, to which Christian theology has long been tied. The pluralist says that two affirmations may be logically

[1]W. Griffith Thomas, *Christianity Is Christ* (1948; reprint, New Canaan, Conn.: Keats, 1981), 1.

[2]Lesslie Newbigin, *The Open Secret: Sketches for a Missionary Theology* (Grand Rapids, Mich.: Eerdmans, 1978), reprinted in *Mission Trends No. 5: Faith Meets Faith*, eds. Gerald H. Anderson and Thomas F. Stransky (New York: Paulist; Grand Rapids, Mich.: Eerdmans, 1981), 7.

[3]Harold Netland, *Dissonant Voices: Religious Pluralism and the Question of Truth* (Grand Rapids, Mich.: Eerdmans; Leicester: InterVarsity Press, 1991), 142. See especially pages 141-50 of Netland's book.

contradictory, but if they produce helpful experiences to their adherents, they are both valid. The claim is that the test of validity of an affirmation is its reality in experience and not in logic. Zen Buddhism attempts to free people from the tyranny of the logical world created by words. They believe that this will help people experience an authentic existence. The adherents meditate on highly illogical statements, called koans, like: "When you clap both your hands together, a sound results. Now listen to the sound of one hand clapping."

Indeed, linear logical thinking is not the only legitimate way to express theological truth. I agree that many of the formulations of Christian theology throughout history have been influenced by logical thinking, derived from Greek philosophy, that forms the basis of western thinking. Ways of expressing truth will vary in the different cultures.

However, the ability to distinguish between truth and falsehood, between right and wrong, is a human trait given by the Creator as a basic ingredient of human morality. It cannot be viewed as the exclusive property of those who practice linear logical thinking. We must not try to transcend that, for by doing so we will violate our humanity.

Most careful students of religions recognize that the different religions move on different axes. We simply cannot say that they teach essentially the same thing. The similarities between Christianity and other religions are often on peripheral things, not on the essentials of the faith.

IS EXCLUSIVISM A PRODUCT OF THE "CHRISTIAN" WEST?

Many who have rejected the traditional Christian claim of uniqueness to the exclusion of other faiths blame the West for this exclusivistic approach. They say that this doctrine was cultivated in the West where people had very little contact with adherents of other faiths. They say that until recently the perception about the world religions in the West was a grossly misrepresented view associated with phrases like "savage heathens."

Then in the last few decades of the eighteenth century serious studies were made of these religions, and a rich religious literature was discovered. As Stephen Neill puts it, "As these 'treasures of darkness' penetrated the consciousness of educated men and women, something of a gasp of astonishment arose. Surprise was followed by appreciation, and even by admiration."[4] The Vatican Council II (1962-65) of the Roman Catholic Church viewed other faiths in a much more appreciative light, as is evidenced by one of its documents, *Lumen Gentium*, "the light of the Gentiles."

Not only the students of comparative religions but also the general Christian public in the West are made to question their earlier views as they encounter adherents of other faiths in their own neighborhoods and see much that is good and admirable in them. It is said that we in the East, having been used to this situation, were naturally pluralist in attitude.

In answer to this we must say that whatever the situation in the West may have been, the early church grew in a strongly pluralistic environment. As David Wells puts it, "Pluralism was the stuff of everyday life in biblical times."[5] Don Carson says that the situation was not that of "a conglomeration of mutually exclusive religious groups, each damning all the others." "Rather," says Carson, "the opinion of the overwhelming majority was that the competing religions had more or less merit to them. True, many religious adherents judged that their favored brand was the best; but probably most saw no problem in participating in many religions." Carson goes on to say, "The Jews were viewed as an intransigent exception." So the Roman Empire "made a grudging exception in their case, and it extended that exception to Christians as well, at least as long as the imperial powers thought of Christianity as a sect within Judaism."[6]

The New Testament preachers and writers responded to this pluralism with strong affirmation of the exclusiveness and supremacy of Christ. Paul's ministry in Athens (Acts 17:16-34) and the Epistles to

---

[4]Stephen Neill, *Crises of Belief* (London: Hodder and Stoughton, 1984), 10 (North American edition, *Christian Faith and Other Faiths* [Downers Grove, Ill.: InterVarsity Press]). For a description of this process of discovery of other faiths, see pp. 9-13 (British edition) of this book.

[5]David F. Wells, *No Place for Truth* (Grand Rapids, Mich.: Eerdmans, 1993), 263.

[6]D. A. Carson, "Christian Witness in an Age of Pluralism," in *God and Culture*, eds. D. A. Carson and John D. Woodbridge (Grand Rapids, Mich.: Eerdmans; Carlisle: Paternoster Press, 1993), 44.

Colosse and Ephesus are good examples of this. So those pushing pluralism today must reckon with the fact that they are adopting a completely opposite attitude to a very similar situation by the New Testament church. In fact, a pantheism similar to that of New Age and Hindu thought was very prevalent in New Testament times.[7]

ABSOLUTE TRUTH AND THE SUPPOSED INFERIORITY OF "NATIVE" CULTURES

A false view of the supposed inferiority of so-called native cultures held by earlier proponents of the uniqueness of Christianity has done much to undermine the Gospel's claim to absolute authority. When motivating people to missionary involvement, emphasis was placed on the "peculiar" and the "inferior" cultures of "the natives." I encountered this occasionally when I traveled to missionary conferences as a student in America in the mid-seventies. The cry was to Christianize the world. But to many, "Christianize" meant "westernize." "We must teach them the wonderful heritage of the West," they said. In Sri Lanka, for example, Christianity was always regarded as a western religion during the centuries of colonial rule by western powers. In fact, even some Christians viewed western cultural forms of expression as the Christian form, so that when other Christians attempted to introduce eastern styles in worship and evangelism, they were accused of departing from the fundamentals of the faith.

Recently the West has been discovering the richness of these cultures. Many sensitive westerners are embarrassed by their older attitudes, and they are saying they were wrong in their claim to uniqueness. And that is partly correct! They were wrong about western superiority, but not about the supremacy of the Gospel, which incidentally did not originate in the West!

It has been disconcerting to me to discover that in the minds of many conservative Christians in the West there is still a strong sense of the superiority of the West. I keep hearing Americans call their country the greatest country in the world. Often their concept of the supremacy of Christ is closely tied to the supremacy of western soci-

---

[7]The similarity between the modern pagan mind and ancient paganism is described by Wells in *No Place for Truth*, 264-70.

ety with its capitalist political system. It is assumed that in wars fought by western countries God is on the side of the western armies. And Christians in some non-western countries have suffered much because they are identified with the views of the western Christians. I am told that innocent Christians in some Muslim countries were murdered during the Gulf War of 1990.

One of the strongest points repeatedly brought up by the Buddhists in their polemic against Christian evangelism in Sri Lanka is the so-called moral decay of the West. We are asked whether we are trying to spread Christianity in the East because Christianity has failed in the West. Parents are warned about letting their children go to Christian programs because they may become contaminated with western immorality through contact with the Christians. Sri Lanka is sending scores of missionaries to the West out of the conviction that the discipline of Buddhism is the answer to the West's lack of moral discipline.

Therefore, the sooner the identification of Christianity with western culture is dropped, the better it will be for the cause of Christ, who Himself was not a westerner.

Unfortunately, this problem is compounded by the fact that the Christian message was introduced in some countries along with the arrival of colonial conquerors. In Sri Lanka we are often told that the first Christians came with the sword in one hand and the Bible in the other. In my book *The Christian's Attitude Toward World Religions* I have shown that colonialism was not necessarily a help to evangelism and that the spirit of colonialism is very contrary to the spirit of the biblical evangelist.[8]

These are sad things about our past that we must acknowledge with humility. But the wrong practices of an earlier generation, who interpreted the truth wrongly, should not cause us to put aside the truth of the Gospel that does not change.

THE CALL FOR RADICAL CONVERSION

Another reason for the rejection of the Christian claim that the Gospel is absolute truth is the call for radical conversion to it once truth is

---

[8]Ajith Fernando, "Conversion and Proselytism," in *The Christian's Attitude Toward World Religions* (Wheaton, Ill.: Tyndale House, 1987), 171-82.

found. To call people to such conversion sounds very arrogant. The step of conversion may involve much unpleasantness because one has to leave behind one's religion. Most people don't have the commitment or the inclination to subscribe to such a costly viewpoint.

I trust that in our ministry we have tried to be as polite, respectful, friendly, helpful, and humble as we can possibly be with the people in the areas where we work. Usually they have responded favorably to this friendliness. But the moment people started to convert, there were some who reacted with anger and opposed our work. Some of these people were once very friendly with us; but when some of their own people converted to Christianity, their attitude toward us changed completely. Others remained friends while vehemently opposing our work.

That is an inevitable thing that happens when you preach a unique Gospel. Truth has a way of dividing people. When Jesus made certain unique claims about Himself, the people took up stones to throw at Him or made plans to put Him to death. When the Gospel was preached in Acts, it elicited an angry response from many hearers. We should not expect it to be different with us. Jesus said, "Remember the words I spoke to you: 'No servant is greater than his master.' If they persecuted me, they will persecute you also" (John 15:20).

In Sri Lanka, where the opposition to evangelism has been mounting recently, there have been people in some churches who have been asking their denominations to make an official statement that the denomination does not attempt to convert others. The leaders of most denominations have resisted this, but some leaders have stated that they are not the ones who are converting others to Christianity. They have distanced themselves from those ministries that are experiencing growth through conversion, calling them "fundamentalists" and telling the persecutors that they too are having trouble with the fundamentalists. It has been very painful for us to feel betrayed by fellow Christians in this way.

Let's face it. Being a true Christian involves proclaiming the message of salvation to others with the goal of conversion in view. That goal has invited opposition throughout the centuries, and it still does so. Evangelism has been associated with bribery and other unethical inducements to conversion throughout history, and this still happens today.

A THREAT TO NATIONAL AND FAMILY HARMONY?

Those who preach an exclusive Gospel are also accused of being a threat to national and family harmony. This is claimed by leaders from Christian backgrounds too. Indian ecumenical theologian Stanley Samartha says, "In contemporary India a radical change in the Christian stance towards neighbors of other faiths is both an existential demand and a theological necessity. It is desperately needed when the unity and integrity of the country are in danger of being torn apart by forces of separation that are influenced by the claims and counterclaims of diverse religions."[9] Similar accusations are made against Christians in the West who fight against things like abortion, pornography, and the legalizing and condoning of deviant sexual practices.

This claim has been made in places that our ministry is involved in too. We are accused of destroying the peace of villages that had enjoyed harmony for centuries. Yet, we must remember that Jesus Himself said, "Do not suppose that I have come to bring peace to the earth. I did not come to bring peace, but a sword" (Matt. 10:34). He went further to show that families will be divided as a result of His influence on people. "For I have come to turn 'a man against his father, a daughter against her mother, a daughter-in-law against her mother-in-law—a man's enemies will be the members of his own household'" (Matt. 10:35-36).

We have learned that we need to follow the protocol of a society as much as possible. We did not have any relationship with the Buddhist monks in an area where our ministry served until they started making things very difficult for us. At that time we went and met them and explained what we were doing and tried to answer some of their objections to our work, many of which were based on false perceptions. We later felt that we should have gone to meet them earlier. When I met with them, I respectfully sat on the floor while they sat at higher levels on chairs. This is the custom in our country, and I

[9]Stanley J. Samartha, "The Cross and the Rainbow," in *The Myth of Christian Uniqueness*, eds. John Hick and Paul F. Knitter (Maryknoll, N.Y.: Orbis, 1988), 72.

followed it. I had the converts from Buddhism tutor me on the way in which I should address the monks, and I chose forms of address that were respectful but did not compromise my conviction that Jesus was my only Lord.

We must urge converts to be better and more dutiful citizens as well as more conscientious and concerned family members than they were before they met Christ. I have a friend, Samuel Ganesh, who is an effective evangelist in India. He is a convert to Christianity from Hinduism's "highest" caste, the Brahmins. He was rejected by his family for becoming a Christian. But after his father died, he sent financial and other support to his mother for several years before she made contact with him. Today she is proud of her son's concern for her. I know of some non-Christian families where the parents take mean advantage of their Christian children because they are so caring, unselfish, and generous. That may be a price these converts have to pay to help break resistance to the Gospel.

In our work we always establish a relationship with the parents of young people from other faiths whom we contact. Most of those who become Christians also become more dutiful children. On some occasions we have found that when opposition to our work comes from the temple, the parents of the converted children defend us against unfair charges made against us. They know us too well to believe that those charges are true.

We must constantly be reflecting on how we should do all we can to help bring harmony to community and family. These things will help defuse the tension somewhat, but they will not take away the pain of ruptured ties that result from conversion. I believe my visit to the Buddhist temple mentioned above helped take away some misunderstandings, but it did not stop the opposition to our work.

The problem is further complicated in Sri Lanka, which has been torn by ethnic strife. Christians have usually stood for the rights of both communities, and this has invited the rage of extremists in both communities in the conflict. Our stand is another inevitable result of our commitment to the Gospel of peace. The peace the Bible speaks of is a peace that is committed to justice for all.

So, even though love is the great aim in our behavior, we will be accused of being unloving. Stanley Samartha says, "To make exclusive claims for our particular tradition is not the best way to love our neighbors as ourselves."[10] Often in the West today those who speak against such things as abortion, homosexuality, and pornography are accused of hatred. But we claim exactly the opposite. It is love that drives us to show the truthfulness of the Christian claim in contrast to other claims. We believe that others should experience the benefits of what Christ won for us by His saving work. This belief is well expressed by Paul in 2 Corinthians 5:14-15: "For Christ's love compels us, because we are convinced that one died for all, and therefore all died. And he died for all, that those who live should no longer live for themselves but for him who died for them and was raised again."

Note how Paul says that everyone "should." There is a compulsion because this is the way we were made to live by our Creator. We are simply messengers of the Creator and the Lord of the universe, urging people to accept the salvation this Lord has provided for them.

Now we admit with sorrow that in the history of the church some who fought for the truth did so in unloving ways. The misbehavior of some pro-life activists in recent years has done immeasurable damage to the cause that movement promotes. We must pray for our enemies and ask God to help us love them. The Bible clearly asks us to love our enemies. I found that I was developing a hatred toward the enemies of the work of the Gospel in Sri Lanka and of our work in particular. This year I included those people in my prayer list. It is liberating to know, amidst all the fear and anger, that these are people we love and for whose conversion we long.

---

[10]Ibid., 76.

CHAPTER EIGHT

THE JOY OF
TRUTH

T HE TOPIC OF God's revelation has occupied the mind of Carl
F. H. Henry for a long time. He has written a three-thousand-
page, six-volume work just on the topics of *God, Revelation, and
Authority.* Henry says, "Truth is Christianity's most enduring asset.
When all other things—the picketing and the protesting—pass away, it
is the question of the truth of Christianity that will ultimately determine its endurance."[1] And we affirm that Christianity is true.

This gives us a tremendous security amidst all the confusion of this
age that denies the reality of absolutes. And that security causes us great
joy. This is why the psalmists wrote so often of joy in the law of God.
Psalm 119, for example, mentions delighting in the law nine times.

C. S. Lewis in his book *Reflections on the Psalms* says that he can
understand people's *respecting* the law. But he says it is a mystery to him
that people can *rejoice* in this way in the Law.[2] After delving into possible reasons for this, he concludes, "Their delight in the law is a delight
in having touched firmness; like the pedestrian's delight in feeling the
hard road beneath his feet after a false shortcut has long entangled him

---

[1]Carl F. H. Henry, "Why We Need Christian Think Tanks," *Christianity Today,*
quoted in *Carl Henry at His Best* (Portland: Multnomah Press, 1989), 203.
[2]C. S. Lewis, *Reflections on the Psalms* (New York: Harcourt, Brace and World, 1958), 55.

in muddy fields."[3] I sensed this once when I was hiking with some friends in the mountains. We decided to take a shortcut and got lost. Along the way we saw droppings of a leopard, which frightened us, but we continued in what we thought was the direction of the town. What a relief and joy it was when we finally found a well-traveled road!

This joy over truth is more intense in the era of the New Covenant. When we come to Jesus, when we enter into a relationship with the truth, we realize that we are in touch with the Absolute. This is firm ground. This is what people are thirsting for. What a joy the discovery of such truth is. What a joy to feast on such truth daily as we read the Scriptures.

In his autobiography Carl Henry mentions a statement his professor, Gordon Haddon Clark, made when he was a student at Wheaton College: "A satisfactory religion must satisfy. But satisfy *what* and *why?* The Greek mysteries satisfied the emotions; brute force can satisfy the will; but Christianity satisfies the *intellect* because it is *true*, and truth is the only everlasting satisfaction."[4] This is one reason we are so excited about the Gospel. It is the Good News—the meaning of the word *gospel.*

William Tyndale lived in the sixteenth century and translated the Bible into English. In the preface to his New Testament, he describes the word *gospel.* To him it "signified good, merry, glad and joyful tidings, that makes a person's heart glad, and makes him sing, dance and leap for joy."[5] The Gospel is a word from the Creator of the world that contains the answer to the human dilemma. If it is that important, the cause of the Gospel is something worth dying for, which William Tyndale did at the age of forty-two.

Ours is a sensual generation that derives pleasure primarily from experiences through the use of our five senses: touch, sight, sound, smell, and taste. We need things that are more enduring to give us true satisfaction. Truth is one of those things.

The evangelical movement of a few generations ago made a signif-

---

[3]Ibid., 62.
[4]Carl F. H. Henry, *Confessions of a Theologian* (Waco, Tex.: Word, 1986), 67 (italics his).
[5]Quoted in R. H. Mounce, "Gospel," in *The Evangelical Dictionary of Theology*, ed. Walter A. Elwell (Grand Rapids, Mich.: Baker, 1984), 472. (I have modernized Tyndale's archaic English language.)

icant contribution to realizing the joy of truth when it popularized the gospel song. One of the most popular gospel songs says,

We have heard a joyful sound:
 Jesus saves!
Spread the tidings all around:
 Jesus saves!
Bear the news to every land,
 climb the steeps and cross the waves;
Onward! 'tis our Lord's command:
 Jesus saves!

Priscilla Owens (1829-1907)

THE LOSS OF THIS JOY IN EVANGELICALISM

I believe that today's evangelical church has lost some of this joy over truth. We have become so influenced by the fast-moving lifestyle of today that we find it difficult to slow down sufficiently to enjoy truth. The joy of truth is experienced best when we stop our feverish activity to reflect on truth, to meditate on joy. Our lives are too rushed for this.

This is actually a vicious cycle. Having lost the security of being rooted in the eternal reality of the Word of God, we are looking to busy activity to fill the void that has been created in our lives. And under that bondage to activity we find it difficult to linger with the Word simply for the joy of it. In fact, we may be afraid to stop our busyness lest it expose the shallowness of our lives. So we go on from activity to activity, from project to project. But activity is a dangerous source of fulfillment. Instead of finding our identity, our sense of self-worth, from our relationship with God, we begin to look to success in programs and other earthly indicators of success for our self-worth. But these will never satisfy. This will only enslave us more in our bondage to activity.

The result of this is burnout. The lust for success makes us so uncontrolled in our drivenness that we drive ourselves into the ground. After a time our bodies and minds say, "That is enough. I cannot stand it anymore." I think the current epidemic of burnout in the ministry is an indication of our loss of security in the Word.

Another sign of the loss of the joy of truth in evangelicalism is the low place that Bible exposition has as a method of preaching. I think our ministers are too busy to devote the time that is needed to study the Word in order to expound it. In addition, the Bible has lost its place of supreme authority in practice. When Christian leaders want an authoritative guide to issues pertaining to life and ministry, they turn to the findings of psychological and sociological research, not to the Scriptures. Here they are able to get the quick answers they need.

Testimonies have replaced preaching and expounding the truth as the most popular style of verbal proclamation. I think testimony is a very effective means of communicating the message. Because it is relevant, it wins many hearers. It encourages us, and it teaches us about God's dealings. I am convinced that it is a vital part of Christian worship. In fact, I have recently gotten into a lot of trouble because I introduced it into the Sunday service of our church.

But expounding the truth relevantly is, in the long run, more effective in changing lives. Because the truth is expounded relevantly, the attention of the hearer is won. The truth gives an eternal foundation on which to build one's life. This, in turn, gives us great security in our pilgrimage through life. Such security is the springboard to a lasting joy. I believe that in its attempt to win a hearing, the contemporary pulpit has been guilty of depriving our generation of lasting joy. They have had the responsibility of feeding a people craving for solid meat, but perhaps not realizing what they are craving for, they have kept feeding them dessert. It may have given the people instant satisfaction, but it has left them unhealthy and not really able to be salt and light for Christ in this world.

Perhaps the most alarming shift in the church is the fact that evangelical leaders themselves have lost touch with the art of using Scripture as their primary source of authority. Look at the typical book of practical advice for Christian leaders that is being published today. It will contain the usual statistics on the issues being discussed and then move on to practical advice from an expert in the field. There will be a smattering of Scripture here and there, but the supreme authority for the book is the experience and the study of the expert. He or she knows how the issues are tackled, and therefore his or her authority is what is important. This is one of the many indications of a major shift that has taken place in western evangelicalism where truth has been replaced by pragmatism as the major influencer of thought and life. This path is suicidal.

It is heartening, however, to see that contemporary western evangelicals, like Charles Colson,[6] Carl Henry,[7] J. I. Packer,[8] John Piper,[9] and David Wells[10] are sounding alarm bells and seeking to call the evangelical movement back to its dependence on the glory of truth. However, I feel that many evangelical leaders are so caught up in and blinded by this bondage to pragmatism that even though they may heartily endorse pleas to return to greater dependence on truth, endorsements make minimal inroads into their ministry styles and strategies.

It is also heartening to see books being written on specific topics pertaining to our lives and ministries that make use of the findings of psychological and sociological research but are firmly founded on the Scriptures.[11] Such books not only inform, instruct, and inspire, but also feed the soul with living bread. Such food leaves the reader equipped with spiritual resources to handle the challenges of life and ministry. One of the great seductions of pragmatism is to convince us that what we need most is to have the proper resources and to know the necessary techniques to respond to the challenges we face. What we need most is the Spirit and the wisdom of the Lord of creation. With that we can face any challenge that comes to us in this world. That is

---

[6]See Charles Colson, *The Body* (Waco, Tex.: Word, 1992).

[7]See Carl F. H. Henry's works, including *God, Revelation and Authority* (Waco, Tex.: Word, 1976-1983); *Twilight of a Great Civilization* (Wheaton, Ill.: Crossway Books, 1988); *The Christian Mindset in a Secular Society* (Portland: Multnomah Press, 1986); and *Christian Countermoves in a Decadent Culture* (Portland: Multnomah Press, 1985).

[8]See J. I. Packer, *The Quest for Godliness* (Wheaton, Ill.: Crossway Books; Eastbourne: Kingsway, 1990).

[9]See John Piper, *The Supremacy of God in Preaching* (Grand Rapids, Mich.: Baker, 1990).

[10]See David F. Wells, *No Place for Truth* (Grand Rapids, Mich.: Eerdmans, 1993); and *God in the Wasteland* (Grand Rapids, Mich.: Eerdmans, 1994).

[11]Books of this nature that I have read recently are: Leighton Ford, *Transforming Leadership* (Downers Grove, Ill.: InterVarsity Press, 1991; British edition: *Jesus: The Transforming Leader* [London: Hodder and Stoughton, 1992]); R. Kent Hughes, *Disciplines of a Godly Man* (Wheaton, Ill.: Crossway Books, 1991); and John Stott, *Decisive Issues Facing Christians Today* (Old Tappan, N.J.: Revell; London: Marshall Pickering, 1990) and *Between Two Worlds: The Art of Preaching in the Twentieth Century* (Grand Rapids, Mich.: Eerdmans, 1982; British edition: *I Believe in Preaching* [London: Hodder and Stoughton, 1982]).

attained by lingering in His presence and in His Word and disciplin-
ing ourselves to applying what we receive from the Word to the situations that we face.

When psychology, sociology, and pragmatism rather than biblically
based theology determine the strategy of ministry for the church, the
church becomes an expression of the prevailing culture, only in
Christian dress. God has not called us to mimic culture; He has called
us to transform it, to be a prophetic presence in it. So the church should
always be countercultural. If psychological and statistical studies show
that people prefer to listen to testimonies rather than to expositions of
truth, then our challenge is to make our exposition so challenging and
relevant that people will want to listen to it. Instead, many Christian
groups have dropped exposition as being the principal means of
Christian communication. By doing that they are guilty of producing a
generation of anemic Christians.

I must say that relevant exposition of truth is hard work. You have
to study the Scriptures and ascertain the truth it is teaching. Then you
have to work hard to apply it to the practical and intellectual challenges
of the day. And you have to present it in a way that is understandable,
attractive, relevant, and practical. All this calls for hard work—for both
long hours at the desk and contact with people. Generalism is difficult
in this era of specialization, and preachers in our activist generation find
it very difficult to sit for a long time grappling with truth.

How much quicker it is to choose a hot topic and look for some
verses from Scripture to buttress your message. And there are so many
resources to help you do this in double-quick time. You don't have to
spend long hours grappling with truth and meditating on it. All that
has been done for you in advance! "No sweat," we say. But no joy
either. We are told that what we need are the proper resources, and
we can take the struggle out of sermon preparation. This may make
us efficient in our work output, but it will also make us shallow ministers who do little to challenge a culture that is headed for destruction because of its warped sense of values. But who cares; everyone
feels good at the end of the sermon. And isn't feeling good what life
is all about?

I am not against the use of resources in the preparation of sermons.
We should make use of the many resources available today to reduce

the time we spend finding details. But may the time saved release us to spend more time for grappling with truth and theological reflection.

In a recent book of reflections on Christian leadership, *In the Name of Jesus,* Henri Nouwen says that theological reflection is one of the most important disciplines for today's minister. But he also says that this is difficult for today's Christian leader.

> Few ministers and priests think theologically. Most of them have been educated in a climate in which the behavioral sciences, such as psychology and sociology, so dominated the educational milieu that no true theology was being learned. Most Christian leaders today raise psychological and sociological questions even though they frame them in scriptural terms. Real theological thinking, which is thinking with the mind of Christ, is hard to find in the practice of ministry. Without solid theological reflection, future leaders will be little more than pseudo-psychologists, pseudo-sociologists, pseudo-social workers. They will think of themselves as enablers, facilitators, role models, father or mother figures, big brothers or big sisters, and so on, and thus join the countless men and women trying to help their fellow human beings to cope with the stresses and strains of everyday living. But that has little to do with Christian leadership.[12]

Related to this is the fact that often in evangelical circles programs are the main method of attracting people to the church, rather than the glorious Gospel of the Lord Jesus. Often an evangelical program will have brilliant music, drama, and the like, followed by a very inferior spoken presentation of the message.

Entertainment has taken over as a way of attracting people to church. Now, I am not against entertainment. I work for Youth for Christ, and entertainment is one the main ways we make contact with young people. But it is a *point of contact;* it is not our message. I fear that somewhere along the way the medium has succeeded in obscuring the message.

God told Jeremiah, "I will make my words in your mouth a fire and

---

[12]Henri Nouwen, *In the Name of Jesus* (New York: Crossroad, 1993), 65-66.

these people the wood it consumes" (Jer. 5:14). It was not a popular message, but it accomplished what God wanted it to accomplish. (Incidentally, if Jeremiah were to apply for a pastor's job today, the search committee would probably not only reject him, but would recommend that he be sent for psychiatric treatment.)

My homiletics teacher, Dr. Donald Demaray, in his beautiful little book *Preacher Aflame* refers to a statement about John Wesley: "At Aldersgate [that's where he had his heart-warming conversion experience] God took a stuffy Oxford don and transformed him into a holy incendiary who went up and down the British Isles spreading the fire of revival wherever he went." Demaray also reminds us that "Benjamin Franklin said he often went to hear George Whitefield because there before his eyes he could watch a man burn."[13]

Today's generation is afraid of intensity. They have seen too many urgent people lead others astray. They feel uncomfortable when people burn with passion over a given topic, especially if it belongs to the religious sphere. But we mustn't discard a biblical concept because of the misuse of intensity by unworthy people like Jim Jones, David Koresh, and Adolf Hitler. Intensity has worked throughout history, and I believe that a person with loving, holy, and informed intensity would be considered to be health-giving and thus attractive even by this bewildered generation.

In missiological studies there is much work being done on the nature of mission and on strategy, but much less work done on the message. Much work is being done on church growth, signs and wonders, missionary anthropology, sociology, and history. I praise God for that. But we must not forget to study our message and how best to communicate it. Shall we call this "kerygmology"? Our message is our greatest resource. It is still the greatest attraction about Christianity.

HOW JOY HELPS US PERSEVERE AMIDST HARDSHIP

The Christian ministry has many elements to it that drains us emotionally. We are misunderstood, maligned, and persecuted. Our status in society gets lower and lower as people lose their esteem for the Gospel. Evangelism has rarely won respectability in any society. We

---

[13]Donald E. Demaray, *Preacher Aflame* (Grand Rapids, Mich.: Baker, 1972), 14.

face failure as programs and people fail to live up to our expectations. All these can have a draining effect on us, especially because we have made so many sacrifices to be in this work. They can leave us emotionally cold and without a spark in our ministries.

Often what God uses to charge our spiritual and emotional batteries is the thrilling reality that the Word of God we handle is true. As Psalm 119:92 puts it, "If your law had not been my delight, I would have perished in my affliction." We find delight as we are reading the Scriptures, and that great sense that we are living in the sphere of eternal security overwhelms us. We reason, "This is God's Word, it is eternally true, and look at how relevantly it speaks to our situation! This is a great sphere to dwell in—the sphere of the Spirit of truth." A freshness comes upon us.

The year 1989 was one of the most tragic years in Sri Lanka's history. Possibly as many as fifty thousand people were killed in an insurgency. And most of them were young people. I struggled much with despair that year. Sometimes my moods would affect my family adversely, and that is not good. Once when my wife saw me in a bad mood, she told our children, "Father is in a bad mood. Let's hope he goes and reads his Bible." She knew that when I spend time with my Bible I emerge with the joy of the Lord.

Jeremiah's confession at a time of deep discouragement is very revealing. Jeremiah 20:1-2 says, "When the priest Pashhur son of Immer, the chief officer in the temple of the Lord, heard Jeremiah prophesying these things, he had Jeremiah the prophet beaten and put in the stocks at the Upper Gate of Benjamin at the Lord's temple." The chief officer of the temple of God is persecuting the prophet of God! The biggest pain that a Christian worker has is not from attacks from outside the church. Attacks from within the church are always more painful than serious persecution. After all we have sacrificed for others for such meager material rewards, we are misunderstood, slandered, and ignored in our time of need. That we will experience this is as sure as the sunrise in the morning. We'd better be prepared to face it!

Jeremiah's personal reaction to all this is quite predictable. After his release the next day he says, "O Lord, you deceived me, and I was deceived; you overpowered me and prevailed. I am ridiculed all day long; everyone mocks me. Whenever I speak, I cry out proclaiming violence and destruction. So the word of the Lord has brought me insult and reproach all day long" (Jer. 20:7-8). He considers giving up this ministry, but he finds that he cannot. "But if I say, 'I will not mention him or speak any more in his name,' his word is in my heart like a burning fire, shut up in my bones. I am weary of holding it in; indeed, I cannot" (Jer. 20:9).

There's the key to continuing urgency. The Word is like a fire crying out for release; it simply must be shared. In fact, Jeremiah says he is weary of holding it in. Most of us get tired from preaching. Jeremiah is tired because of the strain of holding it in, of not preaching. You remember how the two disciples felt on the road to Emmaus? They asked each other, "Were not our hearts burning within us while he talked with us on the road and opened the Scriptures to us?" (Luke 24:32). Truth has a way of burning in our hearts. And as we go to the Scriptures bewildered by the challenges we are facing in life, such an experience awaits us too.

David faced severe crises with enemies on all sides when he wrote Psalm 27. In this psalm he gives a hint as to how he weathered these terrible experiences and came out as a radiant singer of songs of praise. He says, "One thing I ask of the Lord, this is what I seek: that I may dwell in the house of the Lord all the days of my life, to gaze upon the beauty of the Lord and to seek him in his temple" (Ps. 27:4). How does one gaze at the beauty of the Lord? By reflecting lovingly over His message; by meditating on the truths of the Gospel.

Truth, then, is an essential feature of our relationship with God. When we think of commitment to truth, we must not think only of a dogged orthodoxy. It involves that and more. The heart of Christianity is our love relationship with Jesus, the truth. Truths about one we are deeply in love with are things that cause ecstasy in our minds. There's the glow of love in them. So when we think of commitment to truth, we must also think of loving ecstasy. It's just like in a marriage relationship. Dogged commitment is the springboard for truly ecstatic romance.

But to know this ecstasy, we must stop our mad rush and linger in loving contemplation of truth. As the psalmist says, "I delight in your commandments because I love them. I reach out my hands for your commandments because I love them, and I meditate on your decrees"

(Ps. 119:47-48). Meditation is an expression of love, and delight is its reward.

I believe that when we lose this wonder over the Word, we also lose the spark and freshness in our ministries. Gypsy Smith (1860-1947) was a British evangelist who preached the Gospel for seventy years. He died of a heart attack at sea at age eighty-seven en route to the United States. When earlier asked the secret of his freshness and vigor, he responded, "I never lost the wonder."

What is this wonder over the Word? I think it is the amazement over its contents and the thought that the Gospel reached out to us and made us its bearers. It is a thrill to think that we are heralds of such a great Gospel. Paul expresses this beautifully in the first chapter of 1 Timothy. The ecstatic reflection found here is sparked by a simple reference to the Gospel. He says, "and for whatever else is contrary to the sound doctrine that conforms to the glorious gospel of the blessed God, which he entrusted to me." (1 Tim. 1:10b-11). This makes him go on a tangent about his call. Paul would not do too well with a term paper assignment today. He gets too excited and creates too many rapturous tangents. About half of 2 Corinthians is a tangent. Tangents are one of the hazards of discovering the joy of truth. But isn't that what Christian meditation is? It defies our neatly and logically built-up systems and bursts forth with a new entity called delight.

Paul's tangent begins with a word of thanks:

> I thank Christ Jesus our Lord, who has given me strength, that he considered me faithful, appointing me to his service. Even though I was once a blasphemer and a persecutor and a violent man, I was shown mercy because I acted in ignorance and unbelief. The grace of our Lord was poured out on me abundantly, along with the faith and love that are in Christ Jesus. (1 Tim. 1:12-14)

From his call to preach this Gospel he has moved to the fact that this Gospel has reached out to him despite his unworthiness. He continues on this theme:

> Here is a trustworthy saying that deserves full acceptance: Christ Jesus came into the world to save sinners—of whom I am the worst. But for that very reason I was shown mercy so that in me, the worst

of sinners, Christ Jesus might display his unlimited patience as an example for those who would believe on him and receive eternal life. (1 Tim. 1 15-16)

This is too much for Paul. All he can do now is burst forth into an ecstatic doxology (which happens to be my favorite verse in the Bible): "Now to the King eternal, immortal, invisible, the only God, be honor and glory for ever and ever. Amen" (1 Tim. 1:17). He has reached the heights of ecstasy. And he was writing from prison! God would not have given us the capacity for ecstasy if he had not intended us to experience it. And as the Psalms tell us, the Word of God is one of those things that triggers ecstasy.

Jesus succinctly described the experience that Paul was struggling to explain here when he said, "You will know the truth, and the truth will set you free" (John 8:32). As we experience the truth, we find freedom from dependence on this unstable world for fulfillment, freedom from the dehumanizing power of sin, freedom to dwell in the sphere of eternity where there are springs of eternal joy (Ps. 16:11) that will satisfy our deepest aspirations. So, as Jesus said, we must continue in His Word (John 8:31).

When we continue in the Word, we will find that it ministers to us when things go wrong in our lives. To be sure, we don't always feel ecstatic at such times, for our minds are clouded by the troubles we face. Our attitude is more one of anger or anxiety or fear or perplexity. And that is natural. Thank God, the Bible records the perplexity of many of the saints in times of crisis. We realize we are not abnormal when we react like that. But the Bible also gives us many instances when these perplexed saints went to God and grappled with the apparent contradiction between their temporal situation and the eternal truths of the Word. They realized that their mind needed to address their heart, that their theology needed to address their experience. So they preached to themselves until the eternal truths got down to their hearts.

Psalms 42 and 43 were written when the Psalmist was in a desperate situation. Three times in these Psalms we find him saying the same thing: "Why are you downcast, O my soul? Why so disturbed within me? Put your hope in God, for I will yet praise him, my Savior and my God" (Ps. 42:5; see also verse 11 and 43:5). Why three times? It must be because he is like us! It takes some time for the gloom to leave and the vision of eternal truth to come back.

In fact, at such times it may be helpful for us to rely on the thoughts of others, as our thoughts are clouded by the problems we face. This is what Paul and Silas did in the jail in Philippi. I don't think they felt particularly joyful or like praising God at that time. They had been unjustly beaten and imprisoned. Later, when they were released, they protested about the treatment they had received. But still they rejoiced. They used the thoughts of others to help them fix their mind on God. Acts 16.25 says, "About midnight Paul and Silas were praying and singing hymns to God, and the other prisoners were listening to them." They sang hymns—songs of praise written by others. We, too, should not let the actions of bad people ruin our joy.

I have found that in some of my darkest moments my hymnbook really ministers to me. I sit down at the piano and begin to go through the hymn book. At first I can read the hymns only silently. I don't feel like singing. But soon the truths I have been reading about travel from the mind to the heart, and I want to sing. Indeed, I have great joy as I realize that the eternal truth of God is greater than my temporal problems.

This is how truth ministers joy to us. In this fast-moving, efficient society that finds security in its technology and in the marvels of its entertainment, may we look to eternal truth for our security and also for our ecstasy! What place does all of this have in a discussion on the supremacy of Christ? It tells us of the glorious experience we have from realizing that Jesus is the Truth. This is an experience unmatched by other faiths. It is an experience of the eternal God, and only the eternal God can give us eternal joy.

Part Two

JESUS IS THE WAY

CHAPTER NINE

THE MEANING OF THE CROSS

T HE FIRST PART of this book presented Christ as the truth, and a great theme that ran through it is that Christianity is Christ. If Christianity is Christ, then His cross is the key to understanding Him. The space given to the last week before the Crucifixion is evidence of how important the disciples considered His death to be. It occupies about 30 percent of Matthew, 37 percent of Mark, 25 percent of Luke, and 41 percent of John.[1] The English theologian P. T. Forsyth says, "Christ is to us just what his cross is. All that Christ was in heaven or on earth was put into what he did there.... You do not understand Christ till you understand his cross."[2] The church's first great theologian, the apostle Paul, would have agreed with Forsyth. Listen to how he describes his life and ministry: "We preach Christ crucified" (1 Cor. 1:23); "For I resolved to know nothing while I was with you except Jesus Christ and him crucified" (1 Cor. 2:2); "May I never boast except in the cross of our Lord Jesus Christ, through which the world has been crucified to me, and I to the world" (Gal. 6:14).

---

[1] Calculated from figures provided in W. Griffith Thomas, *Christianity Is Christ* (1948; reprint, New Canaan, Conn.: Keats Publishing, 1981), 34.

[2] P. T. Forsyth, *The Cruciality of the Cross* (London: Hodder and Stoughton, 1909), 44-45, quoted in John Stott, *The Cross of Christ* (Leicester and Downers Grove, Ill.: InterVarsity Press, 1986), 43.

Our discussion of the Cross is done under the general heading, "Jesus Is the way." This is because when Jesus says that He is the way in John 14:6, He means that He will become this through death, as the context of this verse (John 13:33–14:5) reveals. What the Cross of Christ achieved is so vast and so deep that numerous interpretations of it have appeared in the history of the Church.[3] Here we will present the three main streams of interpretation: the objective approach, the subjective approach, and the dramatic approach. These approaches are not mutually exclusive. Each brings to light a facet of the meaning of this great event, the depths of which we could never fully plumb.

THE OBJECTIVE APPROACH: SATISFYING THE DEMANDS OF JUSTICE

In the objective approach, the emphasis is on God who satisfies Himself and the demands of justice by fulfilling the necessary requirements for humanity's forgiveness. This approach was championed by Anselm (1033-1109), the Archbishop of Canterbury who has been acknowledged as the greatest scholar in the history of the church between the times of Augustine and Thomas Aquinas. We will examine the objective approach by introducing seven important concepts found in the New Testament in connection with Christ's death. But first we must look at the term *blood*, which is used very frequently in the New Testament to describe the death of Christ.

THE MEANING OF THE TERM *BLOOD*

British Methodist scholar Vincent Taylor has pointed out that the blood of Christ is mentioned nearly three times as often in the New Testament as is the cross of Christ and five times as often as the death of Christ.[4] In this century, a view was popularized that understood the blood of Christ as referring "not to his death but rather for his life released through death, and thus set free to be used for new purposes,

---

[3]For a comprehensive description of the different views that have emerged in history, see, H. D. McDonald, *The Atonement of the Death of Christ* (Grand Rapids, Mich.: Baker, 1985).

[4]Vincent Taylor, *The Atonement in New Testament Teaching* (London: Epworth, 1949), 177.

and made available for man's appropriation, particularly, as some would say, in the Eucharist."[5] This view has been associated with such past luminaries of British New Testament scholarship as Vincent Taylor, C. H. Dodd, and B. F. Westcott. In the 1950s evangelical scholars like Leon Morris and Alan Stibbs opposed this view and showed that the older view is a more valid understanding of the biblical use of the word *blood*.[6]

After a careful study of the use of the word *blood* in the Bible, Alan Stibbs concludes that the "blood is a visible token of *life violently ended*; it is a sign of life either given or taken in death." Stibbs says that "such giving or taking of life is in this world the extreme, both of gift or price and of crime or penalty. Man knows no greater."[7] Stibbs's brilliant summary of the significance of blood is so good that I will quote from it at length.

> The greatest offering or service one can render is to give one's blood or life. "Greater love has no man than this, that a man lay down his life for his friends" [John 15:13].

> The greatest earthly crime or evil is to take blood or life, that is, manslaughter or murder.

> The great penalty or loss is to have one's blood shed or life taken. "The wages of sin is death" [Rom. 6:23].

> The only possible or adequate expiation or atonement is life for life and blood for blood. This expiation man cannot give [see Psa. 49:7-8; Mark 8:36-37]. Not only is his own life already forfeit as a sinner. But also all life is God's. So man has no "blood" that he can give. This necessary but otherwise unobtainable gift God has given.[8]

---

[5]This is Alan M. Stibbs's explanation of this view in *The Meaning of the Word Blood in Scripture* (London: Tyndale, 1954), 4.
[6]See Leon Morris, *The Apostolic Preaching of the Cross* (Grand Rapids, Mich.: Eerdmans, 1955), 108-24 and Stibbs, *The Meaning of the Word Blood*.
[7]Stibbs, *The Meaning of the Word Blood*, 30 (italics mine).
[8]Ibid.

SUBSTITUTION

The first important concept found in the New Testament in connection with Christ's death and perhaps the most basic feature about Jesus' death is that He took our place and bore the punishment for our sin. He was our substitute. Peter, who first revolted against the idea of Jesus' being crucified, later wrote two significant statements about this: "He himself bore our sins in his body on the tree, so that we might die to sins and live for righteousness; by his wounds you have been healed" (1 Pet. 2:24); "For Christ died for sins once for all, the righteous for the unrighteous, to bring you to God" (1 Pet. 3:18). Some statements of Isaiah 53, which was a prophecy that Jesus and the apostles applied to the death of Christ, present this very clearly:

> Surely he took up our infirmities and carried our sorrows ... he was pierced for our transgressions, he was crushed for our iniquities; the punishment that brought us peace was upon him, and by his wounds we are healed. We all, like sheep, have gone astray, each of us has turned to his own way; and the Lord has laid on him the iniquity of us all. (Isa. 53:4-6)

Perhaps the verse in the Bible that presents the extent of Christ's substitution most vividly is 2 Corinthians 5:21: "God made him who had no sin to be sin for us, so that in him we might become the righteousness of God." This is something we will never fully grasp, for we do not know what it is to not have sin; and though we are all sinners, I do not see how we would be able to bear the sins of anyone else, apart from our own.

I was at a meeting of Christian leaders in Sri Lanka when God's Spirit broke through with great conviction one night. For two days after that I spent all the free time I had counseling with leaders. Many of the appointments included confession of sin. The strain of trying to bear in a small way the pain of these Christians under conviction became so heavy that I could hardly stand it any longer. I got my wife to join me whenever I could, just to share the burden. At that conference it occurred to me that if I found the pain of empathizing with confessing Christian leaders so hard to bear, what utter and absolute agony must Christ have experienced when He bore all the sin of the world.

This is why He was "deeply distressed and troubled" in the garden of Gethsemane and said, "My soul is overwhelmed with sorrow to the point of death" (Mark 14:33-34). This is why He cried, "Abba, Father, everything is possible for you. Take this cup from me. Yet not what I will, but what you will" (Mark 14:36). He was talking about drinking the cup of God's wrath against sin. He knew that this included being forsaken by the Father, as His cry of dereliction from the cross showed (Mark 15:34). John Stott explains this in his glorious book *The Cross of Christ*, saying, "From this contact with human sin his sinless soul recoiled. From the experience of alienation from his Father which the judgment on sin would involve, he hung back in horror."[9]

FORGIVENESS

The immediate result of our appropriating the benefits of the death of Christ is the forgiveness of sins. And that death was necessary for the forgiveness to be granted, as Hebrews 9.22 explains: "In fact, the law requires that nearly everything be cleansed with blood, and without the shedding of blood there is no forgiveness." John describes this by using three important words that explain the way God forgives us: "If we (1) *confess* our sins, he is (2) *faithful* and (3) *just* and will forgive us our sins and purify us from all unrighteousness" (1 John 1:9). On our part, we must confess sin. On God's part He forgives us. In so doing, He is faithful and just. John Stott explains this as meaning, "he is faithful to forgive because he has promised to do so, and just because Jesus died for our sins."[10] His punishment on our behalf fulfilled the demands of justice.

The message of forgiveness is one of the most revolutionary aspects of the Christian Gospel. In the next chapter we will show that fallen humanity in its bid to regain its lost self-esteem tries to offset the affects of its sin by self-effort. But humanity cannot adequately solve the problem of guilt. Only forgiveness can do that. The famous psychiatrist Karl

---

[9]John Stott, *The Cross of Christ* (Leicester and Downers Grove, Ill.: InterVarsity Press, 1986), 77. See pp. 72-83 for a defense of this interpretation of Christ's words in the garden and on the cross.
[10]John Stott, "The Letters of John," *Tyndale New Testament Commentaries*, rev. ed. (Leicester: InterVarsity Press; Grand Rapids, Mich.: Eerdmans , 1988), 83.

Menninger is reported to have said that if he could convince the patients of his psychiatric hospitals that their sins are forgiven, 75 percent of them would walk out the next day.[11] We have found this to be true in our ministry with youth involved in violent terrorism. If we can break through the exterior toughness that they have developed to survive in this hard life, we will discover that they are struggling with guilt over their actions.

Bakht Singh was a convert from the Sikh religion who became one of the most powerful evangelists in India in this century. Missiologist George Peters tells how he once talked with Bakht Singh about what he emphasized in his evangelistic ministry in India. Peters asked him whether it was the love of God or the wrath of God or Christ and Him crucified or eternal life. To all these queries Singh gave a negative answer and showed how they would be misunderstood in the Indian context. When Peters asked him what it was that Singh emphasized, he said, "I have never yet failed to get a hearing if I talk to them about forgiveness of sins and peace and rest in your heart. That's the product that sells well. Soon they ask me how they can get it. Having won their hearing I lead them on to the Savior who alone can meet their deepest needs."[12]

We have found, especially in our work with the very poor, that some people do not have a sense of guilt over sin; so the message of forgiveness does not at first seem to be relevant to them. Many of the things we consider to be sin, such as adultery and lying, they do not consider to be sins. A major reason for this is that these people do not believe in a supreme God who is holy and to whom they are responsible for their actions. Of course, we know that deep down there is a sense of sin in them, as their conscience has not been totally obliterated. This must be brought to the surface before they can understand the grace of God. This is a great challenge to the evangelist.

One way we can help people realize the seriousness of their sinful-

---

[11]Quoted in *Illustrations for Biblical Preaching,* ed. Michael P. Green (Grand Rapids, Mich.: Baker, 1989), 156. Menninger's solution to this problem, as described in his book *Whatever Became of Sin?* (New York: Hawthorn, 1972) falls short of the Christian Gospel somewhat, as John Stott has shown in *The Cross of Christ,* 100.

[12]George W. Peters, "Issues Confronting Evangelical Missions," in *Evangelical Missions Tomorrow,* eds. Wade Coggins and E. L. Frizen (Pasadena, Calif.: William Carey Library, 1977), 167, quoted in David J. Hesselgrave, *Communicating Christ Cross-culturally* (Grand Rapids, Mich.: Zondervan , 1978), 169.

ness is to emphasize the holiness of the supreme God in our preaching. Jesus Himself said, "But I will show you whom you should fear: Fear him who, after the killing of the body, has power to throw you into hell. Yes, I tell you, fear him" (Luke 12:5). Many people who have no sense of sin are nevertheless subject to much fear. Some experts say that fear is the dominant emotion of many people. Some in Sri Lanka, for example, fear to displease the gods and are therefore careful not to break the codes of these gods. Usually these codes are magical or what we would call superstition. Yet the fact that these people are afraid of displeasing the gods could be a stepping stone to telling them about the dangers of displeasing the supreme God. That this has been done effectively in the history of the church by evangelists working among the poor is well known. Preachers who saw many converted through their ministries first preached the holiness of God and warned people to flee from the wrath to come. Once the people were conscious of the seriousness of sin, they were able to respond positively to the message of grace.

I believe that there must surely be a lesson here for those who are evangelizing people in western countries too. Modern westerners generally ignore the reality of sin, as psychiatrist Karl Menninger shows in his book *Whatever Became of Sin?*[23] Much modern evangelism in the West also downplays sin and repentance because these concepts are considered to be hindrances to winning a hearing for the Gospel. But how can we adequately introduce people to the Savior if we do not introduce that from which He saves us? Indeed, we may need to use something else to win a hearing; but once the hearing is won, we must present this basic feature of the human malady.

PURIFICATION

The next five concepts explain, using five figures from daily life, what was achieved through Christ's being our substitute and thereby earning our forgiveness. Each figure is inadequate to totally convey the fullness of the meaning of the Cross. But taken together they give us a rich picture of Christ's work.

The first figure, purification, comes from home life where dirty

---

[13]See footnote 6. Karl Menninger, *Whatever Became of Sin?*

things are cleaned. It appears in 1 John 1:9, which we quoted above. Two verses earlier John describes this even more graphically: "the blood of Jesus, his Son, purifies us from every sin" (1 John 1:7). One important aspect of the cleansing that comes to us through Christ is the cleansing of our consciences. Hebrews 9:14 says, "How much more, then, will the blood of Christ, who through the eternal Spirit offered himself unblemished to God, cleanse our consciences from acts that lead to death, so that we may serve the living God!"

This subjective aspect of forgiveness accounts much for the freedom we receive through forgiving grace. Our essential humanity, with its vestiges of the image of God working though our consciences, says that sin makes us unclean. We try to suppress these thoughts, but they always remain, perhaps hidden but not completely forgotten. The discovery of a cleansed conscience is therefore a liberating experience. When a woman who had previously lived an immoral life understood the meaning of God's cleansing, she happily exclaimed, "In God's sight, I am a virgin." She was right, for God, describing the blessings of the new covenant, said, "For I will forgive their wickedness and will remember their sins no more" (Jer. 31:34).

PROPITIATION

The next figure, propitiation, comes from the temple ritual. This word and its related words are used in the *King James Version* for the Greek words *hilasmos* (noun: 1 John 2:2; 4:10), *hilastērios* (adjective: Rom. 3:25), and *hilaskomai* (verb: Heb. 2:17). The word *propitiation* is related to the rituals of the temple where sacrifices are given to turn away God's wrath against sin. The meaning is well expressed in the rendering of 1 John 2:2 in *The Living Bible:* "He is the one who took God's wrath against our sins upon himself, and brought us into fellowship with God."

However, there is disagreement about the meaning of these Greek words. Evangelical scholars like Leon Morris have shown convincingly (to me) that the traditional interpretation of propitiation, meaning pacifying or turning away God's wrath, is still valid.[14] The NASB and the

---

[14]Morris, *Apostolic Preaching*, 125-85. Morris's ideas are presented in a simpler form in his book *The Atonement* (Leicester and Downers Grove, Ill.: InterVarsity Press, 1983), 151-76.

NKJV are among modern translations that preserve the word *propitiation.* But scholars like C. H. Dodd prefer the idea of expiation, which means to make amends for a wrong.[15] This is reflected in translations like the NEB, REB, and RSV (the NRSV and NIV use the more neutral *atoning sacrifice*).

Propitiation focuses on the seriousness of sin and God's wrath against it, which is borne by Jesus. Perhaps the reason we find this difficult to accept is because the doctrine of God's wrath has been neglected by the church. Today we find it difficult to think that words like the following came from the lips of Jesus: "You snakes! You brood of vipers! How will you escape being condemned to hell?" (Matt. 23:33). We are surprised to read descriptions of God like the following: "Your eyes are too pure to look on evil; you cannot tolerate wrong" (Hab. 1:13). We have lost the abhorrence for sin that is found in the Bible.

Right through church history efforts have been made to tone down the biblical teaching of God's wrath. In the second century, Marcion tried to separate the loving Father of the New Testament from the supposedly vindictive God of the Old Testament. F. D. E. Schleiermacher and A. Ritschl in the nineteenth century and C. H. Dodd and A. T. Hanson in this century tried to divorce wrath from the essential nature of God. Dodd said that wrath is retained in the New Testament "not to describe the attitude of God to man, but to describe the inevitable process of retribution."[16] Hanson looked at wrath as an impersonal character and said that it "does not describe an attitude of God but a condition of men."[17] This view has been ably countered and shown to be not in keeping with the biblical witness.[18] In both the Old and New Testaments wrath is considered part of the essential nature of God.

---

[15]C. H. Dodd, *The Bible and the Greeks* (London: Hodder and Stoughton, 1935); and *The Epistle of Paul to the Romans* (London: Hodder and Stoughton, 1932).

[16]Dodd, *Romans*, 23.

[17]A. T. Hanson, *The Wrath of the Lamb* (London: SPCK, 1959), 110.

[18]See Gustav Stahlin, "*Orge*," in *The Theological Dictionary of the New Testament*, vol. 5, ed. Gerhard Friedrich, trans. and ed. Geoffrey W. Bromiley (Grand Rapids, Mich.: Eerdmans, 1968), 427-29; Morris, *Apostolic Preaching*, 129-36, 161-66; and Ajith Fernando, "Wrath Versus Love," in *Crucial Questions About Hell* (Eastbourne: Kingsway, 1991; Wheaton, Ill.: Crossway Books, 1994), chap. 10.

We will miss so much of the significance of Christ's death if we take wrath out of the reckoning. We will also miss something of the freedom of forgiveness if we do not realize that God's anger against our sin has been fully spent on Jesus.

REDEMPTION

The next figure, redemption (Greek: *apolutrōsis, agorazō, exagorazō*) comes from the marketplace where, in those days, slaves were purchased for a price. It speaks of the purchase of our salvation through the payment of a price for our sins. Ephesians 1:7 says, "In him we have redemption through his blood, the forgiveness of sins, in accordance with the riches of God's grace" (see also Col. 1:14; Heb. 9:12; 1 Cor. 6:20; Rev. 5:9; Gal. 3:13). The New Testament also uses the related figure of ransom (Greek: *lutron, antilutron*), which refers to the price Jesus paid to purchase our salvation (Mark 10:45; 1 Tim 2:6). The focus here is on the freedom we receive from the captivity of sin, through the price paid by Christ.

The story of the boy and his toy boat expresses the biblical idea of redemption beautifully. A boy had a toy boat that he loved very much because he himself had made it. He took it to a lake one day and let it float on the water. Suddenly a gust of wind came and carried the boat beyond his reach. Sadly the boy saw it go away from him until it was finally out of sight. Some days later he passed a shop and was surprised to see his boat on sale there. When he told the person at the shop that it was his boat, he was informed that he needed to pay for it if he was to have it. He worked hard at whatever jobs he could find until he was at last able to buy the boat. When he got the boat back he whispered to it, "You are twice mine. I made you, and now I have bought you." Jesus did something like this for us when He died on the cross.

To whom was the redemption price paid? Early Christian thinkers like Origen (c. 185-c. 254), Gregory of Nyssa (330-c. 395), Gregory the Great (540-604), and Peter Lombard (c. 1095-c. 1164) said that it was to Satan. Bizarre theories of the transaction that took place between God and Satan were proposed.[19] The advice of Leon Morris, perhaps the foremost evangelical expert today on the bibli-

---

[19]See McDonald, *The Atonement of the Death*, 138-46.

cal teaching of the Cross, is pertinent here. He believes that it is illegitimate to look for a recipient of the ransom. This is because "in the New Testament there is never a hint of a recipient." Morris says, "We must understand redemption as a useful metaphor which enables us to see some aspects of Christ's great saving work with clarity but which is not an exact description of the whole process of salvation. We must not press it beyond what the New Testament tells us about it."[20]

JUSTIFICATION

Romans 4:25 says, "He was delivered over to death for our sins and was raised to life for our justification." The word *justification* means "to pronounce, accept and treat as just." The figure comes from the law court, and it denotes "a judicial act of administering the law—in this case by declaring a verdict of acquittal, and so excluding all possibility of condemnation."[21] Romans 5:16, 18 describes what happened in our justification: "The judgment followed one sin and brought condemnation, but the gift followed many trespasses and brought justification. . . . Consequently, just as the result of one trespass was condemnation for all men, so also the result of one act of righteousness was justification that brings life for all men."

Some are reluctant to accept this judicial element as being part of the work of Christ, so they take it to mean "forgiveness." In Sri Lanka *The New Sinhala Bible* gave it the meaning "bringing into relationship with God" (against which I protested vehemently). I was relieved to hear that this has been changed in an upcoming revision. These approaches have been ably countered by people like Leon Morris[22] and John Stott.[23] Judicial language is often used to describe Christ's work on our behalf. One of the clearest instances of this is 1 John 2:1 where Jesus is described as our "advocate with the father" (KJV, NAS, NRSV, etc.) who appears on our behalf when we sin.

---

[20]Morris, *Atonement*, 129.
[21]J. I. Packer, "Justification," in *The Evangelical Dictionary of Theology*, ed. Walter A. Elwell (Grand Rapids, Mich.: Baker, 1984), 593.
[22]Morris, *Apostolic Preaching*, 224-74; *Atonement*, 177-202.
[23]Stott, *Cross of Christ*, 182-92.

RECONCILIATION

The last of the figures is reconciliation, and it comes from family life and friendship. Paul says, "God was reconciling the world to himself in Christ, not counting men's sins against them" (2 Cor. 5:19). Reconciliation is necessary because sin is rebellion against God and results in enmity between God and humankind. Romans 5:10 says, "when we were God's enemies, we were reconciled to him through the death of his Son." The result is "peace with God" (Rom. 5:1) and adoption into His family (John 1:12; 1 John 3:1-10). It is from this act of reconciliation that the word *atonement* comes. It means that we have been made "at one" with God (at-one-ment).

The last four figures describe beautifully and comprehensively what happened at the Cross. "Propitiation invariably comes first," says John Stott, "for until the wrath of God is appeased (that is, until his love has found a way to avert his anger), there can be no salvation of human beings at all."[24] Now God can rescue us by paying a high price (redemption). That is the negative side of salvation. On the positive side He can pronounce a verdict of acquittal (justification) and enter into a relationship of love with us (reconciliation).

There are other terms related to the objective approach that the Bible uses, such as sacrifice (which we will consider in the next chapter) and covenant. I think, however, that the seven we have used give us an adequate glimpse, and it is only a glimpse, of the richness of what Christ achieved on the Cross.

THE SUBJECTIVE APPROACH: THE INSPIRATION OF THE CROSS

Anselm's contemporary, the French theologian Peter Abelard (1079-1142), emphasized the subjective approach of the death of Christ, unfortunately to the exclusion of the idea of substitution. In the subjective approach the emphasis is on how God inspires us through the emotional appeal of divine love as expressed in the death of Christ. The Cross, then, is a demonstration of love. This has come to be called the "moral influence theory." It points to a biblical feature of the results of

---

[24]Ibid., 182.

the death of Christ (see John 13:34; 15:12-14). Although it falls short of explaining the heart of the Cross, if held in conjunction with the objective approach it provides an important dimension of the work of Christ on the cross. We will look at this aspect in greater detail in chapter 12.

THE DRAMATIC APPROACH: THE CROSS AS A VICTORY

The Swedish theologian Gustav Aulen (1879-1978) emphasized, in his influential book *Christus Victor*,[25] that the Cross is the evidence of the victory of God in Christ over the powers of evil. It is called *the dramatic or classic approach* of the Cross. It is dramatic because it sees the atonement as a cosmic drama. This is, of course, a biblical emphasis. Paul said, "having disarmed the powers and authorities, he made a public spectacle of them, triumphing over them by the cross" (Col. 2:13b-15). Aulen calls this view the classic view because he says that this was "the ruling idea of the Atonement for the first thousand years of Christian history."[26]

As we will see in the next chapter, the emphasis on the Cross as a victory is a needed one today. In our culture, which places so much emphasis on success, a cross that does not emphasize the victory of the death of Christ appears to many to be the failure of a man who tried to be good.

THE CROSS IN EVANGELISM

Each of the three approaches to the Cross that we have looked at are helpful in the proclamation of the Gospel. But the objective approach must be considered primary and absolutely essential. The subjective approach elicits from us a response of grateful commitment, and that is very important. But ultimately what wins our salvation is not our commitment but God's act of justifying and regenerating us. We soon see that *our* efforts are feeble and inadequate. If our confidence rests primarily upon our personal response, our faith stands on very shaky, unstable ground. Only Christ's act of substitution on our behalf suffices to win our salvation.

The dramatic approach tells people living under the fear of cosmic

---

[25]Gustav Aulen, *Christus Victor*, trans. A. G. Herbert (London: SPCK, 1931).
[26]Ibid., 22-23.

forces, demons, and deities, which they believe control this world, that Jesus is the conqueror of all. They need fear evil no more. They need not fear reprisals from deities if they change religions and come to Christ. He is Victor and Lord over all these forces. Therefore, the wisest thing would be to have Him as our Lord. Yet, they must know that in order to have a relationship with the holy God, their sins, which are dangerously serious, must be forgiven. Only the objective approach adequately gives that knowledge. Therefore, the focus in our evangelistic proclamation should be on the objective.

Taken together, these three understandings of the Cross present the Creator's basic answer to the human dilemma. All other religious systems fall short in their effort to make things right between the Creator and the human being and to open the door for the rich blessings that the Creator seeks to bestow on His children. This chapter and those that follow will demonstrate the reality of the statement of Jesus that He is the only way to God. As the well-known hymn "There Is a Green Hill Far Away" puts it:

> *There was no other good enough*
> *To pay the price of sin;*
> *He only could unlock the gate*
> *Of heaven, and let us in.*

Cecil Frances Alexander (1823-95).

CHAPTER TEN

THE CROSS
CHALLENGES
HUMANISTIC
SELF-SUFFICIENCY

F ROM THE TIME that Jesus lived and on up to the present day, the doctrine of his atoning death by crucifixion has proved to be one of the most offensive aspects of His message. I will let Jewish author Hans Joachim Schoeps represent the large company who are outside the church and who object to the message of the cross: "It is an impossible article of belief, which detracts from God's sovereignty and absolute otherness—an article which, in fact, destroys the world. . . . If God could not look on in anguish while Abraham sacrificed his son, would he then have suffered his own son to be killed without destroying the entire world?"[1] Let the German New Testament scholar Rudolf Bultmann represent the objectors within the church: "How can the guilt of one man be expiated by the death of another who is sinless . . . ? What

---

[1]Hans Joachim Schoeps, *The Jewish Christian Argument* (London: Faber and Faber, 1965), 23, quoted in Colin Chapman, *Christianity on Trial* (Wheaton, Ill.: Tyndale House, 1975), 499.

a primitive mythology it is, that a divine Being should become incarnate and atone for the sins of men through his own blood!"[2]

I hope to show in the next few chapters that, while the message of the Cross raises many questions in the mind of the inquirer, upon closer scrutiny it will be seen as God's answer to the basic problems of humanity. I hope to demonstrate that the Christian doctrine of the atonement is not as strange as it first appears to the inquirer. This is what I have found when using the type of arguments presented in the pages that follow in my conversations with Buddhists and Hindus. Some have accepted the implications of the message and received the salvation Christ gives. Others have not been willing to pay the price of such a religious revolution in their lives. And many more have at least lost their disdain for the message of the cross.

SALVATION THROUGH CHRIST

In keeping with our practice in this book to let, wherever possible, Jesus' statements expound His supremacy, we will now look at the atonement work of Christ using, as a base for study, Jesus' own explanation of it in John 10:7-18. The disadvantage of this method is that some key issues may be missed. I have compensated for that by including issues that are not mentioned in this passage in chapter 11. The advantage of this method is that we will discuss issues that are not often included in our expositions of the cross, but are nevertheless important to Jesus' understanding of the cross. John 10:7-18 is the passage in which he refers to himself as the gate of the sheep and the Good Shepherd.

In John 10:7 Jesus says, "I tell you the truth, I am the gate for the sheep." This has a similar meaning to the statement, "I am the way." In verse 9 He expands His statement: "I am the gate; whoever enters through me will be saved." In John the word *to save* only occurs six times, in contrast to the other gospel writers who use it more frequently.[3] They often use it for the miracles, but in John the word has a

---

[2]Rudolf Bultmann, "The New Testament and Mythology," in *Kerygma and Myth*, ed. Hans Werner Bartsch, trans. Reginald H. Fuller (London: S.P.C.K., n.d.), 7, quoted in Daniel P. Fuller *The Unity of the Bible* (Grand Rapids, Mich.: Zondervan, 1992), 206.
[3]Matthew and Mark use it fifteen times each, Luke in his gospel uses it seventeen times, and Acts thirteen times.

more limited sense. "It denotes much the same as eternal life (the two are linked in 3:16-17)."[4] So, in John 10:9 Jesus is saying that the way to eternal life is through Himself. Then he says that the result of this salvation is that the believers have a real freedom and provision of their needs: "He will come in and go out, and find pasture" (verse 9b). Verse 10b gives another result of this salvation: "I have come that they may have life, and have it to the full" (verse 10b).

The theme of this paragraph, then, is that Jesus is the way to salvation, that he came to this world in order to bring this salvation to humanity. Implied in this is the fact that we cannot save ourselves and that there is no other way to salvation except through Jesus. In the next paragraph Jesus says that he will win our salvation by dying for us. Christianity, then, is a religion of grace, of God's acting in Christ to save us.

SHOULD WE NOT SAVE OURSELVES?

Many who are confronted with the Christian belief in grace ask, "Should we not save ourselves? Why should another die for us?" Most people would like to save themselves. Stephen Neill has said, "The last thing that modern individuals want is that anyone should do anything for them."[5] The message of the cross cuts at the heart of human pride, which is the essence of sin. Adam and Eve's sin was that they wanted to save themselves, independent of God. They did not want to be dependent on a supreme God for salvation or for anything else. The same thing happens today. People like to think that they are saving themselves. It makes them feel good and helps to temporarily still the voice of insecurity and emptiness that is theirs because they are separated from their Maker.

I believe this is why there is an increasing appeal, even in the West, to Buddhism, Hinduism, and New Age ideas, and also to their doctrine of reincarnation. These religious systems give people a sense of achievement. People have the satisfaction of earning their own salva-

---

[4]Leon Morris, *Reflections on the Gospel of John*, vol. 2 (Grand Rapids, Mich.: Baker, 1987), 374.

[5]Stephen Neill, *The Supremacy of Christ* (London: Hodder and Stoughton, 1984), 147-48.

tion through successive lives. They do not have to humble themselves and confess that they cannot help themselves and admit that their only hope is God's mercy. To accept mercy is a blow to their pride. To say that they can win their salvation by their own efforts makes them feel good. John Bunyan has said that when Jesus said we are to take up our crosses to follow him, the first aspect of this cross is "the destruction of [our] own righteousness for the righteousness of another."[6] Paul said that because salvation is by grace we lose our grounds for boasting (Eph. 2:8-9). And that is not easy for anyone in contemporary society.

Also distant from the biblical idea that we are guilty before God and in need of salvation is the belief of Hinduism and the New Age movements that we are all part of the divine. A statement from Swami Muktananda, who had a great influence on Werner Erhard, founder of est and FORUM, expresses well the mood of many people today: "Kneel to your own self. Honor and worship your own being. God dwells within you as You."[7] New Age analyst Theodore Roszak says that our goal is "to awaken the god who sleeps at the root of the human being."[8] Fallen humanity would, in its natural state of rebellion against God, prefer this approach to salvation.

When someone asks me the question, "Should we not pay for our sins?" I usually respond in the following way: the principle of paying for one's sins is found in every religion. The Bible also says, "Do not be deceived: God cannot be mocked. A man reaps what he sows" (Gal. 6.7). Buddhists and Hindus call this the law of karma. But the effects of a principle or law can be overcome by a more powerful force. Take the law of gravity. According to this law, if I hold a book up and let go of it, it will fall. But I can use another more powerful force and overcome the force that operates through the law of gravity. By catching the falling book and raising my arm, I can overcome the force of gravity and make the book reverse its direction. When I do that I do not break the law of gravity. I use a force that overcomes its effects.

God did something like this with us. He created us to live with

---

[6]John Bunyan, *The Heavenly Footman* (Houston: Christian Focus Publications, n.d.), 36.
[7]Quoted in Douglas R. Groothuis, *Unmasking the New Age* (Downers Grove, Ill.: InterVarsity Press, 1986), 21.
[8]Theodore Roszak, *Unfinished Animal* (New York: Harper and Row, 1977), 225, quoted in Groothuis, *Unmasking*, 21.

Himself. But we chose to live independent of Him. By doing this we heaped a terrible load of guilt upon ourselves. Those who try to offset this by their own efforts soon find that they don't have the strength to do so. However much they try, they are not able to tilt the scales of their lives in the direction of their innocence.

The Christian Gospel says that, seeing our helpless condition, our Creator did not abandon us. He brought into operation the law of love. And He let that save us. But He did so without breaking the law of justice or canceling its demands. What He did in love was to satisfy its demands. The demands of justice were not ignored or canceled. They were fully satisfied. And the only way that God could do that was by having his spotless Son take the punishment that was due to us. What we see here is an amazing love. He did for us what we could not do for ourselves. We call this grace, the result of which is salvation.

We often have situations in life where we cannot help ourselves and our only hope is to receive help from another. This is the case when someone is drowning. His only hope is a savior who will jump into the water to save him. In the religious sphere, however, there is the difficult challenge of getting people to accept that they need help. But those who honestly consider their chances of overcoming the effects of bad karma through their own strength realize what a difficult task this is. This difficulty is expressed in a Hindu story called "The Tale of the Banana Peel." A Brahmin (the highest caste in the Hindu system), while walking, saw a banana peel in the middle of his path. These often cause mishaps because people who trample them can slip and fall. His first thought was to step aside, avoid the peel, and walk on. Then he realized that he would reap the fruit of his actions. So he cleared the path by removing the peel, expecting to be rewarded for it in his next life. But he was born into a lower caste in his next life because he had thought of his own future welfare when he had removed the peel. This shows how difficult it is for one to produce enough good karma to merit salvation.

I know of many, trying to earn their salvation through karma, who find liberation in their understanding the truth about grace. One of these was my grandmother. Her mother died when she was three years old, and her father died when she was eighteen. Then, after eleven years of marriage, her husband died. Her mother was a Buddhist and her father a nominal Christian. She was a nominal Christian for a time, but then she reverted to Buddhism. When her husband was sick, she did all that Buddhism could do to offset her bad karma. Nothing seemed to work. Everyone assumed she was suffering for evil done in previous lives.

Then she heard a voice inside her that said, "Return to the faith you once had." She turned to the God of the Bible. She found that Jesus had died for her karma and that she did not have to suffer for her past actions because He had already suffered. She found salvation. And what a transformation there was in her life! My mother, who was at first quite upset about this change of religion, also found Christ. A whole generation was impacted by my grandmother's conversion. She lived into her eighties. And until the day she died, she radiated the love of Christ. No one observing her would have thought that she was a person who had had so much pain and sorrow in her life.

This is why our message is called the Gospel. It is good news! Jesus did for us what we could not do for ourselves. This makes the Gospel very different compared to the other religions. As someone has said,

> Religion says, "Attain"; the gospel says, "Obtain."
> Religion says, "Attempt"; the gospel says, "Accept."
> Religion says, "Try"; the gospel says, "Trust."
> Religion says, "Do this;" the gospel says, "It is done."[9]

We said in chapter 7 that we cannot accept the view that all the religions teach essentially the same thing. The above discussion should have underscored that fact. Much of the ethical teachings of Christianity are found in other faiths too, but those teachings do not come to the heart of the Christian gospel. Christianity is a religion of grace that has been won through the work of Christ in history, which is not found in other religions. So the similarities are peripheral. On the basics there is a vast difference. If Christianity and the other faiths were represented by circles, we might find that they intersect here and there.

---

[9]John T. Seamands, *Tell It Well: Communicating the Gospel Across Cultures* (Kansas City: Beacon Hill, 1981), 70.

But the centers of the circles will be far apart. Christianity moves on a different axis than the other religions.

Having said this, we must point out that even though many religions, in theory, have no place for salvation through the merits of another, in practice this idea is present. For example, the basic Buddhist scripture, the Dhammapada, says, "Purity and impurity depend on oneself. No one can purify another" (verse 165). There is no place for seeking the assistance of a higher being. Yet, in practice Buddhists seek to transfer merit to those who have died through almsgiving (*dana*). This practice of merit transference (*pattidana*) is present in a more formal way in the less orthodox Mahayana branch of Buddhism.

The idea of meriting from another's action is inherent in the human makeup. We were created to respond to grace, but we asserted our independence and chose to work for our own salvation. Yet, vestiges of that sense of the importance of grace remain and take forms that are unacceptable to God. However, as Sri Lankan theologian Tissa Weerasingha points out, this could be a stepping-stone to presenting the message of God's grace in Christ Jesus.[10]

HIS SACRIFICE FOR SIN

In John 10:11, Jesus changes from the gate metaphor to the shepherd metaphor saying, "I am the good shepherd. The good shepherd lays down his life for the sheep." The gate metaphor presented Jesus as being the way to salvation. Now Jesus says how He is going to become the way. A good shepherd is committed to his sheep, says Jesus. So he will die to save them from danger. Jesus is saying that He is going to die to save the human race.

This statement brings up a question that often emerges from our claim that Christ won our salvation: can one person die for another? Is it valid for one to benefit from the sacrifice of another? This is a question often asked by non-Christians. Jesus answers this by saying that if He is a good shepherd, then He should lay down His life for the sheep. That is what is expected of a good leader.

This principle of sacrifice is found throughout life, even among those

---

[10]On this see Tissa Weerasingha, "Explaining the Meaning of the Cross," in *The Cross and the Bo Tree* (Taichung: Asia Theological Association, 1989).

who revolt against the idea that Christ sacrificed His life for us. The whole of creation breathes the idea of one person dying to save another. Dr. E. Stanley Jones puts it like this: "The cross is in our blood. The white corpuscles circulate through the blood looking for infection. When they find it they absorb it if possible. If not, they throw themselves against the infection and die that the rest of the body might live. The pus that comes off is the corpses of the white corpuscles which have died that the rest might live"[11] Dr. Jones talks of the mother bird who throws herself into the open jaws of the serpent in order to save her young. We regard as heroes those who die in battle fighting for freedom. We think it is normal for a mother to stay awake night after night when her child is ill.

Once I was speaking on the Cross of Christ when the mother of a Buddhist convert from our ministry was present. It was the first time she had attended a Christian meeting. I asked her if she would consider it unusual for her to make great sacrifices when her son was sick. She said, "No." At the end of the meeting she said that the message of the Cross did not make sense to her. She must have eventually understood the message of the Cross because some months later it was my joy to be at a service where that mother and her son were baptized as Christians.

Dr. Jones concludes, "The Cross is inherent. It is not merely written in the Scriptures; it is plowed into the facts of life." Dr. J. T. Seamands, after a similar line of argumentation, says, "Now if this is a universal law—and it seems to be—then when we come to God, the highest being, we would expect to find in him the greatest and noblest expression of sacrificial love in the whole universe. Otherwise the creature would be greater than the Creator."[12]

What we are saying is that if there is a Creator and if this Creator sees His highest creation, the human race, in the mess it is in, without any hope of salvation, then we would expect Him to pay the supreme sacrifice in order to deliver us from this situation. Romans 5.8 says, "God proves his love for us in that while we were still sinners Christ died for us" (NRSV). The fact that Jesus died for us is the proof that He is indeed a loving God.

Dr. Jones speaks of a leading Christian in India who was a Brahmin

---

[11]E. Stanley Jones, *The Word Became Flesh* (Nashville: Abingdon, 1963), 109.
[12]Seamands, *Tell It Well*, 161-62.

before he became a Christian. The Brahmins, the highest caste in the Hindu system, are usually very resistant to the Gospel. When this man heard the message of the Cross for the first time, he said to himself, "If that isn't true, it ought to be true."[13] An old Chinese scholar who heard for the first time the story of God's work of redemption in Christ ran his fingers through his hair, turned to his neighbors, and said, "Didn't I tell you there ought to be a God like that!"[14]

Actually, this concept of sacrificing for others is found even in the religions that are hostile to the idea of Jesus' dying for our sins. Stephen Neill refers to "the immense part that the idea and the practice of sacrifice have played in the thoughts and the worship of the human race as far back as we can trace clearly human consciousness."[15] In Buddhist stories in Sri Lanka, we have many instances of heroes and heroines who sacrificed themselves on behalf of the country, whereupon large calamities like floods were averted because of the merit that accrued from their sacrifices.

In the earliest writings of Hinduism, the Vedas (1500-500 B.C.), the idea of sacrifice for the atonement of sin was very prevalent. Here is a statement from the Rig Veda, which is the oldest and most important of the Vedas: "Prajapati, Lord of creatures gave himself for them—he became their sacrifice."[16] In the Satapada Brahmana, which is a commentary on the second most important of the Vedas, the Yajur Veda, is found the statement, "God would offer himself as a sacrifice and obtain atonement for sins."[17] Stephen Neill says that though "in later days, blood sacrifices ceased to be offered in the great temples of Hinduism; in early times they played almost a central role in worship."[18] The nineteenth-century Indian Christian theologian K. M. Bannerjea used the idea of Prajapati's self-sacrifice in his dialogue with educated Hindus.[19]

---

[13]Jones, *The Word Became Flesh*, 125.
[14]Ibid., 114.
[15]Neill, *The Supremacy of Christ*, 138.
[16]Rig Veda, quoted in Jones, *The Word Became Flesh*, 116.
[17]Yajur Veda, quoted in Seamands, *Tell It Well*, 163.
[18]Neill, *The Supremacy of Christ*, 139.
[19]Noted in Bruce J. Nicholls, "Hinduism," in *The World's Religions*, ed. Sir Norman Anderson (Leicester: InterVarsity Press; Grand Rapids, Mich.: Eerdmans, 1975), 155.

Sadhu Chellappa is an effective Indian evangelist among the Hindus of Asia. Born into a Hindu family, he studied the Vedas of Hinduism in his youth. When he read about Prajapati, the god who will sacrifice himself for the sins of the world, he began a quest to find Prajapati. After a long search, he gave up in frustration and became an atheist. He plunged into the depths of drunkenness and dissipation. Finally, deeply in debt, he decided to commit suicide.

One day when he was returning home by train after work, he heard a voice saying over a nearby loudspeaker, "He that covereth his sins shall not prosper" (Prov. 28:13, KJV). These words struck him so strongly that he decided to disembark at the next station and go to the meeting from which this message came. When he discovered that it was a Christian meeting, he decided that though he would listen to the speaker, he would stay at a distance from the meeting. Soon the speaker began to explain how Jesus came into the world and died for sins. A thought came to Sadhu: "Could this be the Prajapati that I have been looking for?" He went for counseling at the end of the meeting and talked for about three hours, after which he finally accepted Christ's offer of salvation.

Soon Chellappa launched into a careful study of the Bible. After he had completed the first five books of the Old Testament, he became convinced that the early Hindu culture and religion had been derived from these five books, especially the book of Leviticus. Within a year he had led his whole family to Christ. He also began to study the Hindu scriptures deeply and saw more and more evidences that Jesus fulfills the aspirations of the Hindu and that there are many parallels between the Hindu scriptures and the Old Testament. Today these facts have become his method of approach to the Hindus.

Our point, then, is that even though a substitutionary atonement may sound strange to some at first, it is something with which our deepest instincts agree. We can trace these instincts to vestiges of the image of God in each human being and to the original revelation of God to the human race.[20]

---

[20]On this see my book *The Christian's Attitude Toward World Religions* (Wheaton, Ill.: Tyndale House, 1987).

THE DEFEAT OF A GREAT MAN?

Some years ago I spoke at a meeting in Sri Lanka on the topic of Christian witness. Being early for the meeting, I chatted with some of the people in the audience beforehand. One of them was a well-known Buddhist writer. He told me that the Buddha was superior to Jesus because even though Jesus lived a noble life, He was defeated through death in His battle for righteousness.

Paul must have encountered this type of argument often because he said, "but we preach Christ crucified: a stumbling block to Jews and foolishness to Gentiles" (1 Cor. 1:23). It was foolishness to the Gentiles. F. F. Bruce says, "In the eyes of the Gentiles the idea that salvation depended on one who had neither the wit nor the power to save himself from so disreputable a death was the height of folly."[21] And this is the viewpoint of a typical self-sufficient contemporary person.

Many view Jesus as a weakling who was too weak or too afraid to say a word in His defense when He was subjected to the humiliation that surrounded the events of the cross. Today's assertive individual finds this picture repulsive and regards Jesus as totally different than their model of a person they want to follow. But as we showed in our discussion of the life of Christ (chapter 4), Jesus was not the weakling He is often pictured to be. We must remember that the same Jesus who subjected Himself to death on the cross fearlessly drove the money changers out of the temple a few days before His death. He had earlier thundered accusations at the powerful religious leaders of the day. From such a person we would do wrong to expect the passive resignation of defeat at the hands of His opponents. We will have to look elsewhere for the immediate cause for His death.

If the Cross was folly to the Gentiles, it was, says Paul, "a stumbling block to Jews" (1 Cor. 1:23). The word translated "stumbling block" has the idea of something that "gives offense or causes revulsion, [or]

---

[21]F. F. Bruce, "The Epistle to the Galatians," in *The New International Greek Testament Commentary* (Grand Rapids, Mich.: Eerdmans, 1982), 237-38.

which causes opposition."[22] Gordon Fee says that "'Christ crucified' is a contradiction in terms, of the same category as 'fried ice.'"[23] As a Jew, Paul must have been repelled by this idea before his conversion. Quoting Deuteronomy 21:23 he said, "for it is written: 'Cursed is everyone who is hung on a tree'" (Gal. 3:13). When Jesus announced how He was going to die, Peter reacted like a typical Jew: He "took him aside and began to rebuke him. 'Never, Lord!' he said. 'This shall never happen to you!'" (Matt. 16:22). Later Jewry referred to Jesus derogatorily as "the hanged one."[24] The contemporary Jew reacts in a similar way, as the following quote from the *Jewish Encyclopedia* shows: "The very form of his punishment would disprove those claims in Jewish eyes. No Messiah that Jews could recognize could suffer such a death; for 'He that is hanged is accursed of God' (Deut. 21:23), 'an insult to God' (Targum, Rashi)."[25]

The Muslims have a similar attitude. They regard Jesus as a prophet, and according to their thinking a prophet could not die in this way. The Qur'an says, "They denied the truth and uttered a monstrous falsehood against Mary. They declared: 'We have put to death the Messiah Jesus, the son of Mary, the Apostle of Allah.' They did not kill him, nor did they crucify him, but they thought they did" (Sura 4:156).[26]

The Muslims give different interpretations for the story of the Cross. Some say that God cast a spell on the people and someone else was crucified in Jesus' place. They say that at some point he was raptured into heaven and that he returned to earth and visited his disciples and commissioned them to take his teachings into the world. Some say that it was Simon of Cyrene who was killed. The so-called Gospel

---

[22]Walter Bauer, *A Greek-English Lexicon of the New Testament and Other Early Christian Literature*, adapted by W. F. Arndt and F. W. Gingrich, 4th edition revised and augmented by F. W. Danker (Chicago and London: University of Chicago Press, 1979), 753.

[23]Gordon D. Fee, "The First Epistle to the Corinthians," in *The New International Commentary on the New Testament* (Grand Rapids, Mich.: Eerdmans, 1987), 75.

[24]Murray J. Harris, *From Grave to Glory* (Grand Rapids, Mich.: Zondervan, 1990), 166.

[25]*The Jewish Encyclopedia*, vol. 7, ed. Isidore Singer (London: Funk and Wagnalls), 167, quoted in Chapman, *Christianity on Trial*, 499.

[26]Quoted in Chapman, *Christianity on Trial*, 500.

of Barnabas, which was written in Italian in the fourteenth or fifteenth century by a Christian convert to Islam, says that Judas Iscariot was crucified. Recently the idea that Jesus swooned on the cross and recovered has been suggested by the Ahmediya sect, whom other Muslims consider to be heretical.

Because this attitude to the Crucifixion was prevalent in the first century, it would be good to look at how the New Testament evangelists responded to it. Because the Gospels are evangelistic documents and because there are many evangelistic messages recorded in Acts, we have ample material with which to work. What we find is that the New Testament evangelists, without seeking to defend the Crucifixion, took the positive approach of presenting it as a triumph planned by God, rather than as a tragedy.

The preaching in Acts focuses on the fact that this was God's plan from the beginning and was predicted by the prophets. At Pentecost Peter said, "This man was handed over to you *by God's set purpose and foreknowledge*, and you, with the help of wicked men, put him to death by nailing him to the cross" (Acts 2:23). Then, after the healing at the temple, he said, "But this is how God fulfilled what he had foretold through all the prophets, saying that his Christ would suffer" (Acts 3:18). Paul said in Pisidian Antioch, "The people of Jerusalem and their rulers did not recognize Jesus, yet in condemning him they fulfilled the words of the prophets that are read every Sabbath.... When they had carried out all that was written about him, they took him down from the tree and laid him in a tomb" (Acts 13:27, 29).

The Gospels record Jesus as often saying that it was necessary for Him to die and rise again and that all this was fulfilling prophecy.

Jesus took the Twelve aside and told them, "We are going up to Jerusalem, and everything that is written by the prophets about the Son of Man will be fulfilled." (Luke 18:31)

He said to them, "How foolish you are, and how slow of heart to believe all that the prophets have spoken! Did not the Christ have to suffer these things and then enter his glory?" (Luke 24:25-26)

He told them, "This is what is written: The Christ will suffer and rise from the dead on the third day." (Luke 24:46)

Sometimes He said that He could have avoided this death if He wished, as the following passages show:

> "The reason my Father loves me is that I lay down my life—only to take it up again. No one takes it from me, but I lay it down of my own accord. I have authority to lay it down and authority to take it up again. This command I received from my Father." (John 10:17-18)

> "Put your sword back in its place," Jesus said to him, "for all who draw the sword will die by the sword. Do you think I cannot call on my Father, and he will at once put at my disposal more than twelve legions of angels? But how then would the Scriptures be fulfilled that say it must happen in this way?" (Matt. 26:52-54)

In John's gospel the Cross is often equated with glory (John 7:39; 12:23-28; 13:31; 17:5). The word *glory* is used when the nature and character of God has been manifested in its splendor. And that is what happened at the cross. We saw the full expression of his holiness and love, which forms the essence of His nature. His holiness was manifested in his hatred for sin that caused him to punish it so severely. His love was manifested in his giving his only Son to die in our stead. The fullest manifestation of the glory of the Cross, however, is in heaven, where the object of worship and the central figure is the Lamb who had been slain.[27]

The evidence we have presented in this chapter shows us how wrong some of our approaches to the Cross are. Some people don't view Good Friday as a "good" day but as a bad day—a day that commemorates a terrible tragedy. That is not the approach of the Scriptures. If there is mourning, it should be about our sin that caused the spotless Son of God to die in this way. The mourning aspect of Good Friday is eclipsed by the fact that on that day the Lord Jesus cried out from the cross, "It is finished" just before "he bowed his head and gave up his spirit" (John 19:30). Leon Morris, commenting on this verse says, "Jesus died with the cry of the victor on his lips. This is not the moan of the defeated, not the sigh of patient resignation. It is the triumphant recog-

---

[27]On this see chapter 14.

nition that he has now fully accomplished the work he came to do."[28] Paul says that rather than being defeated by His enemies, Jesus defeated His enemies on the cross: "... having disarmed the powers and authorities, he made a public spectacle of them, triumphing over them by the cross" (Col. 2:13b-15).

Each year during Holy Week the newspapers in Sri Lanka carry articles about the bizarre ways in which people commemorate the Crucifixion. Their mourning and their self-inflicted wounds do much to communicate to the world a message that is very different from the victorious message of the Bible.

To those who discover its truth, the message of the Bible becomes a source of pride and joy. Paul, who had been such a vehement opponent of the idea of a crucified Messiah, wrote after discovering this, "May I never boast except in the cross of our Lord Jesus Christ, through which the world has been crucified to me, and I to the world" (Gal. 6:14). Samuel Zwemer (1867-1952) who has been called "the Apostle to Islam," has said regarding the Muslim response to the Cross, "We find that, although the offense of the cross remains, its magnetic power is irresistible."[29]

We will conclude this chapter with a memorable quotation from John Calvin's comment on Colossians 2:15:

> For although in the cross there is nothing but curse, this was nevertheless so swallowed up by the power of the Son of God, that it has put on, as it were, a new nature. For there is no tribunal so magnificent, no kingly throne so stately, no show of triumph so distinguished, no chariot so lofty, as the gibbet on which Christ subdued death and the devil, the prince of death; more, has utterly trodden them under His feet.[30]

---

[28]Leon Morris, "The Gospel According to John," in *The New International Commentary on the New Testament* (Grand Rapids, Mich.: Eerdmans, 1971), 815.

[29]Samuel Zwemer, *The Glory of the Cross* (London: Marshall, Morgan and Scott, 1928), 6, quoted in Stott, *The Cross of Christ* (Leicester and Downers Grove, Ill.: InterVarsity Press, 1986), 42.

[30]John Calvin, "Galatians, Ephesians, Philippians and Colossians," *Calvin's New Testament Commentaries*, vol. 11, trans. T. H. L. Parker (Grand Rapids, Mich.: Eerdmans, 1965), 336.

CHAPTER ELEVEN

THE JUSTICE
OF THE CROSS

ABOUT CHRISTIANITY, the English poet and satirist Lord Byron (1788-1824) said, "The basis of your religion is injustice; the Son of God, the pure, the immaculate, the innocent is sacrificed for the guilty." Byron continued, "This proves *his* heroism; but no more does away with man's guilt than a schoolboy's volunteering to be flogged for another would exculpate the dunce from negligence or preserve him from the rod."[1] Yet, John says that when we receive forgiveness through Jesus' blood, God is just in forgiving us through the blood of Jesus (1 John 1:7, 9). Paul says, "God presented him as a sacrifice of atonement, through faith in his blood. He did this to demonstrate his justice . . . so as to be just and the one who justifies the man who has faith in Jesus (Rom. 3:25-26). The Bible, then, is sensitive to the relationship between justice and the forgiveness God offers through the work of Christ. Abraham expressed his hope in God's justice when he asked, "Will not the Judge of all the earth do right [or do justice[2]]?" (Gen. 18:25). I hope to show below that when God forgives us He does do justice.

The charge of injustice is made from different fronts. Let us look at them one by one.

---

[1] Quoted in Colin Chapman, *Christianity on Trial* (Wheaton, Ill.: Tyndale House, 1975), 495.
[2] Leon Morris, *The Atonement* (Leicester and Downers Grove, Ill.: InterVarsity Press, 1983), 179.

JUDGES CANNOT DO AS THEY LIKE

In our law courts, the idea of one person's being condemned for the wrongdoing of another is not accepted for several reasons. First, judges cannot suspend the laws of the land and do as they like. They are responsible to the state or to the king or queen of the land and are bound by its constitution. Their job is to interpret the constitution, not to create new laws. But when God justifies us, the King of the universe, who created the laws that govern the running of the universe, pronounces a judgment regarding His creatures. He is not failing to carry out His duty to someone else or to a state. As Creator and Lord of the universe, he can decide how His laws are satisfied. Even in national constitutions there is usually a clause that allows for this type of thing. The head of state has the authority to pardon a condemned criminal. This is called the royal pardon or the presidential pardon. H. E. Guillebaud, in his classic book on the death of Christ, *Why the Cross?*, says, "God is not administering someone else's law, but his own."[3] Recently in Sri Lanka we have seen presidential pardons given to supporters of presidents that were both unjust and arbitrary. At the cross, however, the demands of justice were satisfied, as we showed earlier.

A Buddhist university student in Sri Lanka went to a Christian meeting on campus with a friend. There he was confronted for the first time with the message of the Cross of Christ. He thought that the idea that someone else should die for us was quite ridiculous. But his Christian friends persisted in presenting the claims of Christ to him. Then he realized that the one who died was the Creator of the world. That settled the matter for him. He reasoned that if there is a Creator, he has the authority to enforce the laws of justice—which he himself created—in the way He thinks best. He became a Christian and was baptized in our church some years ago.

DOES THIS NOT DISHONOR GOD AND HIS SOVEREIGNTY?

But, says our objector, if someone brings dishonor to a state by doing wrong, and if the state in its attempt to help that person were to pardon

---

[3] H. E. Guillebaud, *Why the Cross?* (London: Tyndale Press, n.d.), 147.

him, then the state would greatly jeopardize its honor and stability. Those who harm the state must be punished for the greater good of everyone else. Not to do so would be to harm the state further by encouraging criminal behavior. Then, as Daniel P. Fuller shows, the state fails in that which brings it glory—namely, its ability "to be benevolent to everyone"[4] by protecting them and providing for their welfare a stable and favorable environment. But Jesus viewed His death as bringing honor to God. Looking forward to His death, he said, "Now is the Son of Man glorified and God is glorified in him" (John 13:31; see also 12:27-28).

How does His death bring honor to God? For one thing it showed fully God's glorious nature as being loving and holy, as we saw in the previous chapter. But what about the stability of the state? If criminals were pardoned and simply set free, the door would be opened to unrestrained damage to the stability and honor of the state. But this does not happen with those who benefit from the death of Christ. As Fuller points out, once forgiven they begin "to glorify God and uphold his integrity by exerting an 'obedience that comes by faith.'"[5] Their lives are changed. Forgiveness opens the door to their becoming people who live the way God made them to live—trusting him and obeying his ways. This they did not do before. In fact, the refusal to acknowledge God is the most serious sin one could commit. It is treason against the government God set to run the world. Treason is the most serious sin in a system of government. When we repent of this and turn to God, our lives bring glory to God and also help restore the goodness of creation that was lost in the Fall.

In fact, rather than being a source of dishonor to God and His rule, the death of Christ is the key to restoring His honor and His rule in the hearts of persons and, through that, in the whole world. Habakkuk 2:14 predicted that "the earth will be filled with the knowledge of the glory of the LORD, as the waters cover the sea." When Jesus died, He opened the door for the fulfilling of that prophecy. Until the crown of creation, the human race, aligns itself with God's purpose for the world, there is

---

[4]Daniel P. Fuller, *The Unity of the Bible* (Grand Rapids, Mich.: Zondervan, 1992), 209. I am indebted to Fuller's treatment for much of what I say on this issue.
[5]Ibid.

no hope of His glory being manifested on earth. Through the grace that flowed from Christ's death, people will be able to truly glorify God through lives of obedient faith.

IS IT NOT UNFAIR TO THE SUBSTITUTE?

The comment of Lord Byron quoted above implies that if Christ was punished for our sins, it was very unfair to Him. It is true that judges can't order an innocent person to be punished for the crimes of another. But here the Judge is the one who is being punished. Guillebaud says, "The Substitute who died on Calvary expressly declared himself to be the Judge of the world (Matt. 12:41-42; 25:31-46)."[6] So this is an instance of the Judge pronouncing the sentence against Himself. Paul describes "the church of God" as one "*which he bought with his own blood*" (Acts 20:28).[7] In His death the Substitute was purchasing the church for Himself. Jesus said, "The reason my Father loves me is that I lay down my life—only to take it up again. No one takes it from me, but I lay it down of my own accord. I have authority to lay it down and authority to take it up again" (John 10:17-18). He did this because He wanted to do it.

This does not mean that anyone who voluntarily offers himself up can be a substitute for another's sin. Psalm 49:7-8 says, "No man can redeem the life of another or give to God a ransom for him—the ransom for a life is costly, no payment is ever enough." The only payment that suffices is that of the spotless Son of Man who was also the eternal God. The sovereign God took the initiative in redeeming the world. As Paul says, "God was reconciling the world to himself in Christ, not counting men's sins against them" (2 Cor. 5:19). We see again that the primary case for the supremacy of Christ lies in His deity. It was only because Jesus was God that He could make a sacrifice that could suffice to save us.

---

[6]Guillebaud, *Why the Cross?*, 147.
[7]Some manuscripts have, ". . . the church of God that he obtained with the blood of his own Son" (NRSV). But that does not take away the force of our argument. Because of the Trinity, what God did was what Jesus did.

IS IT NOT UNFAIR TO THE WRONGED PARTY?

When an offender is set scot-free for an offense committed against someone else, that wronged party would feel cheated and could legitimately complain that justice has not been done by him or her. There is a plausible explanation for this apparent injustice also.

Regarding Christ's death, firstly, the sins we commit are primarily against God. And it is in regard to this that He justifies us. After committing adultery, David said, "Against you, you only, have I sinned and done what is evil in your sight" (Psa. 51:4). This too springs from the doctrine of creation. God created us and is Lord of the universe. Therefore, we are ultimately responsible to Him. So He is the wronged party. And if He, seeing our genuinely repentant spirit, takes the initiative to forgive us, then there is no injustice committed against Him.

Secondly, that this is not cheap forgiveness is evidenced by the fact that one who does not show genuine repentance is not saved. For example, Jesus said, "For if you forgive men when they sin against you, your heavenly Father will also forgive you. But if you do not forgive men their sins, your Father will not forgive your sins" (Matt. 6:14-15). There are conditions for receiving this salvation. It is free, and there is no work that we can do to merit it; but we must come with a humble heart that makes no claim to being worthy of it, while thinking that those whom we refuse to forgive are unworthy of our forgiveness.

Thirdly, while God forgives us, He does not immediately take away all the earthly consequences of our sin. For example, though David was forgiven for his adultery, he had to suffer the earthly consequences of it for the rest of his life, as Nathan told him when he announced the forgiveness (2 Sam. 12:7-12). Similarly, a person who gets pregnant out of wedlock has to live with the child who is born and bring that child up or offer the child up for adoption. She cannot simply absolve herself of responsibility by having an abortion.

Fourthly, the Bible talks of the fruit of repentance (Luke 3:8). This would include restitution, such as paying back money that was stolen, as Zacchaeus did (Luke 19:8). It would also include subjecting ourselves to the legal procedures of the land. This is what Charles Colson did after his conversion. He pleaded guilty for crimes related to the

Watergate scandal and served a jail sentence for those crimes.[8] The one who has hurt another must apologize to that person. The father who has repented of ruining the joy of his family through alcoholism must seek the forgiveness of his wife and children and seek to do all he can to make his home a happy place in which to live. The mother who hurt her son by unkind scolding must apologize to him and ask his forgiveness. The clerk who defrauded his company must work on paying back the money he took wrongly. I have counseled with many people who, convicted of sins they have committed, have sought God's forgiveness. But when I talk to them about restitution, some are not willing to follow through completely with that implication of being forgiven by God.

COULDN'T GOD SIMPLY PRONOUNCE FORGIVENESS?

Another question relating to the justice of forgiveness has been asked of me by the more westernized people in Sri Lanka. It is typical of the lightness with which modern western people regard sin. They ask, "Couldn't God simply pronounce forgiveness? Was it necessary for Christ to go through the painful process of dying?" A French cynic has said, "The good God will forgive me, that's his job [or his specialty]."[9]

If God simply pronounced forgiveness, that would make forgiveness cheap. Our sin is too serious for such a response. We are too significant for our wrongdoing to be taken so lightly. People who have not been corrected during their childhood, whose wrongdoing has been regarded lightly, will invariably be insecure people. Subconsciously they reason that if they were significant individuals, their actions would be taken seriously. The failure of their parents and others to punish them in their childhood communicated to them the message that they are insignificant. Some of these people become very rebellious in their effort to win the attention of people. This point has been emphasized by specialists in child psychiatry like Dr. James Dobson.[10]

There is an epidemic of low self-esteem today. There must be many reasons for this. But one of them must be that people's sins have not

[8]This story is told in Charles Colson, *Born Again* (Old Tappan, N.J.: Revell, 1976).
[9]Quoted in John Stott, *The Cross of Christ* (Leicester and Downers Grove, Ill.: InterVarsity Press, 1986), 87.
[10]See James Dobson, *Hide or Seek* (Old Tappan, N.J.: Revell, 1974), 81-88.

been regarded seriously. It unconsciously gives them a message that they are not significant. A person who has been punished by just and loving parents in childhood will invariably be a secure person.

Because God regards us as significant people, He cannot simply pronounce forgiveness for our sins. They must be punished adequately. And Jesus took the punishment because God knew that if we were to take it on ourselves, there would be no hope for us.

Besides, to simply forgive would make a mockery of justice. A world without justice is an insecure and chaotic world. There is right, and there is wrong. And when wrong is done, it is serious. So something serious must be done about it.

Early in this century, C. A. Dinsmore wrote a book called *Atonement in Literature and Life*. He examined the writings of the some of the deepest thinkers in history—people like Homer, Aeschylus, Sophocles, Dante, Shakespeare, Milton, George Eliot, Hawthorne, and Tennyson. He came to the conclusion that "It is an axiom in life and in religious thought that there is no reconciliation without satisfaction"—that is, the satisfaction of justice.[11] He would have come to the same conclusion if he looked at the great literature of the so-called Third World too. After citing Dinsmore's conclusion, Leon Morris asks, "Should we not see this as something God has implanted deep down in the human heart?" Then Morris says, "Faced with a revolting crime even the most careless among us are apt to say, 'That deserves to be punished.'"[12] In the same way, our sin needed to be punished; and because there would be no hope for us if we were punished, Jesus was punished in our place.

One of the facts that has been emerging over and over in our discussion of the Cross is that the message of the Cross agrees with our deepest instincts. That is to be expected, for we were made in the image of God. Therefore, God's answer to humanity's biggest problem would be in harmony with our essential humanness. The problem is that sin has tainted every part of our being and clouded our minds from listening to our instincts. Our job as evangelists is to help resurface those thoughts that have been clouded by sin. That is the work of persuasion.

---

[11]C. A. Dinsmore, *Atonement in Literature and Life* (New York: Houghton Mifflin, 1906), 226, quoted in Leon Morris, *The Cross of Jesus* (Exeter: Paternoster; Grand Rapids, Mich.: Eerdmans, 1988), 9.
[12]Morris, *The Cross of Jesus*, 9, 10.

We will seek to persuade and will leave it to the Holy Spirit to do His work in helping the person accept this truth and yield to its implications.

DOES THE DEATH OF ONE PERSON SUFFICE TO PAY FOR THE SINS OF SO MANY?

If we accept that sin must be punished, then the question arises as to whether the death of one person could pay for the sins of the millions of people who are forgiven. Daniel Fuller, in his book *The Unity of the Bible*, has a helpful discussion on this, to which I am indebted for much of what is written here.[13] Fuller uses an insight from the great American theologian Jonathan Edwards (1703-58), who in his book of doctrinal sermons published after his death, *A History of the Work of Redemption*, shows that the sufferings of Christ began from His incarnation. Edwards argues that "the purchase of redemption was made . . . during the time of Christ's humiliation, from his incarnation to his resurrection."[14] That price paid through condescension was infinite in proportion.

Fuller observes that "it is virtually impossible for any us to understand how transcendentally high God, the creator of the universe, is in comparison with us people on earth."[15] He refers to the description of God in Isaiah 40:15, 22: "Surely the nations are like a drop in a bucket; they are regarded as dust on the scales; he weighs the islands as though they were fine dust. . . . He sits enthroned above the circle of the earth, and its people are like grasshoppers. He stretches out the heavens like a canopy, and spreads them out like a tent to live in." He came, then, from a height that we could never comprehend. Fuller speaks of Jesus "traversing the vast distance from the ivory palaces to experiencing the omnipotent fury of God's wrath."[16]

This journey of Christ began with the Incarnation. Fuller says that it would help to picture this as if Jesus were "descending a winding staircase stretching for a very long distance from the glory of heaven

---

[13]Fuller, *Unity of the Bible*, 209-14.

[14]Jonathan Edwards, *A History of the Work of Redemption*, vol. 1 of *The Works of Jonathan Edwards* (1834; reprint, Edinburgh: Banner of Truth, 1974), 572. Edwards expounds this theme on pp. 272-80.

[15]Fuller, *Unity of the Bible*, 210.

[16]Ibid., 211.

above far down into a world of wretched misery. Each downward step in leaving this glory increased the pain Jesus underwent to pay for our sins." His point is that "a good part of the severity of the punishment Jesus suffered for us consisted in coming down this staircase, whose length cannot be exaggerated since it spanned the infinite distance between the Creator and the creature."[17]

Though the pain Christ suffered when he lived on earth is well-known to us, it too could never be fully comprehended. He experienced the pain of deprivation, the pain of disappointment as those near to Him failed Him, the pain of rejection and of facing hatred after He had given so much love, and finally the pain of death. Paul says, "he humbled himself and became obedient to death—even death on a cross!" (Phil. 2:8). That thought is an amazing paradox. The sovereign God of all creation has become *obedient* to the wages of sin, the last enemy of fallen humanity! But more serious than this was the eternal chasm that was bridged by His actually becoming sin for us. As Paul exclaimed, "God made him who had no sin to be sin for us, so that in him we might become the righteousness of God" (2 Cor. 5:21). As He hung on the cross, having become sin for us, it seemed as if God the Father, whose "eyes are too pure to look on evil; [who] cannot tolerate wrong" (Hab. 1:13), had to forsake His Son. So "Jesus cried out in a loud voice, . . . 'My God, my God, why have you forsaken me?'" (Matt. 27:46). Martin Luther once pondered this thought alone and at great length while he fasted. He finally arose to say, "God forsaken by God . . . who can understand it?"[18]

In the Incarnation and Crucifixion of Jesus an infinite condescension, an infinite loss of glory, was made; and we argue this sufficed to pay for the sins of the finite beings who receive forgiveness from Christ throughout all ages.

STILL EFFECTIVE AFTER TWO THOUSAND YEARS?

Many people have asked me how the death of Christ, which took place almost 2,000 years ago, can still be effective and forgive us for sins that had not been committed at the time He died. This is a paradox and a

[17]Ibid., 210-11.
[18]Quoted in *The Vance Havner Quote Book*, comp. Dennis J. Hester (Grand Rapids, Mich.: Baker, 1986), 59.

problem to us because we live confined by time and space. But God is the Creator of time and space and lives beyond these in the realm of eternity. As Psalm 90:2 says, "From everlasting to everlasting you are God." Then a little later it says, "A thousand years in your sight are like a day that has just gone by, or like a watch in the night [that is, six hours]" (verse 4).

Recent science fiction has tried to delve into the meaning of transcending the barriers of time. Thus, we have movies like *Back to the Future* and TV programs such as the old series *The Time Tunnel*. But eternity is something that we find difficult to understand because we are confined to the restrictions of time. Not so for God.

In addition to the fact that God is eternal is the fact that He is all-knowing. Because He is all-knowing, He knew all the sins that were to be committed in history. Because He is eternal, He could make provision for them even before they were committed. And that is what He did at the cross. He transcended the barrier of time and made provision for sins even before they were committed.

While this concept of eternity is hard for us to fathom, we know that concerned people often make provision for others long before they face an anticipated crisis. We give vaccinations to infants to immunize them from infections to which they may be exposed. When our children were quite small, my wife and I opened a savings account in anticipation of expenses, such as college educations, that would be incurred when they were much older. God did something like this for us when He made provision for the sins He knew we would commit.

So the book of Hebrews says that our High Priest, Jesus, "had offered for all time one sacrifice for sins" (Heb. 10:12), referring to "the blood of the eternal covenant" (Heb. 13:20). In fact, Revelation 13:8 describes Jesus as "the Lamb that was slain from the creation of the world." First Peter 1:20 calls Him the Lamb "chosen before the creation of the world, but . . . revealed in these last times." At the time God created the world there was a cross in the heart of God. Implied in all of this is the fact that provision was made for sins committed even before Jesus died. People were making sacrifices in an attitude of repentance, and God was forgiving them through the merits of the blood of Christ's eternal covenant.

All this tells us that when Jesus died on that cross, there is a sense in which we also were there. A famous American preacher of a previous generation, Robert G. Lee, tells of an unforgettable experience he had the first time he visited Calvary while on a tour of Israel. His excitement was such that he soon outdistanced his guide in climbing the hill. When he reached the spot where Christ had been crucified, his body started to tremble. When the guide caught up with him, he asked, "Sir, have you been here before?" For a moment there was a throbbing silence. Then, in a whispered tone, Dr. Lee replied, "Yes, I was here nearly two thousand years ago."[19]

We are reminded of the old American Negro spiritual:

> *Were you there when they crucified my Lord?*
> *Were you there when they crucified my Lord?*
> *Oh! Sometimes it causes me to tremble, tremble, tremble.*
> *Were you there when they crucified my Lord?*

THE HEART OF THE GOSPEL

In this and the two previous chapters we have grappled with the meaning of the death of Christ, which makes Jesus the way to salvation. Leon Morris says, "Christianity is a profound religion and its teaching has many aspects. But if we are true to the New Testament we must see the cross as at the very heart of it all."[20]

Like every other aspect of the religion of Jesus, the message of the Cross is both a simple and a profound truth. At the cross our personal arrogance is shattered. We see, on the one hand, the immensely condescending love of God in Christ and, on the other hand, the wretchedness of our sin that took Jesus to a cross. As Isaac Watts (1674-1748) says in his beloved hymn:

> *When I survey the wondrous cross*
> *On which the prince of glory died,*
> *My richest gain I count but loss,*
> *And pour contempt on all my pride.*

---

[19]Narrated in Robert E. Coleman, *The Great Commission Lifestyle* (Grand Rapids, Mich.: Revell, 1992), 32.
[20]Morris, *The Cross of Jesus*, 2.

At the cross our theological arrogance is also shattered as we see, on the one hand, that the benefits of this cross are appropriated by all in the same way: the way of childlike trust. But on the other hand, we realize that however much we try, we cannot fully grasp the meaning of the Cross. As Charles Wesley (1707-88) wrote:

> *'Tis mystery all! The immortal dies:*
>   *Who can explore His strange design?*
> *In vain the firstborn seraph tries*
>   *To sound the depths of love divine.*
> *'Tis mercy all! let earth adore,*
>   *Let angel minds inquire no more.*

Dr. Robert Coleman tells the story of Dr. Charles Berry, who was also was an eminent preacher of a previous generation. Trained in a theologically liberal environment, he struggled with the concept of the atoning, substitutionary sacrifice of Christ. He viewed Christ more as a great moral teacher. He viewed Christianity essentially as living a good life.

Late one night in his first pastorate in England, while sitting in his study, he heard a knock. Opening the door he found a poorly dressed Lancashire girl. She asked, "Are you a minister?" When he said, "Yes," she said, "You must come with me quickly. I want you to get my mother in." He thought it was a case of a drunken woman out on the streets. He said, "Why, go and get a policeman." She replied, "No, my mother is dying, and you must come with me quickly and get her into heaven."

The young minister went with her to her mother's side. He knelt down beside her and began to describe the kindness of Jesus, explaining that He had come to show us how to live unselfishly. Suddenly the desperate woman said, "Mister, that's no use for the likes of me. I am a sinner. I have lived my life. Can't you tell me of someone who can have mercy on me and save my poor soul?"

Dr. Berry says, "I stood there in the presence of a dying woman, and I had nothing to tell her. In order to bring something to that dying woman, I leaped back to my mother's knee, to my cradle faith, and I told her of the Cross, and the Christ who was able to save."

Tears began running down the cheeks of the woman. She said, "Now you are getting at it, now you are helping me." This is how Dr.

Berry concluded the story: "I want you to know that I got her in, and blessed be God, I got in myself."[21]

Paul said, regarding his evangelistic ministry in Corinth, "For I resolved to know nothing while I was with you except Jesus Christ and him crucified" (1 Cor 2:2). In our evangelistic ministry we will use many things to win the attention of people; we will spend much effort attempting to answer the questions people have about the faith. But as soon as we possibly can, we must come to the heart of the Gospel: Jesus Christ and Him crucified.

---

[21]Narrated in Robert E. Coleman, *The Heartbeat of Evangelism* (Colorado Springs, Colo.: NavPress, 1985), 16, 17.

Part Three

JESUS IS THE LIFE

CHAPTER TWELVE

THE GIFT OF ETERNAL LIFE

T HE INFLUENCE CHRIST HAS on our daily life is so great that Paul said, "For to me, to live is Christ" (Phil. 1:21). The Gospel is not simply a philosophy of life or a legal means of securing a place in heaven for men and women. It transforms our life so radically that Paul views conversion to Christ as the birth of a new creation. He says, "Therefore, if anyone is in Christ, he is a new creation; the old has gone, the new has come!" (2 Cor. 5:17). The way in which Christ changes our life here and now is another important aspect of the supremacy of Christ, and we will look at it under the general heading, "Jesus Is the Life."

Jesus describes the way that He changes our life in the passage that we used as our base for looking at the description of His work: John 10:7-18 (see chapter 10 of this book). In John 10:10 He said, "I have come that they may have life, and have it to the full." He is referring here to the eternal life that He gives, and He says it is completely fulfilling. Yet this fulfillment is not an impersonal pleasure or "kick" that He gives us through specific experiences. Jesus says in this passage that this life has to do with a relationship we have with Him. So, we will first look at Jesus' description of the relationship and then consider the nature of the fulfillment it gives.

A LOVE RELATIONSHIP THAT GOES
DEEPER THAN OUR HURTS

In John 10:11 Jesus teaches that the relationship we have with Him is based on His commitment to us: "I am the good shepherd. The good shepherd lays down his life for the sheep." Then Jesus immediately goes on to refer to selfish people who fail us, people who do not have such a commitment to us. They desert us in our time of need rather than care for us as Jesus does. He says, "The hired hand is not the shepherd who owns the sheep. So when he sees the wolf coming, he abandons the sheep and runs away. Then the wolf attacks the flock and scatters it. The man runs away because he is a hired hand and cares nothing for the sheep" (John 10:12-13). Jesus knows that this world is full of relationships that fail. In fact, the deep wounds that have been caused by people who have disappointed us have a very powerful place in our emotional lives.

So when Jesus, the Great Physician, describes His commitment, He first contrasts Himself with the disappointing people who have caused this dominant "felt need" in our lives. We can infer that He is presenting His love as the cure to those wounds. And that, as we shall see, is indeed the case. Christ's statement reminds us of Isaiah 49:15: "Can a mother forget the baby at her breast and have no compassion on the child she has borne? Though she may forget, I will not forget you!"

Jesus goes on to say that His commitment to us leads to a personal relationship with us: "I am the good shepherd; I know my sheep and my sheep know me—just as the Father knows me and I know the Father" (John 10:14-15). Then again He gives the proof of His concern for us by saying, "and I lay down my life for the sheep." It is in this relationship that God brings His healing to us for the hurts that have come to us from all the ugliness caused by "the hired hands" who have failed us. There is something ugly about the selfishness and wickedness of people. Sacrificial love is beautiful in comparison.

The Greek word for *good* used in John 10 is *kalos*, and it means more than "good" as opposed to "bad." It has the idea of "beautiful" as well as "good." So a classical Greek scholar, E. V. Rieu, translated the statement of Christ as, "I am the shepherd, the Shepherd Beautiful."[1]

---

[1] Quoted in Leon Morris, *Reflections on the Gospel of John* (Grand Rapids, Mich.: Baker, 1986-88), 377.

In the beauty of the sacrificial love of Jesus lies the key to the healing of the hurts inflicted on us by people who fail us. David found this out, and I believe that is how he was able to be a radiant poet of praise even though he faced so much opposition and hatred in his life. In Psalm 27, which he wrote when he faced the ugly hatred of his enemies, he said, "One thing I ask of the Lord, this is what I seek: that I may dwell in the house of the Lord all the days of my life, to gaze upon the beauty of the Lord and to seek him in his temple" (Psalm 27:4). In his time of deep disappointment, there was nothing he needed more than a vision of the beauty of God. And this vision ministered healing to him for the hurts of life.

This is a world that is rapidly forgetting the appeal of wholesome biblical beauty. A cynicism has spread throughout the world. We cannot think of goodness as being possible, and so we think that beauty also is not possible. Sports are often done for money and not for the love of the sport; many preachers have proved to be hypocrites; political leaders have failed to keep their promises; altruism is considered an impossible, unnecessary, and foolish ideal. The world is asking, "Is goodness possible?" Worse than that, it is asking, "Is goodness necessary?"

With the loss of goodness, beauty has also become outdated. In the fashion world, beauty has been replaced by sensuality and seductiveness. In serious literature, a cynicism has replaced heroism. In novels, adultery has replaced that beautiful thing called love. In art and music, we see and hear clashing chords, despair-filled minor keys, jarring noise, and violent lyrics taking the place of beauty. Many people are too impatient to sit through a beautiful movie because their senses have been numbed by repeated doses of sex, violence, and cynicism. Some people, revolting against this and desperately searching for beauty, have chosen to worship nature or find satisfaction through a pet dog or cat who can be trusted not to betray us.

When God created us human, He gave us the capacity to enjoy beauty. And the greatest experience of beauty is in relationships of love. We have the joy of knowing that Jesus is beautiful and that He expressed His beauty in the most vivid way possible: by dying for us. Now we can taste of that beauty by having a love-relationship with Him that is deeper and sweeter than all the ugliness of the world. This too is a result of the work of Christ. It restores the beauty of life that was lost as a result of the Fall.

The British preacher F. B. Meyer (1847-1929) was traveling on a train when a miserable-looking woman recognized him and shared her burden with him. For years she had cared for a crippled daughter who had brought great joy to her life. She had made tea for her each morning, then left for work, knowing that in the evening the daughter would be there when she arrived home. But the daughter had died, and the grieving mother was alone and miserable. Home was not "home" anymore.

This was the advice Dr. Meyer gave her: "When you get home and put the key in the door, say aloud, 'Jesus, I know You are here!' And be ready to greet Him directly when you open the door. And as you light the fire, tell Him what happened during the day; if anybody has been kind, tell Him; if anybody has been unkind, tell Him, just as you would have told your daughter. At night, stretch your hand out into the darkness and say, 'Jesus, I know You are here!'"

Some months later Dr. Meyer was back in the neighborhood and met the woman again, but he did not recognize her. Her face radiated joy instead of announcing misery. She said, "I did as you told me, and it has made all the difference in my life, and now I feel I know Him."[2] Contact with the beautiful Shepherd brings beauty into our scarred lives.

Some may think that what I have just written is out of place in a book on the supremacy of Christ. I do not agree. A vital test of any faith is the way it helps its adherents tackle the problems that come their way. What we have just said shows that the Christian Gospel emerges from that test with flying colors.

ETERNAL LIFE IS COMPLETELY FULFILLING

The Bible describes our relationship with God in Christ as eternal life. Jesus says, "Now this is eternal life: that they may know you, the only true God, and Jesus Christ, whom you have sent" (John 17:3). Eternal

---

[2]From W. Y Fullerton, *F. B. Meyer: A Biography* (London: Marshall, Morgan and Scott, n.d.), 182-83, quoted in Warren W. Wiersbe and Lloyd M. Perry, *The Wycliffe Handbook of Preaching and Preachers* (Chicago: Moody Press, 1984), 194.

life is the primary result of Christ's saving work (John 3:16; 5:24). This relationship is the source of the fulfillment Jesus spoke about when He said, "I have come that they may have life, and have it to the full" (John 10:10). It is the fulfillment of a love-relationship with God.

By describing this as "life . . . to the full" He is contrasting the life that He gives with all other ways of life. Those others all fall short of the fullness that only the One who created us can give. This is what Francis of Assisi (1182-1226) found out. He was the son of a wealthy cloth merchant. After Francis's spiritual awakening in his twenties, his father was convinced that he was insane and denounced him. Francis took on a lifestyle of poverty. But he did not miss the riches he gave up. He said, "To him who tastes God, all the sweetness of the world will be but bitterness." Jesus explained this same kind of fulfillment saying, "I am the bread of life. He who comes to me will never go hungry, and he who believes in me will never be thirsty" (John 6:35). After we come to Him, healthy ambition and restlessness is not lost. That would make life boring. In fact, we have a new thirst for God, for His glory and for His ways. But the world's hunger that takes away our joy and peace is gone for good.

Let us explore how this eternal life gives an experience that is completely fulfilling.

It gives us that purpose for which God created us: a relationship with Him. Without that we are as good as dead. As John said, "He who has the Son has life; he who does not have the Son of God does not have life" (1 John 5:12). When people who are created for life do not have it, they are restless. St. Augustine (354-430) said, "You have made us for yourself, and our hearts are restless until they find rest in you." The noted French inventor and mathematician Blaise Pascal (1623-62) referred to this restlessness as the God-shaped vacuum found in every human being. The work of Christ in us takes away that restlessness and gives us the fulfillment that we seek from life.

All this is the result of Christ's work on our behalf. It is the outflow of grace, and our receiving such grace fills our hearts with thanksgiving. This is why Paul bursts forth into statements of praise when he is reminded of the grace of Christ to him (see 1 Tim. 1: 12-17). Gratitude is a key to the joy we experience. Another key to our joy is the fact that we have a love-relationship with God. Love and joy are closely linked, which is why the face of a person glows when he or she falls in love. But human experiences of love will always disappoint because humans are fallible. God, on the other hand, never disappoints, as we saw above. So in this relationship with God we can have unmixed joy. It is called the joy of the Lord, and that is our strength as we go through various experiences in this fallen world (Neh. 8:10). This, then, is the heart of Christian spirituality: a joy emerging out of deep gratitude to God for His grace so freely given, and our receiving its vigor from the love-relationship we enjoy with God.

Eternal life gives us freedom from the bondage of sin in this life. Jesus describes this in a discourse with the Jews. He says, "you will know the truth, and the truth will set you free" (John 8:32). Explaining this further Jesus says, "I tell you the truth, everyone who sins is a slave to sin.... So if the Son sets you free, you will be free indeed" (John 8:34, 36). Sin is what ruined life for humanity, and Jesus dealt with it through His work. How we overcome sin in our lives is explained in our discussion of the power of Christ's resurrection in chapter 15.

In the full life that Christ gives us, all our needs are met. In John 10:9 Jesus says, "I am the gate; whoever enters through me will be saved. He will come in and go out, and find pasture." In this new life we find the pasture we need. Because the Good Shepherd is committed to looking after us, we can affirm with David, "The Lord is my shepherd, I shall lack nothing" (Psa. 23:1). Thus Paul is able to say, "And my God will meet all your needs according to his glorious riches in Christ Jesus" (Phil. 4:19); and, "Do not be anxious about anything, but in everything, by prayer and petition, with thanksgiving, present your requests to God" (Phil. 4:6). We keep believing in God when things seem to go wrong, and we express that belief in prayers of thanksgiving and petition. Paul gives the result of this lifestyle in the next verse: "And the peace of God, which transcends all understanding, will guard your hearts and your minds in Christ Jesus" (Phil. 4:7). The assurance of provision gives peace in the heart.

Note that implied in the above passage is the fact that we could miss out on this peace if we do not believe in God's goodness to us. This is expressed more clearly in Romans 15:13: "May the God of hope fill you with all joy and peace as you trust in him, so that you may overflow with hope by the power of the Holy Spirit." If we do not trust in Christ, we do not experience the abundant life of Christ with its joy and peace. This is why many who call themselves Christians do not have this peace and joy.

ETERNAL LIFE COMPARED WITH NON-CHRISTIAN SPIRITUAL DISCIPLES

What an unbeatable combination this joy and peace is! It is the result of the abundant life that Christ gives us. All other schemes fall short of this. Many people have reached heights of spiritual experience without Christ. In achieving this they may have used their God-given thirst for the divine that could produce numerous expressions of spirituality (see Acts 17:27). Many religious systems claim to be pathways to serenity. And there is a sense in which they do produce serenity and joy. Spirituality is a legitimate aspect of the human makeup, and giving expression to it does yield some satisfaction. These experiences, however, are but the gropings of fallen humans after what only a relationship with God can give.

I have a friend who lived for some years alone in a jungle as a Buddhist monk. He told me of some amazing mystical experiences of spirituality and of endurance that he achieved through meditation. But he said that he intensely disliked having to come to civilization to ask for food, as is customary of Buddhist monks. He felt that contact with humanity took away the peace of mind that he had cultivated in the jungle. It was only since meeting Christ that he has been able to have a peace of mind that can weather the rigors of the real world.

The Indian evangelist Sadhu Sundar Singh (1889-c. 1929) came into Christianity with a wide experience in the rigorous spiritual disciplines of the religions of India. He had "attained a mastery of the Yoga technique and became oblivious to the external world for short spells." Bishop A. J. Appasamy, in his biography of Sundar Singh, says that "during those moments he experienced in some measure the peace and joy for which his soul craved. But when he returned to consciousness, he was again plunged into the turmoil of unrest and discontent."[3] This is because these experiences could not really satisfy the thirst that a relationship with God alone can satisfy. But once Sundar Singh became a

---

[3] A. J. Appasamy, *Sundar Singh: A Biography* (1958; reprint, Madras: CLS, 1966), 19.

Christian and experienced the peace of God, he used his skills, acquired while a non-Christian, to experience ecstatic heights of joy in his relationship with God. And this joy helped him endure untold hardship as he took the Gospel to hostile places.

This "spirituality" aspect of eternal life is one of the weakest areas of evangelical Christianity today. There seems to be an epidemic of activism that keeps most evangelicals from truly lingering in the presence of God. Instead of finding our greatest joy from the worship of God, we are finding it in the service of God. Many of us confine our spiritual disciplines to the "quickie devotions" fostered by the "one-minute" Bibles and devotionals that are so popular today. Christian serenity and a true depth of security in Christ comes to those who wait on the Lord and by so doing "renew their strength" (Isa. 40:31). We act as if we are looking to busy activism to still the restlessness that comes from our spiritual poverty. Only spiritual strength can do that, and there are no shortcuts in the path to such strength. We must wait on the Lord. The sad result of this evangelical hyperactivity is that we do not experience the fullness of the joy of the Lord. If we don't take the time to enjoy God, we simply will not enjoy Him.

The spiritual disciplines of other religions could be used as stepping-stones to reach other people with the message of Christ, for they represent the soul's quest that only God can satisfy. Islam has traditionally been a religion where God is so distant that He is not personally involved in human experience in the sense of His having an intimate relationship with us. The mystical branch of Islam known as Sufism is seeking such a relationship with God. Phil Parshall, in his book *Bridges to Islam*, has shown that this mystical element of Islam could be the bridge by which to communicate the Gospel to Muslims.[4]

On my first visit to a new chapter of Youth for Christ in Sri Lanka I was surprised to find that the evangelistic youth program they had organized started with about half an hour of worship. This was very different from the usual "crowd-breaker" used by Youth for Christ at such programs. It usually consisted of a game or some other lively activity that made the non-Christian youth feel at home. I held back commenting on this departure from the usual practice as I wanted to

---

[4]Phil Parshall, *Bridges to Islam* (Grand Rapids, Mich.: Baker, 1983).

understand their logic for doing this. I soon found that vibrant worship was a great means of attracting the Hindu youth of the area. They have a deep respect for the spiritual disciplines, but their religion did not satisfy the hunger for the divine that is in their hearts. Watching the Christans worship God in such a personal way, using indigenous music that appealed to them greatly, made them desire to know this God and the religion that can produce such attractive forms of spirituality. Since we made this discovery through a new program uncontaminated by our preconceived notions about how to attract youth, worship has become a key part of our evangelistic strategy among non-Christian youth.

Those who have practiced the spiritual disciplines of other religions sometimes have a head start when they begin their pilgrimage in Christian spirituality. The Protestant Christian tradition has been very weak until recently in giving due place to the spiritual disciplines. Evangelical Christians, in particular, have not been trained in the art of lingering in the presence of God. A person who is accustomed to the discipline of stillness through the disciplines of other religions may take to Christian spirituality with relish. This is what happened to a devout Hindu, Nadarajah Satchithanandakumar, who was sent to audit our ministry's books by the accountants that we use. Someone in our office spoke to him about Christ, and this began a process that ultimately led to his conversion. I had the happy privilege of discipling him for many years and of seeing him grow to be the leader of our Tamil language ministry in Colombo. One of the surprising things that I found out about him was that he spent extended times in prayer. In fact, I soon realized that his most important ministry strategy was prayer, and that it was very effective in producing leaders from his ministry. The disciplines he had developed as a Hindu stood him in good stead when he experienced the liberation of regeneration by the Spirit of God. The indwelling Spirit took his habit of spiritual discipline and made it into a wonderful pathway to spiritual power.

ETERNAL LIFE BATTLES IRRESPONSIBLE BEHAVIOR

Many times Buddhists and Hindus have told me that the idea that God forgives us because of what Christ did on the cross is not acceptable to them because it opens the door to irresponsible living. "Your forgiveness is so cheap," they say. "All you have to do when you sin is to ask

God to forgive you, and then you are free to sin again." Gandhi held this view and believed that the Christian idea of grace opened the door to moral license. He would cite examples of people who had become morally lax after they converted to Christianity.[5] Our answer to this objection is that the eternal life that results from Christ's death battles such irresponsible behavior. As John says, "No one who lives in him keeps on sinning. No one who continues to sin has either seen him or known him.... No one who is born of God will continue to sin, because God's seed remains in him; he cannot go on sinning, because he has been born of God" (1 John 3.6, 9). Let us now see how the Gospel battles irresponsibility.

PROCLAIMING JESUS AS SAVIOR AND LORD

We must first admit that often in the evangelical movement there has been gospel preaching that has left room for the above criticism. At Amsterdam '86, which was possibly the largest international gathering of evangelists in history, Kenyan evangelist Stephen Mung'oma said, "I feel that in many of our [evangelistic] meetings, we have given half the picture;"[6] that is, we have presented Jesus as Savior, but not as Lord. In support of Jesus being Lord, he pointed to Peter's affirmation in the first evangelistic message in Acts: "Therefore let all Israel be assured of this: God has made this Jesus, whom you crucified, both Lord and Christ" (Acts 2:36).

When Jesus described the message that the disciples were to preach, He told them, "This is what is written: The Christ will suffer and rise from the dead on the third day, and repentance and forgiveness of sins will be preached in his name to all nations, beginning at Jerusalem" (Luke 24:46-47). A call to repentance is a call to put aside our sin in order to follow the way of righteousness. When Jesus describes the evangelistic task in Matthew 28:19-20 He says, "Therefore go and make disciples of all nations, baptizing them in the name of the

---

[5]See M. M. Thomas, *The Acknowledged Christ of the Indian Renaissance* (London: SCM Press, 1969), 201.

[6]Stephen Mung'oma, "The Evangelist's Message: The Response of Faith," in *The Calling of an Evangelist*, ed. J. D. Douglas (Minneapolis: World Wide Publications, 1987), 169.

Father and of the Son and of the Holy Spirit, and *teaching them to obey everything I have commanded you.*" Obedience is a part of the basic message.

Often in the history of the church, people have fallen into the heresy of works righteousness and have insisted that some works are necessary for salvation in addition to or in place of faith. Therefore, many Christians today are hesitant to associate the message of lordship with that of salvation. While this is too big an issue to tackle here, I will nevertheless make a few remarks about it.

1. We must always insist that there is nothing we can do of ourselves to merit salvation. Salvation is "by grace . . . through faith" (Ephesians 2:8).
2. But when we accept His gift of salvation by faith we must know what this gift includes. We must know that it includes following Jesus as Lord. Otherwise people will think they have been tricked into accepting a way without being told what that way is.
3. It is the grace of God that enables us to follow this way. It is all of grace.
4. But it is a way in which sin is left behind and a righteous life is taken on. And when people accept the salvation that Christ offers, they must know that this is what they are accepting. Otherwise they would not be putting their faith in the Jesus of the Bible.

HE GIVES US STRENGTH TO BE HOLY

Once we receive Christ's forgiveness, we enter a brand-new life in which sin is not welcome. Our new nature revolts against sin and battles it so that we cannot continue in sin. Besides, by living with us, Jesus gives us the strength to do things that we earlier considered impossible. So Paul says, "I can do everything through him who gives me strength" (Phil. 4:13). Accepting God's salvation means that we are regenerated. We are given a new life, in which is included the strength to overcome sin if we in faith avail ourselves of God's sanctifying grace (see chapter 15).

This change, wrought within us at conversion, is well expressed in a statement made by a Muslim university student who after studying the New Testament became a Christian. Shortly after he was baptized as a Christian, some of his student friends met him and asked, "Ahmed, we hear you have changed your religion. Is that so?" Quick as a flash he answered, "Oh no, you've got it all wrong. I haven't simply changed my religion. My religion has changed me!"[7]

THE SACRAMENTS ARE REMINDERS

Jesus instituted two sacraments, baptism and the Lord's Supper, which remind us that our coming to Jesus is an awesome act that should elicit from us a commitment to righteousness that does not tolerate irresponsible behavior.

In Romans 6 Paul talks about baptism when dealing with the same objection we are considering. He asks, "What shall we say, then? Shall we go on sinning so that grace may increase?" He answers by saying that that is impossible: "By no means! We died to sin; how can we live in it any longer?" (Rom. 6:2). Then he gives his reason for that strong reaction: "Or don't you know that all of us who were baptized into Christ Jesus were baptized into his death? We were therefore buried with him through baptism into death in order that, just as Christ was raised from the dead through the glory of the Father, we too may live a new life" (Rom. 6:3-4). Baptism is a sign of death to our old life and rising to live a new life.

Similarly, the Lord's Supper is an awesome meal that emphasizes the seriousness of accepting the benefits of Christ's death. Paul is very forthright in his words to the morally lax Corinthians:

> Therefore, whoever eats the bread or drinks the cup of the Lord in an unworthy manner will be guilty of sinning against the body and blood of the Lord. A man ought to examine himself before he eats of the bread and drinks of the cup. For anyone who eats and drinks without recognizing the body of the Lord eats and drinks judgment on himself. That is why many among you are weak and sick, and a number of you have fallen asleep. (1 Cor. 11:27-30)

How sad it is that to many, the sacraments have become mere rituals without much connection with holy living. Some even think that

---

[7]From John T. Seamands, *Tell It Well: Communicating the Gospel Across Cultures* (Kansas City: Beacon Hill, 1981), 62.

by participating in sacraments like the Lord's Supper they can erase their responsibility before God for the sins they have committed. According to the Bible, however, the sacraments were instituted in order that they may be aids to holiness.

CHRISTIAN COMMUNITY LIFE IS A DETERRENT TO SIN

John says, "But if we walk in the light, as he is in the light, we have fellowship with one another, and the blood of Jesus, his Son, purifies us from every sin" (1 John 1:7). The blood of Jesus does cleanse from sin; but part of this cleansing process is walking in the light so that we may have fellowship with each other. This is true spiritual accountability. When we enter into the "in Christ" existence we become one with those who are in Christ. Eternal life is received individually, but it is lived out in community. And the community battles sin in the body by confronting sinners and by requiring spiritual accountability.

I have found that when some converts to Christianity have to face the community-related consequences of sins that they committed after becoming believers they are sometimes tempted to go back to the "karmic" way of their former religion, which does not have such a strong push for accountability for one's actions. They may prefer to perform some ritual, like giving alms, to cancel the effects of their wrong deeds. They are not willing to walk in the light so that there can be true fellowship with other Christians, which is very uncomfortable for one who is persisting in sin.

It is sad that the epidemic of radical individualism has hit many Christian communities so badly that often there isn't this serious spiritual accountability that involves walking in the light with each other and dealing adequately with sin in the body.[8]

THE CHALLENGE OF LOVE SO AMAZING

After all that Christ has done for us, we should find it difficult to persist in dishonoring and disregarding Him by continuing in sin. In chapter 9 we referred to the inspiration of the Cross and the so-called moral influence theory. We said that though this theory falls short of

---

[8]On this, see my book *Reclaiming Friendship* (Leicester: InterVarsity Press; Secunderabad: Living Bibles India, 1991; Scottdale, Penn.: Herald Press, 1993).

explaining the heart of the Cross, if kept in conjunction with the objective view of the substitutionary death of Christ, it provides an important and appealing dimension of the work of Christ on the cross. Jesus' immense commitment to us challenges us to respond appropriately to His Gospel. Isaac Watts (1674-1748) presented this challenge forcefully in his beloved hymn, "When I Survey the Wondrous Cross":

> *Were the whole realm of nature mine,*
> *That were an offering far too small,*
> *Love so amazing, so divine,*
> *Demands my soul, my life, my all.*

Jesus Himself presented this challenge to His disciples at the Last Supper. He said, "Greater love has no one than this, that he lay down his life for his friends" (John 15:13). Immediately after that He said, "You are my friends if you do what I command" (John 15:14).

R. A. Torrey (1856-1928) was a well-known evangelist who, in personal conversation, would often challenge people by getting them to read specific Scripture texts. He tells the story of a conversation he had with "one of the most careless and vile women" he had ever met. Torrey says, "She moved in good society, but in her secret life was as vile as a woman of the street." She told Torrey her story "in a most shameless and unblushing way, half laughing as she did." Without saying much to her, Torrey simply asked her to read John 3:16, to which he had opened his Bible. "Before she had read the passage through, she burst into tears, her heart broken by the love of God to her."[9]

This love of Jesus evokes in us such dedication that we count it a privilege to suffer for Christ and pay whatever price has to be paid in order to honor Him. C. T. Studd (1862-1931) was a famous cricketer who played for the English national cricket team, but caused quite a stir when he went as a missionary to China in 1885 with six other of his fellow students from Cambridge University. (He subsequently founded the Heart of Africa Mission, which later became the Worldwide Evangelization Crusade [WEC].) He once said, "If Jesus Christ be God and gave himself for me, then no sacrifice that I can

---

[9]From R. A. Torrey, *Personal Work* (Old Tappan, N.J.: Revell, n.d.), 52.

make for him is too great." The martyrs of the early church counted it a privilege to identify themselves with Christ in martyrdom. Papylus of Thyatira, who was martyred either in the late-second or the early-third century, said before his death, "Blessed are you, Lord Jesus Christ, Son of God, for you have, in your mercy, been so kind as to allow me a death like yours."[10]

It is only a misunderstanding of the gospel of grace that could result in irresponsible living. The message of the Cross, rather, is a great attraction to sacrificial living. Toyohiko Kagawa (1888-1960) was a great Japanese evangelist and social reformer. He was disinherited by his family when at age fifteen he became a Christian. When he heard the story of the Crucifixion for the first time, he was overwhelmed with emotion. He asked, "Is it true that cruel men persecuted and whipped and spat upon this man Jesus?" He was told, "Yes, it is true." Then he asked, "And is it true that Jesus, when dying on the cross, forgave them?" He was told that this too was true. Then he burst into prayer: "O God, make me like Christ." And that became his life's prayer.[11]

The challenge of the death of Christ also motivates us to forgive others who have harmed us. Louis XII had many enemies before he became king of France. After becoming king he had a list made of those who had tried to harm him and marked a large black cross against each of their names. When this became known, the enemies of the king fled, taking it as a sign that the king was going to punish them. But the king allayed their fears and assured them of pardon. He said that he had put the crosses beside each name to remind him of the Cross of Christ, so that he might follow the example of Jesus who had prayed for His murderers and had exclaimed, "Father, forgive them, for they know do not what they are doing." The example of the Cross helped him overcome his natural inclination to revenge.

Gandhi said he had seen people who brought disrepute to the Christian doctrine of forgiveness by living careless lives. These are not true disciples of Christ. True disciples would be challenged to give their soul, their life, and their all in response to the amazing, divine love of Christ.

---

[10]From *Prayers of the Martyrs*, comp. and trans. Duane W. H. Arnold (Grand Rapids, Mich.: Zondervan, 1991), 78.
[11]From E. Stanley Jones, *The Word Became Flesh* (Nashville: Abingdon, 1963), 288.

CHAPTER THIRTEEN

THE NEW HUMANITY

O NE OF THE GREAT EFFECTS of the work of Christ is the form-
ing of a new humanity, which Paul called the body of Christ.
Jesus talks about this new humanity in the passage that we have
been using as a base for our discussion of the Cross (John 10). He says,
"I have other sheep that are not of this sheep pen. I must bring them
also. They too will listen to my voice, and there shall be one flock and
one shepherd" (John 10:16). In this short passage are truths that are of
immense significance today, and we will look at some of them in this
chapter.

OTHER SHEEP WHO WILL BE BROUGHT
INTO GOD'S FOLD

Describing the effects of His death Jesus says, "I have other sheep that
are not of this sheep pen. I must bring them also. They too will listen
to my voice." There are some who use this statement to claim that there
will also be salvation for those who remain outside the church. They say
that the work of Christ has won salvation for all, both inside and outside the church.

But it is most unlikely that the book that talks so much of the necessity of believing in Jesus for salvation should teach that it is possible for
people to be saved without such belief. The verb *pisteuō*, "to believe,"

appears ninety-eight times in John.[1] In fact Jesus says here, "they too will listen to my voice." The implication is that they will respond to the Gospel. When Jesus refers to "this sheep pen," he seems to be referring to the Jews. That makes the "other sheep" non-Jews. Jesus is saying that His death is going to bring non-Jews into the flock also. This is a theme that appears elsewhere in John (11:52; 12:20-21). It is implied in the statements that present Jesus as the Savior of the whole world (John 1:29; 3:16-17). The result is a new humanity "in Christ." Paul contrasts the new humanity with the old in Romans 5:10-20 and 1 Corinthians 15:20-22. These passages say that those who are in Adam experience the consequence of Adam's sin, whereas those who are in Christ experience the consequence of Jesus' saving act.

Having said that, we need to discuss an increasingly popular doctrine that the humanity that is in Christ includes the whole human race. According to this view, even those who do not respond to the Gospel will ultimately be saved by virtue of Christ's work.[2] This trend has been associated with one of this century's most influential theologians, Karl Barth. Barth placed a great emphasis on the utter sinfulness of man and his inability to save himself. He also placed a great emphasis on the total sufficiency of the work of Christ for our salvation. These two emphases came as a breath of fresh air into a theological arena that had been dominated by liberalism, which placed a strong emphasis on human ability and effort. Barth's approach to Christ's work has been described as objective, as opposed to the subjective approaches of liberalism.

Barth, however, carried his objectivism to an extreme. In stressing that Christ has done everything that is necessary for our justification, he emphasized the insignificance of the human response in receiving Christ. In a study of Romans 5 he said, "In sovereign anticipation of our faith God has justified [people] through the sacrificial blood of Christ."[3] He explained this idea further by saying, "In his own death [Jesus

---

[1] It is surprising that the noun *pistis* does not appear at all in John.
[2] I have responded comprehensively to universalism in my two books, *A Universal Homecoming?* (Madras: ELS, 1983), and *Crucial Questions About Hell* (Eastbourne: Kingsway, 1991; Wheaton, Ill.: Crossway Books, 1994). The following paragraphs are derived from the latter work.
[3] Karl Barth, *Christ and Adam: Man and Humanity in Romans 5*, trans. T. A. Smail (1957; reprint, New York: Macmillan, 1968), 31.

Christ] makes their peace with God—*before* they themselves have decided for that peace and *quite apart from that decision.*"[4] It is evident from these quotes that Barth does not think that the act of believing is as critical as evangelical theology usually holds.

Barth so emphasizes the fact that Christ bore the punishment for our sins that he can't see people as being under God's wrath anymore. As a result, he says that the godless people are groping for an objective impossibility. They are attempting to expose themselves again "to the threat which has already been executed and consequently removed."[5] He says that "for all their godlessness they are unable to restore the perversity for whose removal [Christ] surrendered himself and so rekindle the fire of divine wrath which he has borne."[6]

It is clear that the logical conclusion of this type of thinking is universalism—the belief that all humanity is automatically saved by virtue of Christ's death. Barth knew this, but he himself refused to take the step that leads finally to universalism. Many others, however, took the step that Barth refused to take, and it is acknowledged that Barth's theology gave impetus to the movement toward universalism within the church.[7]

Those who take the step that Barth refused to take regard everybody in the world as having already been saved. These "everybodies" simply do not yet know of God's salvation and therefore do not experience, in daily life, the benefits that accrue from it. Evangelism, therefore, is telling these people that they *have been* saved and that they can experience the benefits of salvation. At least that was the gist of an Evangelism Day sermon that I heard some years back in Sri Lanka. Some who believe in universalism also argue that many people will repent in hell; but all will ultimately be saved.

Another theological system that has become very influential recently has been pioneered in Roman Catholic circles and is associ-

---

[4]Ibid., 23 (my italics).
[5]Karl Barth, *Church Dogmatics II, 2: The Doctrine of God*, trans. G. W. Bromiley et al. (Edinburgh: T. & T. Clark, 1957), 346.
[6]Ibid., 352.
[7]This point is made in Henri Blocher, "The Lost State of Man," in *Evangelism Alert*, ed. Gilbert W. Kirby (London: World Wide Publications, 1972), 55, 56; and Bernard Ramm, "Will All Men Be Finally Saved?" *Eternity* (August 1964), 23.

ated especially with Karl Rahner,[8] Hans Küng,[9] and Raimundo Panikkar.[10] Like Barth, these people, in stressing the efficacy of the work of Christ, say that salvation extends to people independent of explicit faith in Christ. But they take a further step that Barth would have firmly denounced. They see the sacraments of other religions as being means of salvation.[11] So practices like Buddhist almsgiving and Hindu rites are viewed as sacraments that mediate salvation. Rahner described the saved people of other religions as "anonymous Christians." Küng refers to the non-Christian religions as the "ordinary" way to salvation, whereas Christianity is a "very special and extraordinary" way to salvation.

Into this environment Christians come affirming that the Bible is unmistakably clear that one must believe in Jesus Christ for salvation. The apostles were uncompromising in their claim that Jesus was the only way to salvation (Acts 4:12) and that only those who call on the name of the Lord will be saved (Acts 2:21; Rom. 10:13).

WHY FAITH IS SO CRUCIAL TO SALVATION

THE BIBLICAL INSISTENCE ON THE NECESSITY OF FAITH FOR SALVATION

Does it not sound strange that simply calling on the name of Jesus becomes the means of moving a person from damnation to salvation? In the Bible "calling on the name of the Lord" is equivalent to having faith in Christ. Both Jesus (John 5:24) and the apostles claimed that believing in Christ is the means of salvation. Paul put it succinctly: "For it is by grace you have been saved, through faith—and this not from yourselves, it is the gift of God" (Eph. 2:8). On our part what we must

---

[8]See Karl Rahner, "Christianity and the Non-Christian Religions," in *Christianity and Other Religions*, eds. John Hick and Brian Hebblethwaite (Glasgow: Collins, Fount Paperbacks, 1980), 52-79, and *Theological Investigations*, vol. 5 of *Later Writings* (London: Darton, Longman and Todd, 1966), 115-34.

[9]See Hans Küng, in *Christian Revelation and World Religions*, ed. Joseph Neuner (London: Burns and Oats, 1967), 52-53.

[10]See Raimundo Panikkar, *The Unknown Christ of Hinduism*, rev. ed. (Maryknoll, N.Y.: Orbis, 1981).

[11]See Nihal Abeysingha, *A Theological Evaluation of Non-Christian Rites* (Bangalore: Theological Publications in India, 1979).

do, to receive the grace through which Christ won our salvation, is to exercise faith. And faith is more than merely pronouncing the name of Jesus. Faith is a key requirement in God's answer to the human predicament caused by sin.

THE HEART OF SIN IS UNBELIEF

After Adam and Eve were created, they were totally contented and fulfilled, finding satisfaction in their relationship with nature, with each other, and with God (Gen. 2:7-25). By trusting in and enjoying God's goodness, they glorified God and fulfilled the purpose of their creation. But the Serpent made them question God's goodness. He made them think that God had created them to fulfill His own needs and that He was not really concerned with their welfare.[12] He said, "For God knows that when you eat of [the fruit] your eyes will be opened, and you will be like God, knowing good and evil" (Gen. 3:5). Eve found the fruit attractive: "When the woman saw that the fruit of the tree was good for food and pleasing to the eye, and also desirable for gaining wisdom, she took some and ate it" (Gen. 3:6).

One of the attractions of the fruit was that it was "desirable for gaining wisdom." That is the reason for the name of this tree: "the tree of the knowledge of good and evil" (Gen. 2:17). After a survey of the use of the expression "to know good and evil" in the Old Testament,[13] Daniel Fuller concludes that it means "a maturity in which they were independent and therefore responsible for the decisions they made."[14] Most often this is something good. But when it comes to our relationship with God, it means that we, and not God, decide what is good and bad. Adam and Eve decided that they could have a fulfilled life without God's help if they ate that fruit (Gen. 3:6). And that is the heart of sin: independence from God; believing that we can chart our own path to success without God's help.

What we have been describing is actually unbelief. Jesus has

---

[12]For a theological exposition of the Fall, see Daniel P. Fuller, *The Unity of the Bible* (Grand Rapids, Mich.: Zondervan, 1992), 175-86. I am indebted to this study for many points in this section.

[13]Gen. 3:22; 2 Sam. 14:17; 1 Kings 3:9; Deut. 1:39; Isa. 7:15; 2 Sam. 19:35.

[14]Fuller, *Unity of the Bible*, 182.

defined sin as unbelief. He says that the Holy Spirit will convict the world "in regard to sin, because men do not believe in me" (John 16:9). Hebrews 3:12 succinctly presents what we have been trying to explain: "See to it, brothers, that none of you has a sinful, unbelieving heart that turns away from the living God." Sin means to turn away from God, and that is to have an unbelieving heart.

Paul expounds on this theme in the first chapter of Romans. He gives "godlessness" as the reason why people are under the wrath of God: "The wrath of God is being revealed from heaven against all the godlessness and wickedness of men who suppress the truth by their wickedness" (v. 18). Godlessness is defined in verse 21 as the failure to glorify God and give thanks to Him: "For although they knew God, they neither glorified him as God nor gave thanks to him, but their thinking became futile and their foolish hearts were darkened." This is similar to the unbelief of Adam and Eve. Paul says that the consequence of unbelief is idolatry (v. 25) and the more overt forms of wickedness (vv. 24, 26-27, 29-31). Verse 28 summarizes this process: "Furthermore, since they did not think it worthwhile to retain the knowledge of God, he gave them over to a depraved mind, to do what ought not to be done."

THE OPPOSITE OF SIN IS BELIEF

If unbelief is the heart of sin, then the opposite of sin must be belief. When we believe, we are returning the fruit of the tree of the knowledge of good and evil to God. We are saying that we are ceasing our efforts to rule our lives and save ourselves and are availing ourselves of God's provision of a way of salvation. Christ's work on the cross won our salvation and made it available to us in the form of grace. When we believe, we not only accept that grace, but we also reverse the very process that put humanity in need of salvation: the sin of unbelief.

Faith, then, is not simply pronouncing the name of Jesus. It is an admission of the folly of our sin, of trying to save ourselves. It is committing our destiny to the wisdom of God. It is reversing what took place at the Fall. When Adam and Eve ate of the fruit, they said that they would use their wisdom to determine their destiny. When we exercise faith, we look to God's wisdom to save us, to keep us, and to determine our destiny. Paul says it was to effect such a change in our lives that Jesus died on the cross: "And he died for all, that those who live should no longer live for themselves but for him who died for them and was raised again" (2 Cor. 5:15).

THE MISSIONARY CHALLENGE TO COMMITMENT

So John 10:16 teaches that the death of Christ makes it possible for other sheep to come into Christ's flock. But the way this will happen today is through the church's going out and bringing them in. John 10:16, then, is a missionary verse. William Barclay, commenting on this verse, says, "The dream of Christ depends on us; it is we who can help him make the world one flock with him as its shepherd."[15]

If Jesus is going to fulfill His mission through us, the model we use must be the model of Jesus. As Jesus Himself said in John 20:21: "As the Father has sent me, I am sending you." The model we see is one of costly commitment, even to the point of death. I believe one of the greatest challenges to anyone interested in the mission of the church today is to learn to suffer because of the commitments he or she makes. Commitment and suffering go hand in hand. Paul describes this type of commitment in Colossians 1:24-25: "Now I rejoice in what was suffered for you, and I fill up in my flesh what is still lacking in regard to Christ's afflictions, for the sake of his body, which is the church. I have become its servant by the commission God gave me to present to you the word of God in its fullness."

Presently it seems that Christians, especially in the West, are often not willing to endure suffering because of their commitments. When commitment involves suffering, many give up the relationship. They divorce their spouses, change churches, ignore their small groups, leave their organizations, or drop colleagues who have been wounded in the battle between good and evil. If the church in the West does not change here and give tangible evidence of its ability to stick to commitments, I fear it will disqualify itself from being a missionary-sending region.

---

[15]William Barclay, *The Gospel of John*, vol. 2 of *The Daily Bible Study*, rev. ed. (Philadelphia: Westminster, 1975; British edition, Edinburgh: Saint Andrew Press), 66.

One of the keys to missionary effectiveness is the ability to persevere with one's call when the going gets tough, without giving up and going somewhere else. If we are not prepared to suffer, we will become disillusioned after a time and abandon the call God has given us. And if we are not showing the ability to stick to our commitments at home, it is unlikely that we will be able to do this abroad, where the challenges are even greater.

The problem is compounded by the pragmatism of our age. Success is gauged by measurable results. People value efficiency greatly and seek to get the best yield as quickly as possible. This does not often happen in reaching the unreached, especially when one is called to work with resistant people. Those working in cross-cultural settings will face severe frustration as they seek to identify with a people who are so different from themselves. Modern people, so used to the marvels of technology that eliminate frustration in many spheres, find it very difficult to handle the frustration that comes with Christian ministry. Often they move to another sphere of service, like ministry among a more receptive people. Sometimes they shift the emphasis of their ministry to activities like training programs and seminars that produce measurable results. Some adopt evangelistic methods that elicit quick responses of prayers to receive Christ, which are not very difficult to secure in pluralistic cultures where people will be happy to add Jesus to the list of many gods they go to for help. They have impressive statistics of those who "prayed to receive Christ," but only heaven knows how many of these people's names are written in the Lamb's Book of Life. Others leave the ministry altogether, feeling disillusioned and believing that they have been failures.

Many of the great heroes of the church saw few visible results during their lifetimes. Some had to wait for many years before they saw results. In view of this, it is essential that training for missions and evangelistic ministry should include preparation for frustration. Sending bodies and supporters of those doing pioneering evangelism need to be educated so that they will not have unrealistic expectations from those they send and support. Those who send and those who go must know that commitment to a people-group may involve many years of labor with much suffering, frustration, and minimal visible fruit.

THE CROSS IS THE GREAT EQUALIZER

In the last part of John 10:16, Jesus mentions the result of having these other sheep come in: "and there shall be one flock and one shepherd." What we have here is an initial statement about the universal church that Paul is later going to teach about in some detail. He will use the figure of the body of Christ to refer to the church[16] and views those who are "in Christ" by faith as belonging to it. Here Jesus is saying that the Gentiles will come in, and they will belong to the same flock as the Jews. A significant feature of the biblical description of the work of Christ is its emphasis on how the Cross broke earthly distinctions between people.

If the Jews who were listening understood what Jesus meant by this statement, it would have been a very revolutionary thought for them. They always thought that they were separate and superior to other races because they were the chosen people of God. "Only by becoming a full citizen could a non-Jew find entry into Jewish religious groups."[17] Jesus is implying here that His death would make such a step unnecessary.

In first century Graeco-Roman society, "social status still remained the principal criterion by which people were evaluated and treated."[18] In the early Christian church, however, the barrier between the Jews and the Gentiles was broken. Paul went to the extent of saying, "There is neither Jew nor Greek, slave nor free, male nor female, for you are all one in Christ Jesus" (Gal. 3:28). This statement shows that social distinctions had become insignificant in the church, as the slave-free barrier was broken. It seems that the little epistle to Philemon was included in the Bible to underscore this fact. There we find Paul saying, "Perhaps the reason [Onesimus] was separated from you for a little while was that you might have him back for good—no longer as a slave, but better than a slave, as a dear brother. He is very dear to me but even dearer to you, both as a man and as a brother in the Lord" (Philem. 1:15-16).

In the early churches, the rich and the poor worshiped together. Robert Banks has shown that in the church in Corinth, for example,

---

[16]See 1 Cor. 12:27; Rom. 12:5; Eph. 1:22-23; 4:12, 15; Col. 1:18.
[17]Robert Banks, *Paul's Idea of Community* (Grand Rapids, Mich.: Eerdmans; NSW, Australia: Anzea Publishers, 1988), 116.
[18]Ibid., 114.

"a significant number of people in the church came from the more respected levels of society." Banks says, "No fewer than eight or nine people named in the letters to the community were members of the wealthier class, as hints about their occupation, dependents and/or possessions demonstrate."[19] Yet it was about this church that Paul says, "Not many of you were wise by human standards; not many were influential; not many were of noble birth" (1 Cor 1:26). The majority of the church must have been poor people. But they worshiped together.

There has been a trend, in keeping with the specialization of our age, for churches to specialize for different types of groups. Sometimes this is necessary because of vast linguistic and other cultural differences. But we should be cautious about extending this according to differences like class and educational background. It is not easy at first for the rich to worship with the poor. But the struggle and adjustments that are made in order to do this could result in a deep enriching of the lives of those from both groups. I can testify to the truth of this, as it has happened in the church where I worship.

This new approach to earthly differences also influenced the attitude to women in the first-century church. "By and large women were regarded as second-class citizens during this time."[20] A later rabbinic prayer that was recommended for daily use said, "Blessed be God who has not made me . . . a woman."[21] Paul, on the other hand, said, "There is neither . . . male nor female, for you are all one in Christ Jesus" (Gal. 3:28). Banks says that "the records we possess nowhere contain so explicit a declaration" as this breaking of the barriers of sexism.[22]

The unity of the church had a marked impact on those outside it. It is said that the church was accused of magic and sorcery because that was the only way people outside it could explain the barrier breaking that was evident there.[23] Jesus recognized that the unity of the church was a key aspect of the witness of the church. He prayed: ". . . that all of them may be one, Father, just as you are in me and I am in you. May

---

[19]Ibid., 120.
[20]Ibid., 116.
[21]Quoted in Banks, *Paul's Idea*, 117.
[22]Ibid.
[23]Cited in R. Kent Hughes, *The Disciplines of a Godly Man* (Wheaton, Ill.: Crossway Books, 1991), 198.

they also be in us so that the world may believe that you have sent me. . . . May they be brought to complete unity to let the world know that you sent me and have loved them even as you have loved me" (John 17:21, 23). Christ's ability to break human barriers is an important aspect of His supremacy.

HOW CHRIST BREAKS HUMAN BARRIERS

How does the Cross act as the great equalizer of the human race? It does so, first, by showing us that there is nothing any of us can do to win our salvation. In God's sight, all humans are sinners. All are equally in desperate need of salvation. Paul says, "There is no difference: Jew and Gentile alike have all sinned, and all fall short of God's glory" (Rom 3:22b-23; F. F. Bruce, *Expanded Paraphrase*[24]). In God's sight, "There is no one righteous, not even one" (Rom. 3:10). However great we are on earth, we do not measure up to God's standards. It has been said that the entrance is so low at what is considered the place of Christ's birth that all who wish to enter, whether king or beggar, have to enter kneeling.

A beautiful illustration of this point comes from the classic Christian novel *In His Steps*. Rollin Page was a rich snob who did not care for the things of God or for the poor. But he went to an evangelistic tent meeting that was held in the "worst" part of town. The Spirit of God moved him to come forward at the end of the meeting to commit his life to Christ. There he was, in his expensive clothes, kneeling by the side of poor drunken men, people he probably had never been so close to before. But that evening they were equal: sinners desperately in need of salvation.[25]

We all come to God as sinners, and when we enter the kingdom we all become princes and princesses of the King of kings and the Lord of lords. That is true of the richest and the poorest believer, the most educated and the least educated. The glory of being a prince of God cannot be compared with any earthly glory. Therefore, for the true believer, earthly glory becomes insignificantly small. It is not even

---

[24]F. F. Bruce, *An Expanded Paraphrase of the Epistles of Paul* (Palm Springs, Calif.: Ronald H. Haynes Publishers, 1981; British edition, Exeter: Paternoster), 191.
[25]Charles Sheldon, *In His Steps* (Waco, Tex.: Word, 1988), 78-79.

reckoned when we assess the importance of people. We can think of this like two people who were given $1,000,000 each. One had two cents before, and the other had one cent. The two-cent person cannot say to the one-cent person, "I am richer than you." The money they had earlier is utterly insignificant in comparison to the riches they now have. The Cross destroys our false pride and becomes the basis of our new glorious identity.

Paul expounds how the Cross breaks the barriers between the Jews and Gentiles in Ephesians 2:13-16:

> But now in Christ Jesus you who once were far away have been brought near through the blood of Christ. For he himself is our peace, who has made the two one and has destroyed the barrier, the dividing wall of hostility, by abolishing in his flesh the law with its commandments and regulations. His purpose was to create in himself one new man out of the two, thus making peace, and in this one body to reconcile both of them to God through the cross, by which he put to death their hostility.

The way in which the Cross breaks human barriers is powerfully proclaimed each time the church gathers to celebrate the Lord's Supper. At the Supper, everyone is an equal, seated at the same table, brought together in a "holy communion" through the blood of Christ.

THE PATHETIC RECORD OF THE CONTEMPORARY CHURCH

Despite this revolutionary teaching about how the Cross breaks human barriers, the church has fared very badly in recent years in practicing this truth. In this century, many evangelicals have been guilty of prejudice that goes completely against the grain of this teaching. Perhaps as a reaction to the social gospel, which was popular in the first half of this century, and to liberation theology, which we see in the second half, many evangelicals have become fearful of emphasizing the social implications of the Gospel. Yet, the social implications of the Gospel remain crucial teachings for today's world, torn as it is by ethnic and social strife.

Prejudice has been a problem because we have all imbibed

prejudices from our environment that claim that one group is superior to another group. Coming from a nation where ethnic strife has caused so much chaos, I can say that even with Christians our prejudices are among the last things the process of sanctification touches. The prejudice may pertain to race or class or caste or another of those earthly factors that are not significant in God's sight. Those who claim that they are not prejudiced are often the most prejudiced. Sometimes those who claim to be Bible-believing Christians are the most unbiblical on this issue.

Islam is growing rapidly among people who were once treated as inferior by Christians. And one of the things that they are pushing is what they call the brotherhood of Islam where, they claim, earthly barriers have been broken. In a mosque near our home there was a time when the president of the mosque was a rich businessman who was also a member of the national cabinet. The vice-president was a poor mason who lived in the slums. I have often wondered whether this type of situation could exist in a Christian church. I think what would happen is that a rich businessman and a poor mason would be worshiping in different congregations. And the Muslims would come into that situation and say, "Our religion really makes you one." Perhaps I should add that we see gross inequalities existing in Muslim countries too, even in the oil-rich countries. Certainly Christians have a better record of helping the poor and oppressed. A case in point is the starving people in Somalia, which is a predominantly Muslim country, while oil-rich Saudi Arabia is virtually next door.

A key Indian politician, B. R. Ambedkar, who helped frame the Indian constitution, was the leader of a group of untouchables (Gandhi gave the untouchables the name Harijan, meaning "God's children"). Ambedkar wanted to leave Hinduism because of its caste system, and he considered becoming a Christian. But he found that the Christians perpetuated this system too. So he and thousands of his people became Buddhists. A recent *Time* magazine article on the conversion of low-caste Hindus in India states that they are turning to Islam for the same reason.

Much of my work has been with the poor. And one of the most painful aspects of this work has been trying to incorporate converts from poor backgrounds into the broader church. Our understanding of what is excellent, what is successful, and what is leadership seems to be so influenced by middle-class values that there is little chance of these people becoming full participants in the church. This was not true, for example, of the early church or of the evangelical revival of the eighteenth century. The Oxford-educated aristocrat John Wesley spearheaded a movement many of whose early preachers and leaders were from poorer backgrounds. Some of them, like the coal miner Billy Bray, became world-famous preachers.

We have much work to do here! A key to this problem's solution is to rediscover our identity in Christ. People who treat others as inferior are those who themselves suffer from a sense of inferiority and insecurity. Others are a threat to them because they don't have a sense of being important to the eternal God. They don't have the assurance that this God will look after them more than adequately. When we lose sight of our identity in Christ, lesser identifying features, like race, class, caste, and education, become significant. We try to find our identity by acting more significant than others.

OUR ATTITUDE TOWARD NON-CHRISTIANS

Our identity in Christ destroys racial, class, caste, and educational prejudice toward non-Christians too. When we realize this identity, we are so thrilled with what He has done to us that we want to help others see those riches also. We realize that we are not better than anyone in the ultimate sense of the term, that we are all hell-deserving sinners saved by grace. We realize that God made everyone equal.

Paul expresses this well in 2 Corinthians 5:14-16. First he talks about what Christ did on the Cross: "For Christ's love compels us, because we are convinced that one died for all, and therefore all died. And he died for all, that those who live should no longer live for themselves but for him who died for them and was raised again" (verses 14-15). Then he gives an implication of believing that fact: "So from now on we regard no one from a worldly point of view. Though we once regarded Christ in this way, we do so no longer" (verse 16). Earthly distinctions based on factors like race, class, caste, education, and sex are no longer significant. What is important is their relationship to what Christ has done. And that is explained in the next verse: "Therefore, if anyone is in Christ, he is a new creation; the old has gone, the new has come!" (2 Cor. 5:17). We see all people as individuals. All are equally in need of salvation, and we reach out to them in love, realizing that we too received this gift because of mercy and not because of any merit of ours.

We cannot ignore the revolutionary biblical teaching about the breaking of earthly barriers in our evangelistic preaching. Paul brought the unpopular idea of the unity of the human race into his preaching in Athens when he said, "From one man he made every nation of men, that they should inhabit the whole earth" (Acts 17:26a). This ran counter to a belief the Greeks had that they themselves sprang "from the soil of their native Attica" and therefore "were innately superior to Barbarians."[26] When we ask people to repent of their sin and come to Christ, one of the sins they need to repent of is the sin of prejudice. So the message of equality has a place in our evangelistic proclamation.

If prejudice is condemned in evangelistic ministry, how much more should it be condemned in pastoral ministry. We must affirm with Paul, "There is neither Jew nor Greek, slave nor free, male nor female, for you are all one in Christ Jesus" (Gal. 3:28) and do all we can to see that the church demonstrates the truth of that doctrine. Let us pray that we will be open to the work of the Spirit in our lives so that He will convince us of our identity in Christ and help us overcome the sin of prejudice in our lives, both in the church and in the world.

---

[26]F. F. Bruce, "The Book of the Acts," in *The New International Commentary on the New Testament* (Grand Rapids, Mich.: Eerdmans, 1988), 337.

CHAPTER FOURTEEN

THE CROSS AND THE PROBLEM OF PAIN

I N MY CONVERSATIONS with non-Christians, one of the questions that invariably comes up is about how one can reconcile all the suffering in the world with the existence of a God who is said to be both good and almighty. This is a problem that even biblical characters grappled with, as is reflected in Job's statement, "When a scourge brings sudden death, [God] mocks the despair of the innocent" (Job 9:23). John Stott says that "the fact of suffering undoubtedly constitutes the single greatest challenge to the Christian faith."[1] If Christ is God's ultimate solution to the human dilemma, then His Gospel must adequately face the challenge of the problem of evil and suffering.

THE ANSWERS OF OTHER RELIGIONS

The other religions have answers to this dilemma. The foundation of Buddhism, the Four Noble Truths, begins with an affirmation about suffering: all existence entails suffering or *dukka*. The Buddha's understanding of suffering here is somewhat akin to the biblical

---

[1] John Stott, *The Cross of Christ* (Leicester and Downers Grove, Ill.: InterVarsity Press, 1986), 311.

understanding of frustration or futility as expounded in Ecclesiastes and Romans 8:18-25. Buddha said that suffering is caused by craving or *tanha* (the Second Noble Truth). The misfortunes one faces are the result of negative *karma* accrued in previous and present births. The Buddha saw suffering ceasing when craving ceases at Nirvana (the Third Noble Truth), and he presented his eight-fold path or *magga* as the means to the extinction of craving (the Fourth Noble Truth). As Buddhism is a nontheistic religion,[2] Buddhists do not have to grapple with the theological problem of having to reconcile the problem of evil with the existence of a supreme God.

Hinduism, like Buddhism, explains pain and suffering as being the result of the *karma* one has accrued. There are different understandings of deity within Hinduism (ranging from impersonal pantheistic monism to polytheism to monotheism). But these concepts of the divine are such that they do not give rise to the problem of having to reconcile evil with the goodness of a personal God as does Christianity. The polytheistic Hindus would hold that there are good gods and evil gods. Particularly interesting is the monism of vedantic Hinduism where only one reality (Brahman) is recognized. If one were to view what appears as evil from that perspective, it would be seen not to be evil. What is experienced as evil is so because it is experienced as a part of the whole. The whole is complete and in perfect agreement with itself. Many Buddhists and Hindus feel that the karmic explanation is a more adequate answer to the problem of suffering than the Christian explanation.

We must remember that in practice most Buddhists and Hindus have an animistic element to their religious life wherein good and bad deities are held to be responsible for the good and evil that people encounter. The different gods are appeased or their help is solicited at shrines or in special ceremonies. Typically magical practices are used here. This is true of the various animistic and polytheistic tribal religions in different parts of the world. In Sri Lanka, shrines to the gods are often found beside the Buddhist temples. In Hindu temples and Chinese Buddhist temples, they are part of the temple ritual itself. Most

---

[2]It is nontheistic because God is not a necessary part of its scheme. This should be distinguished from atheism, which says there is no God.

followers of popular Buddhism in Sri Lanka go to a shrine or to an astrologer or exorcist before they go to the Buddhist temple when faced with some evil or fear. So even though in theory the law of *karma* is said to explain the problem of evil, the belief in supernatural powers pervades the activity of Buddhists and Hindus when it comes to responding to evil and pain.

The ancient Persian religion Zoroastrianism held to a thoroughgoing dualism with two beings being virtually equal in power. The wholly Good Creator, known as Ahura Mazda (the wise Lord) is the creator of all things. The evil in the world comes from the Destructive Spirit whose nature is violent and destructive. Situations are said to depend on which god is in control at a given time, place, or circumstance. The Parsis represent what remains of Zoroastrianism today. Most of them are found in India after having moved there from their native Persia because of persecution.

The ancient Greek philosopher Plato and modern philosophers like John Stuart Mill, Edgar Sheffield Brightman, and Peter Bertocci have sought to solve the problem of evil by claiming that though God is good he is finite.

The Muslims' response to the problem of pain has similarities to the Christian response. They see suffering sometimes as a punishment for wrongdoing and sometimes as a test of faith. They also have a place for Satan in their explanation, even though his role is downplayed. He is seen as one operating within the will of God to test people. But the Muslim view is heavily influenced by their concept that God is much beyond anything that we can adequately comprehend. He is generally viewed as being detached from moral responsibility or from any involvement in human suffering. Although everything comes from God, He is not responsible in the sense that He has to answer for what is happening. There is an overwhelming sense of predestination: that which happens is God's will, and it must happen. The name *Islam* itself means "submission to God."

The Muslims show a strong militancy when it comes to struggling for the cause of God and his religion, as their commitment to Jihad, or holy war, shows. But when it comes to things like personal tragedy, sickness, financial reversal, and extreme poverty, an attitude of resignation prevails. This is evidenced by their common use of the Arabic expression, *Insha'llah,* meaning "if God wills." Therefore, there is great reluctance to question the providence of God in permitting tragedies to happen. This attitude may have something to do with the fact that most Muslim countries are very poor, and the vast majority of Muslims in the world are poor. When people are so influenced by an absolute concept of predestination, they may not be sufficiently motivated to do something constructive when they suffer or see others suffering.

THE BIBLE AND THE PROBLEM OF PAIN

THE CAUSES OF EVIL AND SUFFERING

While we would wish for a philosophical response to this problem in the Bible, we do not find one because, as John Stott says, "Its purpose is more practical than philosophical."[3] Yet the Bible does tackle the problem of evil and suffering from different fronts.

It says that evil originated in human history at the Fall in Eden. When God created the universe, he described it as "good" and "very good" (Gen. 1). Humankind was the apex of creation and was given the responsibility of ruling (Gen. 1:26-30). But when humankind sinned, the whole of creation lost its equilibrium. Evil is therefore an intruder into this universe. When Adam sinned and evil entered this world, the whole creation was cursed by God (Gen. 3:14-19), and disease and death entered the world. Paul, echoing the teaching of the book of Ecclesiastes, describes this fallen state of creation as a subjection to frustration (Rom. 8:20). As we said, frustration here is a concept somewhat akin to the Buddhist idea of *dukka*.

Satan obtained a foothold in creation through the rebellion of humanity. He has unleashed his power so forcefully that Paul went to the extent of calling him "the god of this age" (2 Cor. 4:4). In the book of Job, we see Satan having the power to torment Job. Jesus described a woman who had been sick as "a daughter of Abraham, whom Satan has kept bound for eighteen long years" (Luke 13:16). Paul says, "there was given me a thorn in my flesh, a messenger of Satan, to torment me" (2 Cor. 12:7).

Sometimes, however, suffering is directly due to human sin. Each year drunk drivers inflict much suffering on innocent people. The poor

---

[3]Stott, *Cross of Christ*, 312.

often suffer deprivation and exploitation because of unjust economic systems. Those who drink excessively suffer from liver ailments in their later years. Selfish people who hurt other people and show no kindness in their younger years often suffer from bitter loneliness when they are old and sick.

The Bible says that sometimes the suffering of individuals is a punishment from God for their own sin. Writing on the abuses of the Lord's Supper, Paul says, "For anyone who eats and drinks without recognizing the body of the Lord eats and drinks judgment on himself. That is why many among you are weak and sick, and a number of you have fallen asleep" (1 Cor. 11:29-30). But that does not mean that *all* that we suffer is because of our own sins. That is what the doctrine of *karma* says. Jesus explicitly denied that anyone's sin had caused the blindness of the person they encountered: "Neither this man nor his parents sinned, but this happened so that the work of God might be displayed in his life" (John 9:3).

Many people struggle today with the dilemma of why the righteous suffer so much while the wicked seem to prosper. According to the law of *karma*, this would be because of evil done in previous lives. But to me it seems extremely unfair that good people should be punished for evil done by a person about whom they know nothing and whose actions they themselves strongly condemn.[4] A Japanese professor who was a Buddhist lost his sight because of a detached retina. He simply could not agree with what his religion taught about this tragedy, that it happened because of what he had done in a previous life. He was encouraged to look at the Christian answer to his problem, and he found the story about Jesus and the man who had been born blind (John 9). Jesus refused to accept the typical *karmic* explanation for suffering and said that the works of God would be manifested through the man's blindness. The professor asked, "Could the works of God be manifest through my blindness? Then that is the answer: I'll use this blindness." Not only did this man become a Christian—he also became an effective evangelist. He went to Scotland for theological studies and then taught theology in Kobe Theological College in Japan.[5]

---

[4]On the injustice of reincarnation, see my book *Crucial Questions About Hell* (Eastbourne: Kingsway, 1991; Wheaton, Ill.: Crossway, 1994).
[5]From E. Stanley Jones, *A Song of Ascents* (Nashville: Abingdon, 1968), 182.

CHRIST'S DECISIVE BLOW AGAINST THE CAUSES
OF EVIL AND SUFFERING

The Bible, then, teaches that the world is under a curse and that all of life in the present is darkened by the reality of frustration. But Paul says, "The creation was subjected to frustration . . . *in hope*" (Rom. 8:20). Even at the time of the curse, God was looking forward to restoring creation to the glory he had intended for it. This will eventually become a reality because of the work of Christ. Christ's death dealt a decisive blow on both of the causative agents of suffering in the world: human sin and satanic power and authority. Paul says, "He forgave us all *our sins*, having canceled the written code, with its regulations, that was against us and that stood opposed to us; he took it away, nailing it to the cross. And having disarmed the *powers and authorities*, he made a public spectacle of them, triumphing over them by the cross" (Col. 2:13-15).

The French-born biblical theologian at the University of Basel, Oscar Cullmann, uses language from war to describe the decisiveness of the blow of Christ upon the forces of evil. He says, "The decisive battle in a war may already have occurred in a relatively early stage of the war, and yet the war still continues." A thing like this happened in the Second World War when the decisive turn took place on what became known as D day in June 1944. On June 6 a huge Allied force from Britain landed in Normandy in northern France, and soon the Allies liberated Paris. The Germans began a retreat that was never reversed. After that, only mopping-up operations needed to be done until finally there came the total victory in Europe, V-E day, about a year later. Cullmann says that "the event on the cross, together with the resurrection which followed, was the already concluded decisive battle."[6]

Now we look forward to V day when God will consummate what was begun with Christ's work. Just as the crucial blow was inflicted on evil in connection with Christ's first coming, the final blow will be inflicted in connection with His second coming. George Ladd explains the present age in this way: "The church lives 'between the times,' the old age goes on, but the powers of the new age have irrupted into the

---

[6]Oscar Cullmann, *Christ and Time*, trans. Floyd V. Filson (Philadelphia: Westminster, 1964), 84.

old age."[7] The messianic kingdom of Christ, as anticipated in the Old Testament, has come but is not yet consummated. Ladd captured this idea well when he named his book on Jesus and the kingdom *The Presence of the Future.*[8]

Satan is therefore still "alive and well on planet earth" as the title of one book put it.[9] But he is bound with a rope that can be lengthened or shortened.[10] He cannot do that which God does not permit him to do, and even his evil schemes will be finally used by the sovereign God to achieve ultimate good.

DIVINE AND CHRISTIAN ACTION IN OPPOSITION TO EVIL

While the Bible says that evil is the result of God's curse upon sin, it also presents God as being opposed to evil and its effects on creation and as acting in compassion to liberate humanity from them. This was clearly shown in the life and work of Jesus. And this is why we pray to God for deliverance in times of suffering. Reflecting God's attitude toward evil, the Christian opposes all evil and actively seeks to alleviate suffering. Therefore, serving the needy is a vital aspect of the Christian religion. Such service is often misinterpreted when it is associated with evangelism. People think that the only reason we are so active in serving the needy is the desire to "buy up" converts through our generosity. Why else would we care so much about insignificant people who have been ignored for so long by the leaders of their own religion (until the Christians show them special concern, after which the other religions also get involved in these communities)?

The biblical idea of the solidarity of the human race because we are all created by God also influences our attitude toward suffering. In Hinduism and Buddhism, suffering is a result of one's own misdeeds. It

---

[7]George Eldon Ladd, *A Theology of the New Testament*, rev. ed., ed. Donald A. Hagner (Grand Rapids, Mich.: Eerdmans, 1993), 67.

[8]G. E. Ladd *The Presence of the Future* (a revision of his *Jesus and the Kingdom*) (Grand Rapids, Mich.: Eerdmans, 1974).

[9]Hal Lindsey, *Satan Is Alive and Well on Planet Earth* (Grand Rapids, Mich.: Zondervan, 1972).

[10]Oscar Cullmann, *The State in the New Testament* (New York: Scribner's, 1956), 69, quoted in Ladd, *The Presence of the Future*, 152.

is something you bear on your own and for which you are responsible. In Christianity, human suffering becomes the responsibility of all Christians because of the idea of solidarity. In fact, corporate solidarity is so important to the Christian approach to life that Christians share the responsibility for evils done by their fellow humans. In the famous prayer in Daniel 9, Daniel repeatedly confesses as his own the sins of his people. There was a terrible week of violence in Sri Lanka in July 1983 when the Sinhala people attacked the Tamils following the killing of thirteen Sinhala soldiers by Tamil militants. Thousands were killed, scarred, and left homeless. A Sinhala Anglican Bishop, Lakshman Wickremasinghe, was in England for a heart operation at the time. In his first sermon after returning to Sri Lanka, he used the words, "We have killed … ," even though he had not been in the country at the time.

This sense of corporate solidarity also motivates Christians to take on voluntary suffering: that is, not suffering we deserve—the result of *karma*—but what we choose to undergo—the result of a call to service. The basic call of Christ to His followers included a call to voluntary suffering. He said, "If anyone would come after me, he must deny himself and take up his cross and follow me. For whoever wants to save his life will lose it, but whoever loses his life for me will find it" (Matt. 16:24-25). So the Christian tradition has motivated many to take on the cup of suffering for the sake of serving needy humanity.

Whatever one may say in criticism of the Christian answer to the problem of evil, he or she cannot dispute the unrivaled record of Christians in history in the alleviation of suffering. Following the example of their servant Lord, Christians have distinguished themselves in sacrificial and powerfully effective service to humanity. The proof of the validity of a system of thought is the way it influences the lives of its adherents. Christianity passes this test with flying colors.

THE FINAL DEFEAT OF EVIL

But why doesn't God immediately take away evil from the face of this earth? Evil is too integral a part of humanity and nature for Him to do that. He cannot destroy evil without at the same time destroying humanity. Some physical diseases are allowed to run their course because an immediate cure could kill the patient. A friend of mine had a skin ailment for a long period of time. His doctor felt that it was an ailment that needed to be controlled rather than eradicated. Another doctor said that he knew of a drug that would completely heal the skin. My friend eagerly took this medicine, and in a few days his skin was as smooth as a baby's skin. But he also got some side effects that were even more serious than the skin ailment. He had to immediately stop taking the so-called miracle drug.

Yet, the Bible says that Jesus will finally defeat His enemies and complete the work He began at the cross. Paul says, "Then the end will come, when he hands over the kingdom to God the Father after he has destroyed all dominion, authority and power ... so that God may be all in all" (1 Cor. 15:24, 28). But before this happens Christ "must reign until he has put all his enemies under his feet" (1 Cor. 15:25). Elsewhere Paul says, "The creation itself will be liberated from its bondage to decay and brought into the glorious freedom of the children of God" (Rom. 8:21). This teaching about Christ's battle against and final victory over evil finds its most graphic and detailed exposition in the book of Revelation.

Paul says that in the meantime, "the whole creation has been groaning as in the pains of childbirth. ... Not only so," says Paul, "but we ourselves, who have the firstfruits of the Spirit, groan inwardly as we wait eagerly for our adoption as sons, the redemption of our bodies" (Rom. 8:22-23). Believers in Jesus are not immune to the pain of this world. We share in it, and through that sharing we become a redemptive community in this hurting world. This method of ministering through identifying with suffering reached its climax in the life and ministry of Jesus, the Suffering Servant. "He was despised and rejected by men, a man of sorrows, and familiar with suffering. Like one from whom men hide their faces he was despised, and we esteemed him not" (Isa. 53:3). If that was what Christ experienced, His followers cannot expect an easy life removed from pain and sorrow.

So we look forward to the glorious destiny of creation. It was with this destiny in mind that God created the world. This destiny is described in the book of Revelation as the new heaven and the new earth (Rev. 21–22). Revelation describes this glory not as one achieved in a vacuum but as one achieved through triumph over evil and pain. In glory, God "will wipe every tear from their eyes. There will be no more death or mourning or crying or pain" (Rev. 21:4; see also 7:17). In fact, Revelation often talks of a special place given on this final day to those who have suffered for righteousness (see, e.g., Rev. 7:13-17). In the new heaven and the new earth the effects of evil will be eradicated, and those who were victims of evil will be vindicated.

What is most interesting is that the center of this final redemptive activity is Jesus, and that he is most often referred to in Revelation as the Lamb, or the Lamb who was slain (thirty-one times). In the glorious description of the worship of heaven in Revelation 5, we have one tense moment when a question is asked about the opening of the book that probably contained the world's destiny:[11] "'Who is worthy to break the seals and open the scroll?' But no one in heaven or on earth or under the earth could open the scroll or even look inside it" (v. 2). John writes, "I wept and wept because no one was found who was worthy to open the scroll or look inside" (v. 4). He then receives the reassuring message, "Do not weep! See, the Lion of the tribe of Judah, the Root of David, has triumphed. He is able to open the scroll and its seven seals" (v. 5). And who is this great personage who is able to open the scroll? John says, "Then I saw a Lamb, *looking as if it had been slain*, standing in the center of the throne" (v. 6). The central figure in heaven is the Lamb! There we will see the Cross in all its glory, and we will fully understand what Jesus meant when he described His cross as being His glory.[12]

The rest of Revelation 5 describes the worship given to this Lamb and to God the Father. It says that Christ is worthy to open the scroll because of His death: "You are worthy to take the scroll and to open its seals, *because you were slain*, and with your blood you purchased men for God from every tribe and language and people and nation" (v. 9). It records the song of "many angels, numbering thousands upon thousands, and ten thousand times ten thousand" (v. 11) who sang in a loud voice, "Worthy is the Lamb, *who was slain*, to receive power and wealth and wisdom and strength and honor and glory and praise" (v. 12). William Dyrness says, "The Crucifixion, an obvious result of evil and injustice, will not have been passed over and overcome; it will actually be featured—an object of eternal wonder and devotion."[13]

---

[11]Leon Morris, "Revelation," *Tyndale New Testament Commentaries*, rev. ed. (Leicester: InterVarsity Press; Grand Rapids, Mich.: Eerdmans, 1987), 92.

[12]See John 7:39; 12:23-28; 13:31; 17:5

[13]William Dyrness, *Christian Apologetics in a World Community* (Downers Grove, Ill.: InterVarsity Press, 1983), 163.

So, in Jesus and His work we see God's answer to the problem of evil, an answer that was in His mind before the creation of the world. His death was going to start a process of triumph over evil that would culminate in its total destruction. And as Sir Norman Anderson says, "It must be that the final end will be so wonderful as to outweigh all the intervening 'groaning,' frustration and suffering."[14]

THE CROSS AS A SYMBOL OF GOD'S SOVEREIGNTY OVER EVIL

THE SCRIPTURAL PERSPECTIVE

The apostles viewed the death of Christ as a symbol of God's sovereignty over suffering. When they encountered opposition to the work of the Gospel for the first time, their response was to pray. And most of the prayer was a reflection on the sovereignty of God over the forces of evil. As evidence of the outworking of God's sovereignty over evil they presented the death of Christ. They said, "Indeed Herod and Pontius Pilate met together with the Gentiles and the people of Israel in this city to conspire against your holy servant Jesus, whom you anointed. *They did what your power and will had decided beforehand should happen*" (Acts 4:27-28). God had planned to turn the crucifixion of Jesus, which appeared to be a tragic defeat, into a glorious victory.

Jesus presented His death as evidence of the principle that suffering comes before glory, and death before life. Immediately after predicting His death he said, "I tell you the truth, unless a kernel of wheat falls to the ground and dies, it remains only a single seed. But if it dies, it produces many seeds" (John 12:24). So Christians today look at the death of Christ and take note that it was followed by the Resurrection and exaltation. Paul explained it like this: "And being found in appearance as a man, he humbled himself and became obedient to death—even death on a cross! *Therefore* God exalted him to the highest place and gave him the name that is above every name" (Phil. 2:8-9). This evidence of God's sovereignty helps Christians examine their problems and say, "We know that in all things God works for the good of those who love him, who have been called according to his purpose" (Rom. 8:28).

---

[14]Sir Norman Anderson, *Christianity and World Religions* (Leicester and Downers Grove, Ill.: InterVarsity Press, 1984), 132.

E. Stanley Jones presents this perspective in his own inimitable style:

> This dark problem of unmerited suffering lights up as we see what
> happened at the cross. Jesus did not bear the Cross—he used it. The
> Cross was sin, and he turned it into the healing of sin; the Cross was
> hate, and he turned it into a manifestation of the love of God. The
> Cross showed man at his worst, and there Jesus shows God at his
> redemptive best. The cruelest, darkest word that life ever spoke was
> at the Cross, and Jesus took all that cruelty and darkness and turned
> it into pure love and pure light. . . . What a light it sheds upon the
> tragedy of life to find such a fact at the center of our faith.[15]

THE MOLDING OF CHARACTER

What good is achieved from evil and suffering? What immediately
comes to mind is the molding of character that takes place through trials. Both Paul and James point this out:

> Not only so, but we also rejoice in our sufferings, because we know
> that suffering produces perseverance; perseverance, character; and
> character, hope. (Rom. 5:3-4)

> Consider it pure joy, my brothers, whenever you face trials of
> many kinds, because you know that the testing of your faith devel-
> ops perseverance. Perseverance must finish its work so that you may
> be mature and complete, not lacking anything. (James 1:2-4)

Sometimes our troubles are God's chastisements, which may be
compared to the discipline of a father (see Heb. 12:5-11). Martin Luther
understood this well. He once said, "Affliction is the best book in my
library." Another time he said, "My temptations have been my masters
in divinity."[16]

---

[15]E. Stanley Jones, *Along the Indian Road* (London: Hodder and Stoughton, 1939), 258-
59.
[16]Quoted by James S. Stewart, in *Classic Sermons on Suffering*, comp. Warren W.
Wiersbe (Grand Rapids, Mich.: Kregel, 1984), 89.

\

SOVEREIGNTY AND THE ULTIMATE CAUSE OF EVIL

Others have gone further in their speculation to reflect on the ultimate cause of evil. They have tried to show that the sovereign God saw evil as necessary for goodness to exist. According to this understanding, *evil is the necessary backdrop for perfection*. The early church father Irenaeus (130-202) is said to be one of the first to clearly expound this understanding of evil theologically. He described life as "a vale of soul-making." The Eastern (Orthodox) branch of the church has traditionally emphasized this theology. They view evil as a pedagogic tool that leads people to maturity. In this view, "Adam's sin was more an understandable lapse than a great catastrophe, for man was not so much created perfect as created for perfection."[17]

St. Augustine (354-430) has said, "God judged it better to bring good out of evil than to permit no evil to exist." But could not God have created beings capable of real love and also incapable of evil? Oliver Barclay answers, "God preferred to do it another way because, in the long run, it is far, far better, even if, in the short run, it seems worse. The Christian may simply have to trust that God knows best."[18] So essentially this is a matter that Christians will have to accept by faith. We have overwhelming evidence in so many areas related to evil that God is sovereign. We therefore extend that belief to conclude that God was sovereign even when he permitted evil to come into existence.

Others have pointed out that the existence of evil is inevitable because it was necessary if angels and humans were to have a free will. They say that a free agent who can do no evil is a logical impossibility. Logically, God cannot create a world containing moral good but no moral evil. It is difficult to say whether moral freedom could exist in a world where people always choose what is right. People would then be like machines, automatons, or robots. Gordon Lewis says, "Not even omnipotence itself could create a moral being without the possibility of disobedience as well as obedience. Omnipotence can do everything

---

[17]This is how William Dyrness describes this view in *Christian Apologetics*, 160.

[18]Oliver Barclay, *Reasons for Faith* (Leicester and Downers Grove, Ill.: InterVarsity Press, n.d.).

it chooses in the way it chooses, but it cannot do contradictory nothings like creating a will which cannot will."[19]

We end this section without an inerrant explanation about the cause of evil, but with the hope that God, who turned the crucifixion of the Son of God—the biggest evil ever committed—into something glorious, is sovereign. If His sovereignty has been expressed in history, there is nothing to prevent us from believing that it will be expressed in eternity. One day it will be revealed that the very existence of evil has been turned into something good.

THE CHRISTIAN RESPONSE OF PATIENCE

Because we know that God is sovereign over evil and therefore achieves something good out of all situations of suffering, the Christian approaches suffering with an attitude of patience. Paul says, "But if we hope for what we do not yet have, we wait for it patiently" (Rom. 8:25). We wait patiently for the good that will result from the suffering. The Greek word for "patience" is one of those great Christian words: *hupomonē*. It does not mean what usually comes to our mind when we think of patience. Stoics, who steel themselves against suffering, as expressed in the statement, "My head might be bloody, but it will be unbowed under the bludgeonings of chance,"[20] have a kind of patience. Biblical patience is different. Muslims who meekly submit to suffering, saying it is the will of God, have a kind of patience. Biblical patience is different. Christian patience is an active thing. It conveys the idea of positive endurance rather than quiet acceptance. Leon Morris says, "It is the attitude of the soldier who in the thick of the battle is not dismayed but fights on stoutly whatever the difficulties."[21]

The British Methodist preacher W. E. Sangster was told he was dying of progressive muscular atrophy when he was in his prime as a preacher. His voice was one of the first things that he lost. When he found out how serious his sickness was, however, he made four resolutions: (1) I will never complain, (2) I will keep the home bright, (3) I will

---

[19]Gordon R. Lewis, *Judge for Yourself* (Downers Grove, Ill.: InterVarsity Press, 1974), 40.

[20]Quoted in E. Stanley Jones, *Along the Indian Road*, 259.

[21]Leon Morris, *The Epistle to the Romans* (Grand Rapids, Mich.: Eerdmans; Leicester: InterVarsity Press, 1988), 325.

count my blessings, (4) I will try to turn it to gain.[22] He kept himself busy. His last book was written with two fingers and was sent to the publisher one or two days before he died.[23]

This is the active endurance that the biblical concept of patience involves. We endure hardship because we are faithful to God and His ways. But we don't just give up the fight. We actively seek to make the best of the situation, knowing that the sovereign God will turn this into something good. In fact, this helps us have joy in the midst of pain, as the statements from Romans and James quoted above show (Rom. 5:3; Jas. 1:2). James goes to the extent of saying that we must "consider it *pure* joy ... whenever [we] face trials of many kinds." When we consider the thing that causes us pain, the hope that God will sovereignly turn it to good fills us with unmixed joy. Even the pain cannot take away the brightness of this joy.

We turn to E. Stanley Jones again to vividly describe the biblical idea of patience:

> Don't bear trouble, use it. Take whatever happens—justice and injustice, pleasure and pain, compliment and criticism—take it up into the purpose of your life and make something out of it. Turn it into testimony. Don't explain evil, exploit evil; make it serve you. Just as the Lotus flower reaches down and takes up the mud and mire into the purposes of its life and produces the lotus flower out of them, so you are to take whatever happens and make something out of it.[24]

THE PAIN OF GOD

A GOD WHO SUFFERS PAIN

John Stott has said that "the real sting of suffering is not misfortune itself, nor even the pain of it or the injustice of it, but the apparent God-forsakenness of it." He says, "Pain is endurable, but the seeming indifference of God is not." Most of us have faced the situation of struggling to comfort a suffering friend who asks us why God does not look at his

---

[22]Paul Sangster, *Dr. Sangster* (London: Epworth Press, 1962), 54, quoted in Warren W. Wiersbe and Lloyd M. Perry, *The Wycliffe Handbook of Preaching and Preachers* (Chicago: Moody Press, 1984), 217.

[23]W. E. Sangster, *Westminster Sermons*, vol. 2 of *At Fast and Festival* (London: Epworth Press, 1961), Foreword.

[24]E. Stanley Jones, *A Song of Ascents*, 180.

or her pain and do something to relieve it. Stott says, "We think of him as an armchair spectator, almost gloating over the world's suffering, and enjoying his own insulation from it." Then Stott says, "It is this terrible caricature of God that the cross smashes to smithereens."[25] At the cross we see the immensity of God's pain as He endured the sacrifice of Jesus. And God experienced that pain of the cross from the time he created the world, for the Bible describes Jesus as "the Lamb that was slain from the creation of the world" (Rev. 13:8; see also 1 Pet. 1:20).

The Bible often presents God as suffering over the pain and dis-obedience of His creation, as the following texts show:

> The Lord saw how great man's wickedness on the earth had become, and that every inclination of the thoughts of his heart was only evil all the time. The Lord was grieved that he had made man on the earth, and his heart was filled with pain. (Gen. 6:5-6)

> And [the Lord] could bear Israel's misery no longer. (Judg. 10:16)

> "Is not Ephraim my dear son, the child in whom I delight? Though I often speak against him, I still remember him. Therefore my heart yearns for him; I have great compassion for him," declares the Lord. (Jer. 31:20)

> "How can I give you up, Ephraim? . . . My heart is changed within me; all my compassion is aroused." (Hos. 11:8)

Jesus experienced this same pain when He lived on earth, and He often gave expression to it. Once when the Jews remained silent when Jesus asked them about healing on the Sabbath in the synagogue, "He looked around at them in anger . . . deeply distressed at their stubborn hearts" (Mark 3:5). He lamented over Jerusalem saying, "O Jerusalem, Jerusalem, you who kill the prophets and stone those sent to you, how often I have longed to gather your children together, as a hen gathers her chicks under her wings, but you were not willing!" (Luke 13:34). Later "as he approached Jerusalem and saw the city, he wept over it" (Luke 19:41). We can imagine that He felt deep pain when His family

---

[25]Stott, *Cross of Christ*, 329.

pronounced Him insane and when His disciples disappointed Him time after time. And then there was the tremendous pain in the Garden of Gethsemane and at the cross when He bore the sins of the world. Truly He matched Isaiah's description of Him: "He was ... a man of sorrows, and familiar with suffering" (53:3).

I believe this pain still remains in God's heart. While it is true that Christ's sacrifice for our sin is complete, because God has a relationship of love with us, He still suffers when we sin. The writer to the Hebrews says that those who commit apostasy "are crucifying the Son of God all over again and subjecting him to public disgrace" (Heb. 6:6). Part of the agony of this re-crucifixion must be the agony of seeing a loved one leave the path of righteousness.

The idea that God suffers with the world is alien to Hindu thought because the ultimate reality is impersonal and without attributes. Muslims see God as too exalted to suffer and be affected in the way described above. This may be one reason why they find the idea of a crucified prophet so repulsive. But this is a very important aspect of the Christian message, especially as it responds to the problem of pain. Kazoh Kitamori, who was professor of systematic theology at Union Theological Seminary in Tokyo, wrote a book, *Theology of the Pain of God*, in 1945, shortly after the Second World War. The book is said to have been influenced in part by the blinding heat of Hiroshima. He speaks of how God's wrath is manifested against the sin of those He loves. He says the pain of God is manifested in His will to love the object of His wrath. He describes the pain of God as "a synthesis of his wrath and love."[26] Similarly Jürgen Moltmann has written a book, *The Crucified God: The Cross of Christ as the Foundation and Criticism of Christian Theology.*[27]

THE PAIN OF GOD AND SUFFERING HUMANITY

The impact that God's pain makes on suffering humanity is immense. John Stott has said, "I could never myself believe in God, if it were not for the cross. The only God I believe is the One Nietzsche ridiculed as

---

[26]Kazoh Kitamori, *Theology of the Pain of God* (London: SCM Press, 1966), 26.
[27]Jurgen Moltmann, *The Crucified God: The Cross of Christ as the Foundation and Criticism of Christian Theology* (London: SCM Press, 1974).

'God on the cross.'"[28] P. T. Forsyth says, "The cross of Christ ... is God's only self-justification in a world" like ours.[29] John Stott presents the playlet entitled *The Long Silence*, which I have used often when I speak on the problem of suffering in evangelistic settings.

> At the end of time, billions of people were scattered on a great plain before God's throne.
>
> Most shrank back from the brilliant light before them. But some groups near the front talked heatedly—not with cringing shame, but with belligerence.
>
> "Can God judge us? How can he know about suffering?" snapped a pert young brunette. She ripped open a sleeve to reveal a tattooed number from a Nazi concentration camp. "We endured terror ... beatings ... torture ... death!"
>
> In another group [an African-American boy] lowered his collar. "What about this?" he demanded, showing an ugly rope burn. "Lynched ... for no crime but being black!"
>
> In another crowd, a pregnant schoolgirl with sullen eyes. "Why should I suffer?" she murmured. "It wasn't my fault."
>
> Far out across the plain there were hundreds of such groups. Each had a complaint against God for the evil and suffering he permitted in this world. How lucky God was to live in heaven where all is sweetness and light, where there is no weeping or fear, no hunger or hatred. What did God know of all that man had been forced to endure in this world? For God leads a pretty sheltered life, they said.
>
> So each of these groups sent forth their leader, chosen because he had suffered the most. A Jew, a Negro, a person from Hiroshima, a horribly deformed arthritic, a thalidomide child. In the center of the plain they consulted with each other. At last they were ready to present their case. It was rather clever.
>
> Before God could be qualified to be their judge, he must endure what they endured. Their decision was that God should be sentenced to live on earth—as a man!

---

[28]Stott, *Cross of Christ*, 335.
[29]P. T. Forsyth, *The Justification of God* (Duckworth, 1916), 32, quoted in Stott, *Cross of Christ*, 336.

"Let him be born a Jew. Let the legitimacy of his birth be doubted. Give him a work so difficult that even his family will think him out of his mind when he tries to do it. Let him be betrayed by his closest friends. Let him face false charges, be tried by a prejudiced jury and convicted by a cowardly judge. Let him be tortured.

"At the last, let him see what it means to be terribly alone. Then let him die. Let him die so that there can be no doubt that he died. Let there be a great host of witnesses to verify it."

As each leader announced his portion of the sentence, loud murmurs of approval went up from the throng of people assembled.

And when the last had finished pronouncing sentence, there was a long silence. No-one uttered another word. No-one moved. For suddenly all knew that God had already served his sentence.[30]

Jesus' sufferings played a key role in the spiritual awakening of young Joni Eareckson (Tada) after her terrible accident. She was a vivacious, energetic, and athletic girl who dove off a raft into the Chesapeake Bay, hit a stone, and was paralyzed below her neck. When the full realization of what had happened to her dawned on her and she realized that her paralysis would be permanent, she pleaded with a friend to help her end her life by giving her an overdose of pills or cutting her with a razor. When the friend refused, "Joni learned another cruel fact: she was too helpless to die on her own."[31]

As Philip Yancey reports, "The turning to God was slow. Change from bitterness to trust in him dragged out over three years of tears and violent questionings." One night a big breakthrough was made that left her convinced that God did understand. I will let Yancey tell the story.

Pain was streaking through her back in a way that is a unique torment to those paralyzed. Healthy persons can scratch an itch, squeeze an aching muscle, or flex a cramped foot. The paralyzed must lie still, defenseless, and feel the pain.

Cindy, one of Joni's closest friends, was beside her bed, search-

---

[30]Stott, *Cross of Christ*, 336-37.
[31]From Philip Yancey, *Where Is God When It Hurts?* (Grand Rapids, Mich.: Zondervan, 1977), 116. Joni's complete story is told in the book *Joni* by Joni Eareckson (Grand Rapids, Mich.: Zondervan, 1976).

ing desperately for some way to encourage Joni. Finally, she clum-
sily blurted out, "Joni, Jesus knows how you feel—you aren't the
only one—why, he was paralyzed too."

Joni glared at her. "What, what are you talking about?"

Cindy continued, "It's true. Remember he was nailed on a cross.
His back was raw from beatings, and he must have yearned for a
way to move to change positions, or redistribute his weight. But he
couldn't. He was paralyzed by the nails."

The thought intrigued Joni. It had never occurred to her that
God had felt the exact piercing sensations that racked her body.
The idea was profoundly comforting.[32]

THE FELLOWSHIP OF SHARING IN HIS SUFFERINGS

Paul mentions another profound aspect of God's solidarity with suffering humanity when he says, "I want to know Christ ... and the fellowship of sharing in his sufferings, becoming like him in his death"
(Phil. 3:10). Elsewhere he said, "we share in his [that is, Christ's] sufferings" (Rom. 8:17). Christ is a suffering Savior. Because of this fact,
those who follow Him must also suffer. Suffering is an essential ingredient of union with Christ. There is a depth of oneness that we share
with Christ that can only be achieved when we are one with Him in
suffering. The beautiful thing is that when we suffer, He suffers with
us. Paul found out about this on the road to Damascus when Christ
asked Him, "Why do you persecute *me*?" (Acts 9:4). Paul was hitting the
church, but Christ was feeling the pain! Christ and the church had
become one in suffering. To the suffering person there is immense
comfort in this truth.

For the Christian, the most important thing in life and the deepest
source of joy in life is his or her relationship with God. Our highest
ambition is to deepen this relationship. If suffering is going to bring one
closer to God, then we can look at it with bright hope. The Japanese
evangelist and social reformer Toyohiko Kagawa (1888-1960) once
thought that he was going blind. He described what he felt like in this

---

[32]Yancey, *Where Is God?*, 118-19.

way: "The darkness, the darkness is a holy of holies of which no one can rob me. In the darkness I meet God face to face."[33]

There have been times when Christians, in their urgent desire for unity with Christ, have desired the fellowship of participating in Christ's sufferings. We have already seen Paul's expression of his desire to know "the fellowship of sharing in his sufferings" (Phil. 3.10). The most vivid instance of this that I know is that of Ignatius, who was bishop of Antioch in Syria at the end of the second century. He asked the church not to attempt to deprive him of the honor of martyrdom. He said, "Now I begin to be a disciple. I care for nothing, of visible or invisible things, so that I may but win Christ. Let fire and the cross, let the companies of wild beasts, let breaking of bones and tearing of limbs, let the grinding of the whole body, and all the malice of the devil, come upon me; be it so, only may I win Christ Jesus!" After he was sentenced to be thrown to the beasts and when he heard the lions roaring, he said, "I am the wheat of God; I am going to be ground with the teeth of wild beasts, that I may be found pure bread."[34]

The above discussions have shown that while the Bible does not discuss in detail the philosophical issues pertaining to the problems of pain and evil, it certainly gives hints toward an adequate solution to this problem. We will close with another quotation from E. Stanley Jones:

> He cleansed suffering! It was no longer a sign of our being caught in the wheel of existence, as Buddha suggests; no longer the result of our evil deeds of a previous birth, as our Hindu friends tell us; no longer the sign of the displeasure of God, as many of all ages and of all religions have suggested; no longer something to be stoically and doggedly borne. It is more than that. *Suffering is the gift of God.*[35]

---

[33]Stewart, in *Classic Sermons*, 92.

[34]From John Foxe, *Foxe's Book of Martyrs* (1563; reprint, Springdale, Pa.: Whitaker House, 1981), 19-20.

[35]E. Stanley Jones, *Christ and Human Suffering* (New York: Abingdon, 1933), 192-93, quoted in *Selections from E. Stanley Jones*, comp. James K. Matthews and Eunice Jones Matthews (Nashville: Abingdon, 1971), 89-90.

CHAPTER FIFTEEN

THE RESURRECTION IS PROOF

I WILL NEVER FORGET how surprised I was when I heard my beloved professor Dr. Daniel P. Fuller say in class that if anyone were to produce the bones of Jesus, he would give up Christianity. In the twenty or so years since I heard that statement, I have often wondered whether I could make the same statement. Was this the overstatement of a man I had come to recognize as a thoroughgoing scholar who placed so much emphasis on evidence that he would not accept a dogma, however entrenched it may be in the church, without sufficient evidence? Was it the overenthusiasm of a man who had written a book on the relationship between history and faith and how they connect with the Resurrection?[1]

Surely, even if they were to show the bones of Jesus, that would not dislodge my faith in Him. Had I not experienced Jesus in a uniquely wonderful way? Is not that proof enough of the validity of Christianity? Indeed, it is proof. But there are many people today who claim that they have had wonderful experiences through their religions too. Because Christianity is the Creator's own answer to human aspiration, I believe that it is the only truly fulfilling experience. Did not Jesus Himself say,

---

[1] Daniel P. Fuller, *Easter Faith and History* (Grand Rapids, Mich.: Eerdmans, 1965).

"I have come that they may have life, and have it to the full" (John 10:10)? But I know that I sometimes go through times when my experience is extremely discouraging. Certainly experience is not firm enough to be the ultimate ground for the uniqueness of my faith.

The foundation of the Christian Gospel presented in the New Testament is Jesus. And to the New Testament writers, the final proof about Jesus' claims was the Resurrection. Therefore, it was the key message of the early church. When Peter explained to the believers about the need for a replacement for Judas he said, "For one of these must become a witness with us of his resurrection" (Acts 1:22). The evangelistic ministry of the apostles in Jerusalem was described in relation to the Resurrection: "With great power the apostles continued to testify to the resurrection of the Lord Jesus" (Acts 4:33). This was true of Paul's teaching in Athens too, where his ministry was described as "preaching the good news about Jesus and the resurrection" (Acts 17:18). After a survey of the place of the Resurrection in the New Testament, G. E. Ladd concludes, "The cornerstone of the entire New Testament is the resurrection."[2]

Christianity makes claims about the uniqueness and exclusiveness of its founder that no other religion makes. How do we know these claims are true? The apostles would have answered this question by saying that the Resurrection is the proof. At the conclusion of his message to the inquiring Athenians, Paul says, "[God] has given proof of this to all men by raising him [Christ] from the dead" (Acts 17:31). What then does the Resurrection prove?

PROOF ABOUT HIS PERSON

First, it proves the biblical teaching about the person of Christ. We mentioned in chapter 9 that the idea of a crucified Messiah was and is scandalous to a Jew. Despite all Jesus' teaching about His mission, even His disciples were bewildered by His death, as the mood of the two disciples on the road to Emmaus indicates (Luke 24:17-26). All the disciples were paralyzed by fear and were in hiding after the Crucifixion. On Easter Sunday the women came and told them the news of the

---

[2]G. E. Ladd, *I Believe in the Resurrection of Jesus* (London: Hodder and Stoughton; Grand Rapids, Mich.: Eerdmans., 1975), 43.

Resurrection as reported to them by the angels. "But they did not believe the women, because their words seemed to them like nonsense" (Luke 24:11). But once they knew that He was indeed risen, they could not be stopped. They did not start with the more sympathetic audience in Galilee. They went straight to the hostile people in Jerusalem and proclaimed that Jesus was the Messiah (Christ). And surprisingly, the number of disciples grew to 5,000 in a few days (Acts 4:4). The Resurrection was evidence enough for an amazingly large number of people.

The Resurrection was the crucial argument in Peter's message on the day of Pentecost. He said, "But God raised him from the dead, freeing him from the agony of death, because it was impossible for death to keep its hold on him" (Acts 2:24). If He was who Peter believed He was, then it was impossible for death to hold Him. The Messiah, the Son of God, could not possibly remain dead. After expounding at some length on the Resurrection and the Ascension, Peter climaxed his argument with the implication of what he had been expounding: "Therefore let all Israel be assured of this: God has made this Jesus, whom you crucified, both Lord and Christ [Messiah]" (Acts 2:36). In the Greek that verse begins emphatically, stating, "Assuredly therefore . . ." (*asphalos oun*).

Paul makes this same point in connection with Jesus' being the Son of God when he says, "who through the Spirit of holiness was declared with power to be the Son of God by his resurrection from the dead: Jesus Christ our Lord" (Rom. 1:4). The Resurrection was the ground for a declaration to be made about Jesus' person. It is significant that the Resurrection is usually referred to as the work of God in the New Testament. In his speech just quoted, Peter said, "God raised him from the dead" (Acts 2:24). This is part of the New Testament's insistence that the Resurrection was God's authentication of Jesus' mission.

PROOF ABOUT HIS PLAN OF SALVATION

The Resurrection also validates the extraordinary claim made in the Bible that His death is the means by which our sins are forgiven. Many non-Christians have asked me how the death of one man could possibly save other people. I usually answer that question by presenting some of the arguments we have described in this book. But the clincher is that

God raised Jesus from the dead as proof that the sacrifice for sin was accepted. Paul says, "He was delivered over to death for our sins and was raised to life for our justification" (Rom. 4:25). J. A. Schep says, "The resurrection is God's 'Amen' to Jesus' loud cry: 'It is finished,' and therefore the guarantee that by Jesus' death the believer has indeed been reconciled to God and made righteous."[3]

This was a matter of life and death for Paul. God's forgiveness of our sins depended on the Resurrection. Paul says, "And if Christ has not been raised, your faith is futile; you are still in your sins. Then those also who have fallen asleep in Christ are lost" (1 Cor. 15:17-18). The validity of His message depended on this fact: "And if Christ has not been raised, our preaching is useless and so is your faith" (1 Cor. 15:14).

The reality of the Resurrection gives us confidence to proclaim our message with authority, even to audiences who are not interested in or are even hostile to the Gospel. This is what gave Peter the boldness on the day of Pentecost to proclaim, "you, with the help of wicked men, put him to death by nailing him to the cross. But God raised him from the dead.... Therefore let all Israel be assured of this: God has made this Jesus, whom you crucified, both Lord and Christ" (Acts 2:23-24, 36). This statement is all the more significant when we realize that it was said in Jerusalem a few days after the people had demonstrated their great power in putting Jesus to death and that these words came from the lips of Peter who had repeatedly denied knowing Jesus.

The Resurrection also gives us assurance about our own salvation. Jesus was indeed "raised to life for our justification" (Rom. 4:25). Our salvation does not depend on our achievements but on Christ's achievement, which we know is complete. This is one of the great attractions of Christianity to the non-Christian. In Islam there is no such assurance. Muslims faithfully perform their rituals, hoping that God will have mercy on them, but having no assurance of God's acceptance. The Jehovah's Witnesses, despite the confidence with which they proclaim their understanding of the Scriptures, do not have such an assurance.

---

[3] J. A. Schep, "Resurrection of Jesus Christ," in *The Zondervan Pictorial Bible Encyclopedia*, vol. 5, ed. M. C. Tenney et al. (Grand Rapids, Mich.: Zondervan, 1975), 83.

To the Buddhists and Hindus the path to liberation is a long and dreary climb spanning countless numbers of lives, with no assurance of when they will be able to offset all the bad *karma* they have gathered along the way. What good news it can be to such pilgrims, weary of toiling for their salvation, when they hear the words of Paul: "Therefore, there is now no condemnation for those who are in Christ Jesus, because through Christ Jesus the law of the Spirit of life set me free from the law of sin and death" (Rom. 8:1-2).

The Resurrection alone may not be what initially attracts many people to the Gospel. I have found that usually the life, death, and won-der-working power of Christ are initially more attractive to most non-Christians. In fact, many find the doctrine of the Resurrection rather strange and difficult to believe. Therefore, because of the pragmatism typical of today's approach to evangelism, many evangelists and wit-nesses hardly bring up the Resurrection in their witness with non-Christians. According to the records in Acts, however, the earliest evangelists proclaimed this message and used it as their clincher with both Jewish and Gentile audiences, even though in some cases it was a stumbling block. The fact that some of the intellectuals in Athens would sneer about the Resurrection did not prevent Paul from talking about it there (Acts 17:31-32).

I believe that the Resurrection can be a key source of attraction to some intellectually oriented persons. Although at first they may scoff at the idea, they may be provoked to regard the Gospel seriously when presented with the arguments for the Resurrection. If they come to accept that it really took place, their rational approach to truth may urge them to pursue this fact to its logical conclusion. That is what hap-pened to some Chinese graduate students at Emory University when my teacher, Dr. Joseph Wang, was there working on his doctorate. The students came to Wang and asked him about the credibility of the Christian belief in Jesus' resurrection. He presented to them the case for the Resurrection in a way similar to what I present in the next chapter.[4] Once they were convinced by the arguments, they knew that

---

[4] I am indebted to Dr. Wang for introducing me to the approach that forms the basis of the next chapter.

they had to deal with the tremendous implications of this event. This led to their becoming Christians.

The resurrection doctrine is also of vital importance with those who are *not* intellectually oriented. Although other features of the Gospel may make the average person receptive to the message of Jesus, the Resurrection is the feature that gives stability to their faith. It is what gives confidence in the saving and keeping power of God. Those who come because of the miracle-working power of God soon find that some of their prayers for deliverance are answered very differently from the way they expected. At such times they are tempted to go to another source, like an astrologer or the incumbent of a shrine of another "powerful" deity, for a quick answer to their problem. What gives them stability to persevere amidst such discouragement and temptation is the fact that whether their prayers are answered in the way they want or not, Christianity is true, and therefore it would be folly to move away from the truth for the sake of temporary gain. When the author of Hebrews wrote his beloved benediction about God's equipping us, he referred to God as the one who raised Jesus up: "May the God of peace, who through the blood of the eternal covenant *brought back from the dead our Lord Jesus* . . . equip you with everything good for doing his will, and may he work in us what is pleasing to him" (Heb. 13:20-21). The logic here is that if God could bring back the Lord Jesus from the dead, then He can be trusted to equip us for every challenge we face.

So, even though the Resurrection may not be very attractive, it is the foundation of a stable faith. There is in all of us a deep yearning for the stability that truth alone can bring. This may not be realized by many people, as they are overwhelmed by the physical realities of life. But it is there, and in satisfying that alone is there true stability in life. We must therefore emphasize it. Then those who come to Christ initially looking for an answer for some physical need will remain faithful to Christ for a deeper reason: because the Christian Gospel is true.

We all know the pain of seeing people who come to Christ enthusiastically fall away when problems come their way. I believe that this could be reduced greatly if we emphasized the Resurrection more in our preaching and teaching. Certainly it needs to have a key place in our basic new-convert, follow-up material.

PROOF ABOUT HIS LORDSHIP

Not only does the Resurrection give evidence that Christ is Messiah—it also confirms that He is Lord. At Pentecost, at the conclusion of his discussion of the Resurrection, Peter said, "Therefore let all Israel be assured of this: God has made this Jesus, whom you crucified, both Lord and Christ" (Acts 2:36). The title *Lord* was used only sparingly before the Resurrection, but much more frequently after it. This does not mean that He became Lord only after the Resurrection. It means that "what was true of his person essentially, but was only dimly perceived before, was now known demonstrably."[5] So the Jew, Peter, is unafraid to tell a group of Romans at the home of a centurion, Cornelius, "This is the message God sent to the people of Israel, telling the good news of peace through Jesus Christ, who is Lord of all" (Acts 10:36). In the Roman Empire, the famous affirmation was "Caesar is Lord"; but Christians were willing to go to their deaths for refusing to make that affirmation. Here Peter tells these Romans that the one whom the Romans delivered to be crucified is "Lord of all"!

The Christians also recognized that the Resurrection was just the beginning of a process of Jesus' claiming His lordship over all creation. The Resurrection was closely associated in the New Testament with the exaltation of Christ, as the title of Murray Harris's book on the Resurrection, *From Grave to Glory,*[6] suggests. Peter's speech at Pentecost is again illuminating here. He follows his statement about the Resurrection with a reference to the exaltation: "God has raised this Jesus to life, and we are all witnesses of the fact. Exalted to the right hand of God, he has received from the Father the promised Holy Spirit and has poured out what you now see and hear" (Acts 2:32-33).

Immediately after mentioning the exaltation, Peter explains how Jesus is completing His victory in His exalted state: "For David did not ascend to heaven, and yet he said, 'The Lord said to my Lord: "Sit at my right hand until I make your enemies a footstool for your feet"'" (Acts 2:34-35). In his great chapter on the Resurrection, 1 Corinthians 15, Paul explains this process in even more detail. He says that by virtue

---

[5]Everett F. Harrison, *Interpreting Acts* (Grand Rapids, Mich.: Zondervan, 1986), 70.
[6]Murray J. Harris, *From Grave to Glory: Resurrection in the New Testament* (Grand Rapids, Mich.: Zondervan, 1990).

of Jesus' resurrection He is the "firstfruits" of those who will follow (1 Cor. 15:23). Next he explains what will accompany the Resurrection at the end: "Then the end will come, when he hands over the kingdom to God the Father after he has destroyed all dominion, authority and power" (v. 24). But before that final event there is a process of defeating Christ's enemies: "For he must reign until he has put all his enemies under his feet. The last enemy to be destroyed is death" (vv. 25-26).

So the Resurrection has always been associated with the great triumph of Christ. The christological hymn of Philippians 2 presents this victory immediately after presenting the humiliation of Christ: "Therefore God exalted him to the highest place and gave him the name that is above every name, that at the name of Jesus every knee should bow, in heaven and on earth and under the earth, and every tongue confess that Jesus Christ is Lord, to the glory of God the Father" (Phil. 2:9-11).

Christ's victory gives us the boldness to follow Him as Lord of our lives and to pay whatever price needs to be paid to do that. That was seen in the remarkable transformation that took place in the disciples, especially Peter, after they saw the risen Lord. With the victorious Christ as their Lord, they were willing to pay the price of obedience.

This realization of the victory and lordship of Christ also helps us follow Christ as our Lord whatever the cost. It gives us courage amidst discouragement, strength amidst weakness. Martin Niemoller was a courageous German pastor who spent several years in prison because he spoke out against the unhealthy influence Adolf Hitler's regime was having on the church in Germany. He knew that in that bleak period of the history of his people, the Resurrection of Christ would be an encouragement to his people. On Easter morning, March 28, 1937, three months before he was arrested and imprisoned, he preached a sermon of encouragement to his people. In his sermon he spoke of the way in which evil had been manifested in those days and how people ridiculed the Christians. He said, "We may feel frightened about this newly wakened enmity of a whole world; and people do not forget to tell us how few visible guarantees we have for our belief that God will create the new world—or how few guarantees we have for the truth of our faith. . . . Does the Easter message . . . still hold good, they wonder?"

Niemoller faced squarely the temptation to compromise under this pressure. He asked, "Is it not more honest, is it not more fitting to make peace with the old world, the pre-Easter world, which is after all showing itself very much stronger and more enduring than we thought or suspected?" Then he spoke of the folly of such thinking: "It is better for us not to trust what our eyes see, for that will pass away! And he tells us, 'Blessed are they who have not seen, and yet have believed.'" And why is that so?

> Throughout the centuries, the risen Christ has gone before his community, and today too he goes before us. His victory will be our victory also. And just as our fathers in the faith believed in him with that assurance which the risen Christ gave to his first disciples, so we too are sure and will continue to proclaim... what makes us glad deep down in our hearts, in the ups and downs amidst which we live.... I think what makes us glad with a great joy is this: "The Lord is risen; he is really and truly risen!"
>
> *Satan, the World, Death, Sin, and Hell*
> *Are quelled for evermore.*
> *Their rage and power are brought to nought*
> *By Christ whom we adore.*[7]

This Easter faith is what helps us to persevere in preaching also. Our moods go up and down. Often we don't feel like preaching because the world has been bad to us, or because we are tired, sick, or depressed. But our message is not destroyed by these things. The fact remains that Jesus rose from the dead. We have a message of Good News about the one who has been proclaimed Lord of all creation. We have courage, therefore, to go and preach. And we are not hypocrites when we preach with urgency though our hearts may be broken by what we are experiencing. We know that what we preach is true and that the truth of Christianity is a more basic reality than the pain we are experiencing.

PROOF ABOUT OUR NEW LIFE

The Resurrection also helps us in the path of discipleship because we ourselves participate in it by virtue of our union with Christ. In Romans 6:4 Paul says, "We were therefore buried with him through baptism into

---

[7]Martin Niemoller, *God Is My Fuehrer* (New York: n.p., 1941), 191, quoted in Wilbur M. Smith, *Therefore Stand* (New Canaan, Conn.: Keats, 1981), 432-33.

death in order that, just as Christ was raised from the dead through the glory of the Father, we too may live a new life." When we come to Christ we share in the resurrection life. In the next verse Paul says, "If we have been united with him in his death, we will certainly also be united with him in his resurrection" (Rom. 6:5). In this passage Paul is talking about our ability to overcome sin in our daily lives.

This is another of the great features about the Gospel. Jesus gives us the power to live according to the principles of holiness. Whereas a moral code would frustrate sincere people because of their inability to follow it, Christianity brings with it the resurrection life that empowers us for obedience. Included in this life is what Paul calls "the power of his resurrection" (Phil. 3:10). After a careful discussion of this expression, Peter O'Brien concludes that this expression refers to "the life-giving power of God, the power that He manifested in raising Christ from the dead, and that He now manifests in the new life that the Christian receives from the risen Christ and shares with him."[8]

While on a preaching assignment in Peru, I was assigned a security guard to constantly be with me because at that particular time a Peruvian rebel group was assassinating foreigners. During our time together I often talked to him about Christ, but he kept saying that though it was a wonderful Gospel, it was not for him. On the last day of our conference I told him how much I would like to see him commit his life to Christ before I left for Sri Lanka. He told me that he was too big a sinner to be saved. I took a Spanish Bible, turned to 1 Timothy 1:15 and asked him to read it. He read, "Here is a trustworthy saying that deserves full acceptance: Christ Jesus came into the world to save sinners—of whom I am the worst." He said, "But I am the worst of sinners." I told him, "Then it is speaking about you." This gave him some joy.

But he lost heart once more and told me that he would never have the strength to live the Christian life if he became a Christian. I turned to Philippians 4:13 and asked him to read it. And he was thrilled to read, "I can do everything through him who gives me strength." Within two hours of that conversation a Baptist pastor from North America, Bob Mackay, who was another speaker at the conference, led him to com-

---

[8]Peter T. O'Brien, "Commentary on Philippians," in *The New International Greek Testament Commentary* (Grand Rapids, Mich.: Eerdmans, 1991), 404.

mit his life to Christ. What joy he had after that. We gave him a Bible at the closing ceremony of the conference. On receiving it he showed the audience his machine gun and said, "I have hit people with this all these years." Then, raising his Bible, he said, "Now I will hit them with this!" In a few days he had led his brother to Christ.

Before mentioning the power of the Resurrection in Philippians 3:10, Paul mentions his desire to know Christ—that is, to have an intimate relationship with Christ. Peter O'Brien has shown that the Greek in this verse indicates that the power of the Resurrection is actually an aspect of knowing Christ.[9] This intimate relationship with Christ is another consequence of the Resurrection. Shortly before His death He told His disciples, "But I tell you the truth: It is for your good that I am going away. Unless I go away, the Counselor will not come to you; but if I go, I will send him to you" (John 16:7). As long as He was in the world, He was limited by time and space. Once His work was done and He was exalted in heaven, he sent His Spirit to dwell with us. So shortly before His ascension he told His disciples, "surely I will be with you always, to the very end of the age" (Matt. 28:20). Peter gives the sequence of these events in his speech at Pentecost: "God has raised this Jesus to life, and we are all witnesses of the fact. Exalted to the right hand of God, he has received from the Father the promised Holy Spirit and has poured out what you now see and hear" (Acts 2:32-33).

Now, in the person of His Spirit, He is constantly with us, and so Paul said, "the Spirit of God lives in you" (Rom. 8:9). The word translated "lives" (*oikeo*) is from the word *oikos*, which means "to live in as in a house."[10] Paul is saying that "the Spirit is not an occasional visitor; he takes up residence in God's people."[11] The familiar gospel song by A. H. Ackley expresses the experience of the resurrected Savior beautifully:

I serve a risen Savior, He's in the world today;
I know that He is living, whatever men may say;
I see His hand of mercy, I hear His voice of cheer,
And just the time I need Him He's always near.

---

[9]Ibid., 402-04.
[10]Leon Morris, *The Epistle to the Romans* (Grand Rapids, Mich.: Eerdmans; Leicester: InterVarsity Press, 1988), 293, n. 98.
[11]Ibid., 308.

He lives, He lives, Christ Jesus lives today!
　He walks with me and talks with me along life's narrow way,
He lives, He lives, salvation to impart!
　You ask me how I know He lives? He lives within my heart.[12]

There are those who object to the evidence of the Resurrection given at the end—"He lives within my heart"—saying it is too subjective. Indeed, it is subjective. But it is a scripturally authentic experience. We do have a vital relationship with God, but without the foundation of objective facts it would be a shaky source of security. If our relationship with God is built on the firm foundation of the objective truths about Christ, that relationship becomes a joyous reality that makes the Christian Gospel uniquely attractive.

After a Muslim in Africa was converted, his friends asked him why he became a Christian. He answered, "Well, it's like this. Suppose you were going down the road, and suddenly the road forked in two directions, and you didn't know which way to go; and there at the fork were two men, one dead and one alive. Which one would you ask for directions?"[13]

When the Spirit indwells us, He empowers us to live a new life of holiness. Jesus promised His disciples that they would "receive power when the Holy Spirit comes on you" (Acts 1:8). He makes "the power of his resurrection" (Phil. 3:10) available to us. The greater the number of born-again Christians and even prominent Christian leaders who are living defeated lives in their battle against sin, the more the validity of the Christian claim to victory over sin is being questioned today. Therefore, it is necessary for us to look at how the Holy Spirit helps us live a victorious life. He does this in several ways.

The Holy Spirit makes us His temple by indwelling us, and this makes it difficult for us to sin. Paul asks, "Don't you know that you yourselves are God's temple and that God's Spirit lives in you?" (1 Cor. 3:16). He is talking of a relationship, a day-to-day walk. When someone we respect is with us, we usually abstain from dishonorable behavior. People sometimes apologize for obscene language when they realize that it was said

---

[12]Copyright 1938 by Homer Rodeheaver.
[13]John T. Seamands, *Tell It Well* (Kansas City: Beacon Hill, 1981), 69.

in front of a clergyman. Similarly, the realization that the Holy Spirit is right there with us should make us ashamed to indulge in sin. The wonder is that Christians still go on sinning! We often are influenced only by what we see; because we cannot see God, we tend to ignore Him.

A major reason why Christians are not afraid of sinning in the presence of God is that they have not been confronted with the holiness of God. A young man in the small group I lead went back to drugs after having made good progress in his faith for a few months. When another member of the group, who had once been a slave to liquor, heard of it, the first thing he said was, "He has lost his fear of God." (This young man has since returned to Christ and is seeking the way of holiness now.) People who come seeking the love and power of God must soon be taught the truth of Hebrews 12:14: "Make every effort to . . . be holy; without holiness no one will see the Lord."

It is easy to neglect the message of God's holiness in our preaching. We are in such a battle for the attention of people that we tend to emphasize those truths that elicit an immediate favorable response from our hearers. We can unconsciously neglect those truths that are not so pleasant to our hearers, such as God's holiness.

Paul says that "The Spirit himself testifies with our spirit that we are God's children" (Rom. 8:16). *By reminding us of our identity as children of God, He reminds us that sin is below our dignity.* We abstain from sin in order to protect our status. The fear of losing the glorious experience of significance, which is ours because of our adoption into God's family, acts as a deterrent to sin. In fact, it makes sin unnecessary, for it gives us a sense of fulfillment in Christ that reduces the attractiveness of the fulfillment the temptation is supposed to give us.

The Spirit gives us "the peace of God, which transcends all understanding" (Phil. 4:7) *and "an inexpressible and glorious joy"* (1 Pet. 1:8). This wonderful experience "will guard [our] hearts and [our] minds in Christ Jesus" (Phil. 4:7). Ask those who, after living a godly life, backslid for a time and then returned to God, and they will testify that they felt utterly miserable during their time away from God. The fear of losing joy and peace will keep us on the path of righteousness. George Müller said, "The first great and primary business to which I ought to attend every day is to have my soul happy in the Lord." Such commitment to joy will keep us from sin, which takes away our joy.

Of course, sin is attractive to people because of the pleasure it promises. Even Christian leaders have sometimes jeopardized every- thing good in their lives for a moment's pleasure. But those pleasures are "passing" (Heb. 11:24, NASB). They revolt against our humanity and therefore leave us empty and unfulfilled once the initial "kick" is over. The joy of walking with God tells us that fleeting pleasures of sin are nothing in comparison to eternal joy.

The Spirit leads us in different ways along the path of righteousness (Ps. 23:3; Rom. 8:14). He convicts us of sin (John 16:8). He provides a way of escape for us when we are tempted (1 Cor. 10:13). He does this in dif- ferent ways. Sometimes He brings a clear impression in the mind that alerts us to danger. Sometimes He brings to mind a verse that directs us to the path of righteousness. Sometimes we hear a sermon that speaks directly to the temptation we are facing. Sometimes He brings a cir- cumstance to pass that acts as a warning and therefore as a deterrent to sin. For example, a Christian on his way to see an unedifying movie encounters another Christian, and this jolts him into changing his plans.

Vital contact with the Spirit of God results in the nature of God being implanted upon our character so that we begin to think and act like God. Paul expressed this process vividly: "And we, who with unveiled faces all reflect the Lord's glory, are being transformed into his likeness with ever-increasing glory, which comes from the Lord, who is the Spirit" (2 Cor. 3:18). When this happens, we express the fruit of the Spirit in our lives: "love, joy, peace, patience, kindness, goodness, faithfulness, gen- tleness and self-control" (Gal. 5:22-23). We behave like holy people because our very nature is stamped with the holiness of God.

All the activity of the Spirit is useless if we do not have the capac- ity to respond to Him. In our natural state that is how we are. Paul says, "For what the law was powerless to do in that it was weakened by the sinful nature, God did by sending his own Son in the likeness of sinful man to be a sin offering" (Rom. 8:3). Even though the law was good, it was powerless to help us keep its demands. The work of Christ has given us that capacity to be holy. So *the Spirit regenerates us by giving us a new life.* We are "born of the Spirit" (John 3:8).

This spiritual life in us makes us capable of responding to the promptings of God. When we do this, our minds are "controlled by the Spirit," and Paul says this is "life and peace" (Rom. 8:6). With this new

life in us, we are able to live holy lives. So, for example, Paul says that
"by the Spirit [we] put to death the misdeeds of the body" (Rom. 8:13).
He means that the indwelling Spirit gives us the ability to overcome sin.
He does it for us. We are weak; so He holds our hand and gives us the
strength and courage to overcome sin. The Bible speaks of a fullness
that the Holy Spirit gives us to fulfill special tasks. Some call this an
anointing. Peter was filled with the Spirit so he could speak to the rulers
(Acts 4:8). Stephen was filled in order to face the experience of being
stoned to death (Acts 7:55). Paul was filled so that he could confront
Elymas the sorcerer (Acts 13:9). In the same way, we can expect the
Spirit to fill us in order to face temptation triumphantly.

Then why is it that many Christians are living defeated lives, even
though they are supposed to have the Spirit indwelling them? The Bible
says that we can "grieve" the Spirit (Eph. 4:30) and that we can "put out
the Spirit's fire" (1 Thess. 5:19). We can do this in several ways.

1. We can disobey the promptings of the Spirit as He shows us a way
of escape (1 Cor. 10:13) and give in to sin.

2. We can refuse to believe the reality of the transformation that
God has effected in our lives. Paul says, "In the same way, count yourselves dead to sin but alive to God in Christ Jesus" (Rom. 6:11). We can
refuse to do this and believe instead that sin still has mastery over us
and that therefore we are powerless to overcome the temptation. Just as
justification is by faith, so is sanctification. We must accept by faith the
reality of what God has done and will do in us. This gives us the
strength to believe that sin can be overcome.

3. We can believe the lie that the pleasure of sin is greater than the
joy of the Lord and by so doing reject joy for fleeting pleasure.

4. We can believe the lie that we have to commit some sin in order
to succeed in life, like lying or being unkind or being unfair to an
employee.

5. We can refuse to seek first the kingdom of God and His righteousness (Matt. 6:33). We can do this by not taking our spiritual nour-
ishment through reading the Scriptures. Then in our malnourished
state we become susceptible to spiritual illness. We can also do this by
neglecting to spend time in prayer and as a result lose contact with our
source of spiritual strength. As someone has said, "Seven prayerless days
makes one weak." We can also do it by making a decision, like vocation
or marriage, that takes us along the slippery slope of compromise.

All of the above causes can keep us from experiencing the victorious life. God does not force us to obey Him. He provides us with the ability to live a victorious life. It is never necessary for any Christian to sin. Through the power of the Resurrection mediated by the indwelling Holy Spirit, God has opened the door for us to live victorious lives. As John said, "You, dear children, are from God and have overcome them, because the one who is in you is greater than the one who is in the world" (1 John 4:4).

This victory over sin is something that marks the Christian Gospel as supreme. All religions teach us to be good. Many sincere people become frustrated because of their inability to live up to the teaching set before them. The Christian religion, in the person of the Holy Spirit, gives us the companionship of the Savior, who conquered sin. And He enables *us* to conquer sin.

PROOF ABOUT HIS VICTORY OVER DEATH

Perhaps the most obvious triumph of the Resurrection is Christ's victory over death. His resurrection also means that there will be victory over death to those who are in Christ. Paul says, "We believe that Jesus died and rose again and so we believe that God will bring with Jesus those who have fallen asleep in him" (1 Thess. 4:14). The Bible calls death the last enemy of the human race, and we know that Christ has conquered it.

In 1 Corinthians 15, Paul argues that because we are one with Christ, we too will share in this victory. What happens to the Head, Christ, will happen to the body, the believers, too. The "in Christ" motif is one of Paul's favorite themes. The idea comes many times in different ways in this chapter (see vv. 18, 19, 20, 22, 23, 31, 58). In verse 20 he explains it by using the figure of firstfruits: "But Christ has indeed been raised from the dead, the firstfruits of those who have fallen asleep." Firstfruits were given as offerings to God at the start of a harvest. They not only represented the whole harvest but also symbolized the offering of the entire harvest.

The firstfruits principle and the way it operates is explained in the following way: "For since death came through a man, the resurrection of the dead comes also through a man. For as in Adam all die, so in Christ all will be made alive. But each in his own turn: Christ, the firstfruits; then, when he comes, those who belong to him" (vv. 21-23). Jesus, describing this hope, said: "I am the resurrection and the life. He who believes in me will live, even though he dies; and whoever lives and believes in me will never die" (John 11:25-26).

This hope makes it possible for Christians to die well. Sverre Norborg, who was rector of the cathedral in Oslo, tells the story of a young man, Christopher, who was in the hospital along with eight other tuberculosis patients. One day Christopher told Pastor Norborg, "We too are going to have a real Easter this year. Our superintendent says a radio is being brought in; that will make it possible for us to be along in the services." His pale face shone in anticipation.

Good Friday came, and the radio carried the Word to the hospital. It reached Christopher. In the afternoon Pastor Norborg went there, and Christopher beckoned him, more radiant than ever. "It is Easter today," he said. "Indeed," answered Norborg, "it is Good Friday and ..." Christopher became very quiet. Then he said, "I guess you don't understand. It is Easter today." With his emaciated hand, he pointed to his heart. Norborg says, "He had laid hold of those words which created Easter! 'But he was pierced for our transgressions, he was crushed for our iniquities; the punishment that brought us peace was upon him.' ... There in a hospital ward we worshipped together that Good Friday."

At three o'clock the next morning a pastor was hurriedly summoned to the hospital. "Christopher had had a hemorrhage. He lay in a heavy sleep. . . . Just once toward the end he roused himself, and his last word was a greeting: 'It is Easter today.' There he died unto eternal life."[14]

This hope is missing in the Eastern religions with their belief in reincarnation. The person born in the next life does not even have a memory of the person who was previously on earth. The possibility of liberation from the cycle of births and death is always many lives away. And there is nothing truly attractive to look forward to. When I asked a girl who converted to Christianity from Buddhism through our ministry what attracted her to Christianity, the first thing she told me was, "I did not want Nirvana." The prospect of having all her desires snuffed

---

[14]Sverre Norborg, *What Is Christianity?* (Minneapolis: n.p., 1936), 69-70, quoted in Smith, *Therefore Stand*, 433.

out after a long and dreary climb was not attractive to her. Of course, the idea of eternal life may not be appealing to a Buddhist because of the Buddhist understanding of life as suffering. In the Christian hope, however, there is no suffering, and our desires are not snuffed out; they are totally satisfied, for we will desire that which is good. And this goodness is totally joyous. The western forms of reincarnation have tried to improve on this by introducing an element of the hope of liberation in fewer lives. But nothing compares to the Christian certainty of resurrection.

For this reason, the Christian funeral can always be an occasion for effective evangelistic witness. A family from a Hindu village in India came to Christ. As they were the only ones from the village to give up Hinduism, the others in the village warned them that the gods they had discarded would punish them. Shortly after this a child from that family fell very ill. The people took it as the punishment from the gods. The family went to church and earnestly asked the Christians to pray for the healing of the child. But the child got worse and ultimately died. The Christians conducted the first Christian funeral that village had ever had. The testimony for the Gospel through it was so powerful that this village, which had been previously resistant to the Gospel, suddenly became receptive, and some of the villagers became followers of Christ. The death of a child became an opportunity to demonstrate the glorious Christian hope of victory over death.

CHAPTER SIXTEEN

THE EVIDENCE FOR THE RESURRECTION

WE HAVE PINNED MUCH on the reality of the resurrection of Christ. But did the Resurrection really take place? In chapter 6 we argued that the Gospels are historical documents. In chapter 4 we argued for the reasonableness of believing in miracles. That material provides a strong case for believing that the Resurrection actually took place. Of all the miracles of Christ, the Resurrection receives the most careful and extensive coverage in the Bible. If the Gospels are historically accurate, then the most carefully documented event in the Gospels should be accurately reported. But there are other evidences that are uniquely applicable to the Resurrection, and this book would not be complete without at least a brief listing of these evidences.

ALTERNATE THEORIES

Various alternate explanations of the events surrounding the Crucifixion have been presented that do not require belief in the Resurrection. Of these, we will mention three here.

HE DID NOT REALLY DIE

Eighteenth- and nineteenth-century German rationalists like C. H. G. Venturini and H. E. G. Paulus presented the swoon or apparent-death theory, which claimed that Jesus did not really die. Due to pain and the loss of blood, He is said to have swooned and was presumed dead (medical knowledge in those days was not very advanced). Even Pilate was surprised that He had died so soon. He then revived in the cool atmosphere of the sepulchre, escaped from the tomb, and appeared to His disciples. They were convinced that He had really risen from the dead.

More recently a well-known biblical scholar, J. Duncan M. Derrett, proposed that Jesus had been clinically dead when it looked like His breathing and pulse had stopped, but that He revived briefly before He finally suffered brain death and was cremated by the disciples in the place of burning in the Kedron Valley. Here His ashes would have joined that of the numerous Passover animals and become indistinguishable. Derrett says that the word *anastasis*, which we usually translate as resurrection, means something like physical revival, getting up, or waking up.[1]

Sydney University professor Barbara Thiering also proposes a highly imaginative theory that tries to explain her claim that Jesus did not really die on the cross.[2] She says that the vinegar given to Jesus was poisoned wine that made Him unconscious. Medicines were given to Him in the cave that helped expel the poison. "He recovered from the effects of the poison, was helped to escape from the tomb by friends, and stayed with them until He reached Rome, where He was present in A.D. 64."[3]

A similar view is held by the Ahmediya sect of Islam. They say that Jesus spent some time with His disciples, then headed northward and met Paul when he was on his way from Jerusalem to Damascus. He is

[1] J. Duncan M. Derrett, *The Anastasis: The Resurrection of Jesus as an Historical Event* (Shipston-on-Stour: Drinkwater, 1982). For a more detailed examination of this view, see Sir Norman Anderson, *Jesus Christ: The Witness of History* (Leicester and Downers Grove, Ill.: InterVarsity Press, 1985), 158-64.

[2] Barbara Thiering, *Jesus the Man: A New Interpretation of the Dead Sea Scrolls* (London: Corgi Books, 1993; originally published as *Jesus and the Riddle of the Dead Sea Scrolls* [Garden City, N.Y.: Doubleday, 1992]), 153-70.

[3] Ibid., 154.

said to have gone to north India to take His message to the "lost sheep of the house of Israel." He finally died and was buried in Srinagar in Kashmir.[4]

Many points can be given against the view that Jesus did not really die on the cross.

First, the New Testament clearly testifies that Jesus really died and that His corpse was placed in a tomb (e.g., Matt. 27:50, 57-66; Acts 13:28-29; 1 Cor. 15:3-4; 1 Pet. 3:18).[5] Sir Norman Anderson points out that "the Fourth Gospel is emphatic that steps were taken to make certain that Jesus was dead; for that, surely, must have been the reason for the spear thrust in His side (John 19:31-34)."[6] Pilate carefully questioned the centurion about Jesus' dying so quickly before he released the corpse for burial. So the record suggests that care was taken to ensure that He was really dead (Mark 15:44).

Second, Murray Harris points out that "there is unambiguous evidence outside the New Testament that testifies to the actual death of Jesus." He says that "both the Jewish historian Josephus (*Antiquities* 18:63-64, written c. A.D. 93) and the Roman historian Tacitus (*Annals* 15:44, written c. A.D. 93) refer to the execution of Jesus on the orders of Pontius Pilate."[7]

Third, it is improbable that one who had gone through the terrible experience of a Roman scourging and a crucifixion could survive a cold night that was characteristic of the weather during Passover time in Jerusalem. And if He did survive, it is improbable that in His weakened state He would have been able to loose Himself from the yards of grave clothes weighted by many pounds of spices, roll away the stone that three women felt incapable of tackling (Mark 16:1-3), and then walk a few miles on His wounded feet.

Fourth, about thirty times in the New Testament the phrase "from the dead" is added to the expression "God raised Jesus" or "Jesus rose," indicating that the New Testament writers clearly believed that He had died.[8] During the days that Jesus met them after His "death," if they had

---

[4]This view is described in Anderson, *Jesus Christ: The Witness*, 84.
[5]Murray J. Harris, *From Grave to Glory* (Grand Rapids, Mich.: Zondervan, 1990), 115.
[6]Anderson, *Jesus Christ: The Witness*, 85.
[7]Harris, *From Grave to Glory*, 115.
[8]Ibid., 107-8.

a wrong impression would we not expect Jesus, the Truth, to correct it without permitting them to be misled?

Fifth, D. F. Strauss, who himself believed that Jesus' life was presented in the Gospel as a myth, pointed out how impossible it would be that a half-dead person like Jesus, needing medical treatment, "could have given to the disciples the impression that he was a Conqueror over death and the grave, the Prince of Life, an impression which lay at the bottom of their ministry." He says that the type of resuscitation postulated according to this view "could by no possibility have changed their sorrow into enthusiasm, have elevated their enthusiasm into worship."[9]

THE VISION THEORY

The idea that the disciples may have had a vision of Christ or been subject to hallucinations is getting more popular these days. John Hick says, "Some kind of experience of seeing Jesus after his death, an appearance or appearances which came to be known as his resurrection seems virtually certain in view of the survival and growth of the tiny original Jesus movement." He says, "The possibilities range from the resuscitation of Jesus' corpse to visions of the Lord in resplendent glory."[10] A. N. Wilson thinks that the belief in the Resurrection is the result of the disciples' fantasies.[11]

The following points can be made in response to this view:

First, the first reaction when one sees a person who is already dead would be to think that it is a ghost. And that is what the disciples thought at first. Luke says that Jesus Himself demolished that idea by saying, "Look at my hands and my feet. It is I myself! Touch me and see; a ghost does not have flesh and bones, as you see I have" (Luke 24:39). Then He asked them to give Him something to eat, and He ate a piece of broiled fish that they gave Him (vv. 41-43). This also eliminates the idea that this was a vision.

Second, there are limits to what a vision is able to do. A person

[9]D. F. Strauss, *Life of Jesus*, vol. 1 (London: Williams and Norgate, 1864), 412, quoted in Anderson, *Jesus Christ: The Witness*, 85-86.

[10]John Hick in *The Myth of God Incarnate*, ed. John Hick (London: SCM Press, 1977), 170.

[11]A. N. Wilson, *Jesus: A Life* (New York: Ballantine, 1992), 66.

appearing in a vision cannot make food and give it to the disciples to eat, which is what Jesus did (John 21:9-14).

Third, the disciples were not psychologically geared for visions. Colin Chapman says, "Hallucination often takes the form of seeing things one would like to see; but there is no evidence that the disciples were expecting or looking for these appearances."[12] Mary (John 20:14), the two on the road to Emmaus (Luke 24:16), and the disciples who were fishing (John 21:4) did not recognize Jesus at first. Some of the disciples found it hard to believe even after they saw Christ. Thomas refused to believe the report until he saw and touched Christ. And when he saw, he really believed.

Fourth, there were so many people of such diverse psychological makeup who saw Christ. Five hundred saw Him on one occasion. Could five hundred people experience the same kind of hallucination at the same time?

Fifth, visions are normally of short duration. Some of Jesus' appearances were very long, such as the appearance on the road to Emmaus.

Sixth, the reports of Christ's appearances were not of the sort that passed away quickly. Jesus appeared over a period of seven weeks on different days, at different times of the day, and in different places. After seven weeks they did not continue because He ascended to heaven.

WE DON'T KNOW, AND IT DOES NOT MATTER

People like Rudolph Bultmann, who emphasize the subjectivity of truth, say that it is not possible to be certain whether the Resurrection really happened or not. Bultmann says, "The resurrection itself is not an event in past history. All that historical criticism can establish is the fact that the first disciples came to believe in the resurrection." But this is not a big problem to Bultmann. To him it does not really matter whether the event took place or not. He says, "The historical fact is scarcely relevant to Christian belief in the resurrection." What is important is "Easter faith," which is a subjective, personal experience that he describes as "the self-manifestation of the risen Lord."[13] In other words,

---

[12]Colin Chapman, *Christianity on Trial* (Wheaton, Ill.: Tyndale House, 1974), 523.
[13]Rudolph Bultmann, "New Testament and Mythology," in *Kerygma and Myth*, vol. 1, ed. H. W. Bartsch (London: S. P. C. K., 1962), 42.

what is important is not that Jesus rose, but that I experience the living Christ today.

We have critiqued this approach to truth in chapter 8. So we will not devote any more space to it here.[14] But what follows adds to what we said in that chapter in refuting this approach to the historicity of the story of Jesus as presented in the New Testament.

MARKS OF AUTHENTICITY IN THE BIBLICAL RECORD

Some important marks of authenticity are found in the biblical record of the Resurrection.

VARIETY IN THE NEW TESTAMENT RECORD

The way that the New Testament describes the Resurrection is significant. All four gospels record that Jesus rose from the dead and that the tomb was empty. Of course, "multiple attestation is no proof of truth. A falsehood does not become true because it is repeated four times."[15] But it is significant that these four gospel records reflect three or four independent descriptions of the empty-tomb story. Matthew, for example, has special material that is not found in Mark or Luke. Murray Harris identifies the following independent descriptions: Mark 16:1-16, Matt. 28:11-15, John 20:11-18, and probably Luke 24:1-12. Harris says, "When we remember that countless 'facts' of ancient history rest on the testimony of a single literary witness, this fourfold literary testimony to the emptiness of the tomb becomes a powerful argument."[16]

The reports of the post-resurrection appearances of Christ in the Gospels and Acts have Him appearing at different times and in various places and being seen in His glorified body by many persons. Some talked with Him; others broke bread with Him or ate a meal that He had prepared. Some held His hands and feet and perhaps even examined the spear wound in His side. Robert Coleman says, "It is the kind of firsthand, objective evidence that would stand in a

---

[14]For a detailed critique of this approach see Daniel P. Fuller, *Easter Faith and History* (Grand Rapids, Mich.: Eerdmans, 1965).
[15]Harris, *From Grave to Glory*, 107.
[16]Ibid.

court of law. Clearly Jesus wanted his disciples assured of his bodily
resurrection. . . . They are witnesses to a very literal, visible historical reality."[17]

SPECIAL EFFORTS TO SHOW THAT IT REALLY HAPPENED

The New Testament writers make a special effort to show that the
Resurrection was a historical happening. This is not so of the other miracles that are usually simply recorded. Acts 1:3 states this emphatically:
"After his suffering, he showed himself to these men and gave *many convincing proofs* that he was alive. He appeared to them over a period of
forty days and spoke about the kingdom of God."

Let's look at the report of one appearance: Luke 24:36-43. His
appearance was quite unexpected, and it startled the disciples: "While
they were still talking about this, Jesus himself stood among them and
said to them, 'Peace be with you.' They were startled and frightened,
thinking they saw a ghost" (vv. 36-37). So Jesus reassures them, saying,
"'Why are you troubled, and why do doubts rise in your minds? Look
at my hands and my feet. It is I myself! Touch me and see; a ghost does
not have flesh and bones, as you see I have.' When he had said this, he
showed them his hands and feet" (vv. 38-40). All these evidences were
not enough to convince them, and so Jesus gave them more evidence:
"And while they still did not believe it because of joy and amazement,
he asked them, 'Do you have anything here to eat?' They gave him a
piece of broiled fish, and he took it and ate it in their presence" (vv. 41-
43). Luke shows the disciples' coming to a conviction very reluctantly.
This frank, uncensored report implies that Luke was sure that Jesus had
risen from the dead and that he was eager for his readers to know
this fact.

There is an emphasis on witnesses to the truth of the Resurrection.
When a successor for Judas was chosen by the believers, one of the reasons for the choice, according to Peter, was that "one of these must
become a witness with us of his resurrection" (Acts 1:22). In five of the
speeches of Acts the apostles claim to be witnesses to the Resurrection
(Acts 2:32; 3:15; 5:32; 10:39-41 [twice]; 13:30-31).

---

[17]Robert E. Coleman, *The Master Plan of Discipleship* (Old Tappan, N.J.: Revell, 1987),
    28ff.

In 1 Corinthians 15:3-4 Paul describes the Gospel as a series of events: the death, the burial, and the resurrection of Christ. Then, in verses 5-8, he gives a detailed list of the people who saw Him after His resurrection:

> ... and that he appeared to Peter, and then to the Twelve. After that, he appeared to more than five hundred of the brothers at the same time, most of whom are still living, though some have fallen asleep. Then he appeared to James, then to all the apostles, and last of all he appeared to me also, as to one abnormally born.

Notice how he says that most of the 500 brothers to whom He appeared are living, suggesting that, if His readers wanted, they could check on the reality of the Resurrection. A. N. Wilson's claim that Corinth was very far from Jerusalem and therefore no one could check out this statement[18] attributes to Paul motives that are unworthy of the portrait we have about the great apostle.

Paul goes into so much detail because the fact that this event really happened was very important. The whole scheme of salvation through the substitutionary death of Christ depended on whether He really rose from the dead or not. So Paul says later in this chapter:

> And if Christ has not been raised, our preaching is useless and so is your faith. More than that, we are then found to be false witnesses about God, for we have testified about God that he raised Christ from the dead. But he did not raise him if in fact the dead are not raised.... And if Christ has not been raised, your faith is futile; you are still in your sins. (1 Cor. 15:14-15, 17)

When we add to the above evidence the point we made in chapter 6, that the early Christians were very committed to truth, we must conclude that this event that they were trying to present as history was really history. A. N. Wilson agrees. He says that "the New Testament is patently the work of men striving to be good" and that it is unlikely that such men "should concoct such a whopping lie as the story of Jesus's resurrection." He tries to solve this problem by stating that "Human beings

---

[18]A. N. Wilson, *Jesus: A Life*, 22.

have such a boundless capacity to fantasize, particularly in the area of religious experience, that we need not question the sincerity of the evangelists when they describe the reappearance of Jesus from the tomb."[19] Our points in this chapter, especially about the vision theory, and in chapter 6 show that it is extremely unlikely that all the early disciples would have had the same fantasy and that they would let their fantasies determine the very cornerstone of their religion. Actually the record in the Scriptures is not about fantasizing but about doubt and their reluctance to believe that Jesus had really risen (Luke 24:11; John 20:25).

THE FIRST WITNESSES WERE WOMEN

According to Jewish legal principles, the testimony of women was generally inadmissible as evidence in those days. Yet, the Gospels depict women as the first witnesses of the empty tomb (Matt. 28:1-10; Mark 16:1-8; Luke 24:10; and probably also John 20:1-2). Murray Harris says that these women were well-known in the early church, and their names were specifically mentioned. This would have been "a risky procedure if the account had been fabricated."[20] R. T. France points out that no one could be expected to take their story seriously and that even the disciples refused to believe their testimony at first. "The only conceivable reason for claiming that women found the tomb empty is that it was true."[21] Even A. N. Wilson concedes this point, though he does not believe Jesus rose from the dead.[22] He suggests that Mary Magdalene saw not Jesus but His brother James, who looked very much like Jesus![23]

THE EMPTY TOMB

It has undoubtedly already become evident that the empty tomb is powerful evidence for the Resurrection. And the case for believing that the tomb was empty is very strong.

First, when the apostles hinged their argument for the Gospel on the resurrection of Jesus, and did so in Jerusalem, all the authorities had

---

[19]Ibid., 66.
[20]Harris, *From Grave to Glory*, 111.
[21]R. T. France, *Jesus the Radical* (Leicester: InterVarsity Press, 1989), 194.
[22]Wilson, *Jesus*, 241.
[23]Ibid., 244.

to do was to point to the tomb where Jesus' corpse lay. But they could not do this, for the body was missing. So the first Christians continued to proclaim the message of the Resurrection and thrived as a community in Jerusalem. The fact that the first preaching of the Gospel was done in Jerusalem, that so many responded to this message in a few days, and that the church thrived in Jerusalem as a community is strong evidence that the tomb was really empty.

Second, the account of the empty tomb also has marks of authenticity. We showed that the fact that the Gospels record that it was first reported by women suggests that it was authentic.

Many (though not all[24]) scholars believe that Mark was the first gospel to be written. If so, the earliest account of the discovery of the empty tomb is Mark 16:1-8. It is an extraordinarily restrained and unadorned account. Murray Harris says, "If Mark's record were a legendary fabrication, we might have expected the narrative to be adorned with fantastic features befitting an event which, if true, must from any perspective have been the most stupendous occurrence in human history." Harris points out that "legendary features are clearly evident in such later Christian writing about the resurrection as the Gospel of Peter (mid-second century A.D.)." This is also true about great events in other religions. I write this on "Wesak," a holiday commemorating the birth, enlightenment, and death of the Buddha. The records of these events, especially the former two, include legendary features. Harris concludes, "With its extraordinary sobriety, Mark's narrative has the 'ring of truth.'"[25]

Third, in those days the Jews venerated the burial places of prophets and other holy persons, such as righteous martyrs (Matt. 23:29; Acts 2:29; cf. also the apocryphal 1 Maccab. 13:25-30).[26] But there is no evidence that Jesus' tomb was venerated, even though the first Christians viewed Jesus as the Savior of the world. The tomb must really have been empty for such a situation to be.

Fourth, the evidence for the empty tomb is so strong that even modern authors who do not believe in a literal resurrection, including A. N. Wilson and Barbara Thiering, admit that the tomb must really have been

---

[24]See John Wenham, *Redating Matthew, Mark and Luke* (London: Hodder and Stoughton; Downers Grove, Ill.: InterVarsity Press, 1991).
[25]Harris, *From Grave to Glory*, 108.
[26]Ibid., 112.

empty. They, of course, give alternate explanations for this that keep out the Resurrection. The number of professional New Testament scholars convinced of the empty-tomb tradition is on the rise.[27] In a recent article, W. L. Craig gives a list of forty-seven such scholars.[28]

THE SURVIVAL OF CHRISTIANITY

Most other religions are based on their teachings. Christianity is based on the death of Christ and the Resurrection that attests its efficacy. The idea of the Resurrection was scorned by most people, as the response of the philosophical Athenians to Paul indicates: "When they heard about the resurrection of the dead, some of them sneered" (Acts 17:32). But Christianity has stood the test of time. This is significant because Christianity is the only religion that stands or falls on the truthfulness of an event. Its survival is evidence that its unique basis, the Resurrection, is indeed valid.

We have said that the first preaching was done in Jerusalem, where Jesus' enemies were concentrated, and not in Galilee, where He had more friends. Relatively few of Jesus' disciples were from Judea.[29] The principal preacher of the early church, Peter, had an easily distinguishable Galilean accent (Matt. 26:73). This accent was probably because the Galileans were an ethnically mixed group. "The racial mixture, differences in speech, and location caused Judean Jews to view Galilee, and its inhabitants with contempt (John 1:46; 7:41, 52)."[30] The Jewish leaders regarded Peter and John as "unschooled, ordinary men" (Acts 4:13). All this makes Jerusalem look like a most unsuitable place for the church to commence its evangelistic activity. But there was one overriding factor that determined its suitability: Jerusalem is where Jesus rose from the dead. The amazing success of the first few preaching efforts bears this out.

---

[27]Ibid.

[28]W. L. Craig, "The Historicity of the Empty Tomb of Jesus," *New Testament Studies* 31 (1985): 67, n. 88.

[29]D. A. Carson, "Matthew," in *The Expositor's Bible Commentary*, vol. 8 (Grand Rapids, Mich.: Zondervan, 1984), 558

[30]Henry W. Holloman, "Galilee, Galileans," in *The Baker Encyclopedia of the Bible*, vol. 1, ed. Walter A. Elwell et al. (Grand Rapids, Mich.: Baker, 1988), §36.

THE TRANSFORMATION OF THE DISCIPLES

John Stott says, "Perhaps the transformation of the disciples of Jesus is the greatest evidence of all for the resurrection."[31] At the time of His death they were very much afraid. Peter went to the extent of vehemently denying that he knew Christ. But in a few days this same Peter fearlessly proclaimed the Gospel in the same city. Listen to His audacity: "The God of Abraham, Isaac and Jacob, the God of our fathers, has glorified his servant Jesus. You handed him over to be killed, and you disowned him before Pilate, though he had decided to let him go. You disowned the Holy and Righteous One and asked that a murderer be released to you" (Acts 3:13-14). There had to have been a sufficient reason for such a transformation.

Most of these disciples were martyred for their faith. But none of them recanted their affirmations in order to save their lives. Someone surely would have done so if they had even a doubt that the Resurrection was not true.

Some who don't accept the Resurrection have had to reckon with this amazing phenomenon of the changed lives of the disciples. John Hick thinks something special must have happened, and he says, "the possibilities range from the resuscitation of Jesus' corpse to visions of the Lord in resplendent glory."[32] A. N. Wilson says that we do not "know what 'the disciples' were like before they had 'the resurrection experience.'"[33] He can say that because he rejects the historicity of the Gospel records. We have shown that you cannot reject these records so easily. But even so, when you take the survival of the church and the boldness of the disciples together, they combine to present a strong case for the Resurrection.

JEWISH CHRISTIANS DISCARDED THEIR CHERISHED CONVICTIONS

The first Christians were primarily Jews. Within a few days the number of male believers had grown to 5,000 (Acts 4:4); even a large num-

---

[31]John R. W. Stott, *Basic Christianity* (Leicester: InterVarsity Press; Grand Rapids, Mich.: Eerdmans, 1958), 58.

[32]John Hick, in *The Myth of God Incarnate*, 170.

[33]Wilson, *Jesus*, 169.

ber of priests became Christians (Acts 6:7). When they accepted Christianity and accepted the direction in which the church moved, they had to make changes in their thinking and discard some cherished convictions. Their willingness to do this can be best explained by the fact that an event of such magnitude as the Resurrection occurred that forced them to change their thinking.

We have already told how the idea of a crucified Messiah was abhorrent to the Jews. For so many Jews to accept that doctrine, the event that is presented as proof of the doctrine of a crucified Messiah, the Resurrection, must surely have happened.

The Christians soon changed their principal day of worship from the Sabbath to Sunday. There was an almost fanatical commitment among Jews to the keeping of the Sabbath, especially during the intertestamental period (around 200 B.C. to A.D. 100).[34] Jesus Himself regularly attended the synagogue on the Sabbath (Mark 1:21; Luke 4:16). Given the Jewish reverence for the Sabbath and Jesus' example, we would have expected the Jewish Christians to formalize the Sabbath as their day of worship too.[35] But soon the first day of the week, which was called "the Lord's Day," took its place (see John 20:19, 26; Acts 20:7-11; 1 Cor 16:1-2; Rev. 1:10). Early in the second century A.D. Ignatius of Antioch noted that "those who followed ancient customs [that is, the Jews] have come to a new hope, no longer celebrating the Sabbath but observing the Lord's Day, the day on which our life sprang up through Christ."[36]

The Jews were a fiercely monotheistic people. But soon the Jewish Christians were regarding Jesus as God and rendering to Him worship that befits God alone. Larry Hurtado describes six major phenomena of the devotional life of the early Christians that show they really worshiped Jesus as they would God. They are:

> (a) The early Christian hymns concerning Christ and probably sung to Christ, (b) prayer to Christ, (c) liturgical use of the "name" of Christ, such as, "calling upon the name" of Christ (probably cor-

---

[34]Harris, *From Grave to Glory*, 151.

[35]This point is made by Harris, ibid., 152.

[36]*To the Magnesians* 9:1, see also *Epistle of Barnabas* 15:9, quoted in Harris, *From Grave to Glory*, 152.

porate invocation/praise of Christ in the worship setting) and baptizing "in/into the name of Jesus," (d) the understanding of the
Christian common meal as "the Lord's supper," which identifies this
marker of Christian fellowship as belonging to Christ, (e) "confessing" Jesus, another ritual probably set within the Christian community gathered for worship, and (f) prophecy in the name of Jesus
and inspired by the "spirit of Christ."[37]

In 1945 a Jewish archaeologist, Professor E. L. Sukenic, found five
sealed caskets that had not been opened before in Talpioth, a suburb
of Jerusalem. Based on the date of the coins found in them, they were
sealed between A.D. 40 and 50. Two of the five caskets had the following inscriptions: "Jesus, help!" and "Jesus, let him arise!"[38] Within
twenty years of the death of Christ, people in Jerusalem were praying
to Jesus.

For Jews to make such a drastic change in their thinking, there
needed to have been an event of the magnitude of the Resurrection.

We note that in the controversies involving the Jews in the early
church, the battle was not over the person of Christ and His death and
resurrection but over the place of the Jewish law. The strict Jews in the
church, then, had accepted the Christian teaching about Jesus' resurrection and His being Lord and Christ.

Paul's change from a fierce opponent of Christianity to a Christian
missionary is best explained by the fact that Paul really believed that
Jesus had risen from the dead. In the previous chapter we told how
Paul hinged his faith on the reality of the Resurrection (1 Cor. 15:14,
17). He was very close to the Jewish hierarchy prior to his conversion,
and he could have checked the facts regarding the Resurrection. He
had everything he could have asked for in terms of success. He was a
rich Roman citizen and a Pharisee, who had had an outstanding education, outstripping His contemporaries in the knowledge and practice of the Jewish religion (Gal. 1:14). But he gave it all up because of

---

[37]Summarized in L. W. Hurtado, "The Origins of the Worship of Christ," *Themelios* 19,
no. 2 (January 1994): 5, from L. W. Hurtado, *One God, One Lord: Early Christian
Devotion and Ancient Jewish Monotheism* (Philadelphia: Fortress Press; London: SCM
Press, 1988).
[38]See Chapman, *Christianity on Trial*, 546-47.

his encounter with the risen Lord. This encounter converted him from being the most vehement persecutor of the Christians to being their most effective propagandist.

Paul went to the extent of equating Christ with God. In 1 Corinthians 8–10 he instructs his converts concerning idols in the typical Jewish, antipagan, monotheistic style. But in this same passage, written scarcely twenty years after the death of Jesus, Paul is seen equating Jesus with God:

> For even if there are so-called gods, whether in heaven or on earth (as indeed there are many "gods" and many "lords"), yet for us there is but one God, the Father, from whom all things came and for whom we live; and there is but one Lord, Jesus Christ, through whom all things came and through whom we live. (1 Cor. 8:5-6)

As Hurtado points out, "This passage exhibits a most exalted reverence for Christ, reverence expressed in terms normally applied only to God."[39] The wording suggests that Jesus is distinct from the Father but equal in status to Him.

James, the brother of Jesus, did not believe in Jesus during His earthly ministry (John 7:5). Mark says Jesus' family said, "He is out of His mind" (Mark 3:21). That must have included James. He continued to have strong Jewish sympathies even after his conversion. This helped him play a mediating role in the controversy about the place of the Jewish law in the early church. His devotion to the law is seen in the request he and his colleagues made to Paul to participate in Jewish purification rites in Jerusalem (Acts 21:18-25). A late second-century writing by Hegesippus claims that because of James's faithful adherence to the Jewish law and his austere lifestyle, he was given the designation, "the Just."[40] What caused him to become a Christian? Paul gives us a clue when he says that Jesus appeared to James after His Resurrection (1 Cor. 15:7). There needed to be something as big as the Resurrection to cause such a faithful Jew to convert to Christianity.

---

[39]Hurtado, "The Origins," 4.
[40]"James," *Baker Encyclopedia of the Bible*, vol. 1, 1090.

THE CUMULATIVE FORCE OF THE EVIDENCE

The above discussion shows that the case for the Resurrection is a multifaceted one. It is not just one point but many that lead to the conclusion that it can be demonstrated "beyond reasonable doubt" that Jesus was really raised from the dead.

The method of arriving at such a conclusion, of course, is historical. We will not go into the complexities of the types of knowledge available to humankind here. Historical truth does not belong to what may be called the "logical" branch of truth. You can use mathematical type data to prove something by the use of reason through logical argumentation. Historical truth belongs to the "empirical" branch of truth. Here we have scientific truth and historical truth. Scientific truth can be tested under controlled conditions—for example, in a laboratory where experiments can be repeated. But you cannot repeat historical events.

With historical truth, we gather as much data related to the events under study and obtain as comprehensive a picture of it as possible. For example, in the modern era we will look at newspaper reports and also try to get as close as we can to an eyewitness account of the event. Then we try to arrive at a coherent picture with all this data. In our examination of the resurrection of Christ we conclude that the only plausible conclusion, given the available evidence, is that it really took place.

In the modern era, several people who, because of the influence of the prevailing bias against the miraculous, did not believe in the Resurrection have become believers after examining the evidence with an open mind. The British lawyer Frank Morison who, in 1930, wrote the influential book *Who Moved the Stone?* was one of them. He wanted to write a book about what he considered the most important period in Christ's life, His last seven days. He wanted to include "all its quick and pulsating drama, its sharp, clear-cut background of antiquity, and its tremendous psychological and human interest." He was influenced by the mood of the day that is well summarized by Huxley's statement, "miracles do not happen." Morison wanted "to strip [this book] of its primitive beliefs and dogmatic suppositions, and to see this supremely great Person as He really was."[41] He had no place, of course, for the so-called fairly-tale ending that we call the Resurrection.

---

[41]Frank Morison, *Who Moved the Stone?* (1930; reprint, Bromley: STL Books, 1983), 11.

Morison says, "Ten years later, the opportunity came to study the life of Christ, as I had long wanted to study it, to investigate the origins of its literature, to sift some of the evidence at first hand, and to form my own judgment on the problem which it presents." This is how he describes the result: "I can only say that it affected a revolution in my thought. Things emerged from that old-world story which previously I should have thought impossible."[42] He realized that "not only could he no longer write the book as he had once conceived it, but that he would not if he could."[43] The result was a book that is still considered one of the best presentations of the case for the Resurrection. Morison appropriately entitled the first chapter of the book, "The Book That Refused to Be Written."

---

[42]Ibid., 12.
[43]Ibid., 5.

CONCLUSION

GOD'S ANSWER TO HUMANITY

I N THIS BOOK WE have upheld an affirmation that is viewed with disdain by many in this pluralistic age. We have shown that Jesus and his Gospel are supreme. We have said that we can speak in terms of absolute categories when we refer to the Christian Gospel. And why?

- Because it is the Creator's answer for the human predicament. It was God Himself who came down in the form of Jesus. *The identity of the Savior* makes the Gospel of Christ supreme and absolute.

- Because Christ's work of incarnation, death, resurrection, and ascension dealt the decisive blow against the cause for sin and evil in this world. It opened the door for our forgiveness, it began the defeat of evil, and it paved the way for His return to consummate His work of redeeming creation. *The work of the Savior* makes the Gospel of Christ supreme and absolute.

- Because the work of Christ paved the way for us to respond to the grace that flowed from it, and because the way we respond reverses the process that caused our fall in the first place. Saving faith returns the fruit of the tree of the knowledge of good and evil to its rightful owner: God. It also opens the way for the experience of "life ... to the full" (John 10:10), which comes from knowing God (John 17:3). This gives a person fulfillment here and now. And that fulfillment is but "a foretaste of glory divine" that will come at the

consummation. *The way to and experience of salvation provided by the
Savior* makes the Gospel of Christ supreme and absolute.

The Creator of the world has indeed presented the complete solution to the human predicament. As such it is supreme; it is unique; and
it is absolute. So we have the audacity in this pluralistic age to say that
Jesus as He is portrayed in the Bible is not only unique but also
supreme. He is our message to the world. A Hindu once asked Dr. E.
Stanley Jones, "What has Christianity to offer that our religion has not?"
He replied, "Jesus Christ."

Dr. Jones often gave lectures on Christianity to Hindu audiences in
India. At one such meeting the Hindu governor of the state was the
chairman. During his opening introduction this man said, "I shall
reserve my remarks for the close of the address, for no matter what the
speaker says, I will find parallel things in our sacred books." After Dr.
Jones spoke, he was at a loss for words. Dr. Jones had not presented
"things"; he had presented a person, Jesus Christ, and that person was
not found in their sacred books.[1] And the thing that Christ did that no
other religion even claims that their leaders did was to die and rise again
for the sins of the world. In the height of the battle with modernism in
the church earlier in this century, J. Gresham Machen (1881-1937)
wrote a key book called *Christianity and Liberalism.* Here he described
the uniqueness of Christianity in the following words:

> All the ideas of Christianity might be discovered in some other reli-
> gion, yet there would be in that other religion no Christianity. For
> Christianity depends, not upon a complex of ideas, but upon the
> narration of an event. Without that event, the world in the Christian
> view, is altogether dark, and humanity is lost under the guilt of sin.
> There can be no salvation by the discovery of eternal truth, for eter-
> nal truth brings naught but despair, because of sin. But a new face
> has been put upon life by the blessed thing that God did when he
> offered his only begotten son.[2]

---

[1]Quoted in John T. Seamands, *Tell it Well* (Kansas City: Beacon Hill, 1981), 60.
[2]J. Gresham Machen, *Christianity and Liberalism* (New York: Macmillan, 1923), quoted
in Ned B. Stonehouse, *J. Gresham Machen: A Biographical Memoir* (Edinburgh and
Carlisle: The Banner of Truth Trust, 1987), 344.

The apostle Paul said, "I am not ashamed of the gospel, because it is the power of God for the salvation of everyone who believes: first for the Jew, then for the Gentile" (Rom. 1:16).

SELECT BIBLIOGRAPHY

BOOKS FOCUSING ON THE CONTENT OF THE GOSPEL AND THE PERSON AND WORK OF CHRIST

Anderson, Sir Norman. *Jesus Christ: The Witness of History.* Leicester and Downers Grove, Ill.: InterVarsity Press, 1985. The eminent British Professor of Law is at his best here.

Barnett, Paul. *Is the New Testament History?* London: Hodder and Stoughton, 1986. An Australian Anglican bishop defends the historicity of the New Testament.

_____. *The Truth about Jesus: The Challenge of Evidence.* Sydney: Aquila Press, 1994. A well-reasoned response to current skepticism about Christ.

Blomberg, Craig. *The Historical Reliability of the Gospels.* Leicester and Downers Grove, Ill.: InterVarsity Press, 1987. A clear and well-reasoned defense of the reliability of the Gospels.

Brown, Colin, ed. *History, Criticism and Faith.* Leicester and Downers Grove, Ill.: InterVarsity Press, 1976. Four eminent British scholars seek to expound responsible approaches to the historicity of biblical literature.

Bruce, F. F. *The New Testament Documents: Are They Reliable?* Leicester and Downers Grove, Ill.: InterVarsity Press, 1960. A revised edition of the first book-length work (1943) of one of this century's foremost biblical scholars. Still heart-warming, clear, and relevant.

Carson, D. A. "Five Gospels, No Christ." *Christianity Today,* April 25, 1994. A description of and response to some current skeptical views of Jesus.

Chapman, Colin. *Christianity on Trial.* Wheaton, Ill.: Tyndale House, 1974. An invaluable apologetic handbook. This has been revised and reset as *The Eerdmans Handbook for the Case for Christianity.* Grand Rapids, Mich.: Wm. B. Eerdmans.

Craig, William Lane. *Reasonable Faith: Christian Truth and Apologetics.* Wheaton, Ill.: Crossway Books, 1994. This book by an eminent evangelical theologian has convincing treatments of many issues related to Jesus and history.

Crossan, J. D. *The Historical Jesus: The Life of a Mediterranean Jewish Peasant.* San Francisco and Edinburgh: HarperSan Francisco and T & T Clark, 1991. A member of "the Jesus Seminar" reconstructs the life of Christ using sources other than the canonical gospels and presenting Jesus as a somewhat un-Jewish Jew.

Derrett, J. Duncan M. *The Anastasis: The Resurrection of Jesus as an Historical Event.* Shipston-on-Stour: Drinkwater, 1982. Argues that Jesus was clinically dead but not brain dead.

France, R. T. *Jesus the Radical.* Leicester: InterVarsity Press, 1989. An easy-to-read life of Christ by an outstanding New Testament scholar.

_____. *The Evidence for Jesus.* London and Downers Grove, Ill.: Hodder and Stoughton and InterVarsity Press, 1986. Defends the authenticity of the New Testament record of Jesus' life.

Fuller, Daniel P. *Easter Faith and History.* Grand Rapids, Mich.: Wm. B. Eerdmans, 1965. Shows that the Resurrection is subject to historical verification and discusses how this fact relates to faith.

_____. *The Unity of the Bible.* Grand Rapids, Mich.: Zondervan, 1992. Expounds the message of the whole Bible and demonstrates its uniqueness and supremacy.

Groothuis, Douglas. *Revealing the New Age Jesus: Challenges to the Orthodox Views of Christ.* Leicester and Downers Grove, Ill.: InterVarsity Press, 1990. By an outstanding younger evangelical apologist.

Guillebaud, H. E. *Why the Cross?* London: Inter-Varsity Fellowship, 1937. Answers many questions asked by unbelievers about the Cross.

Guthrie, Donald. *New Testament Theology.* Leicester and Downers Grove, Ill.: InterVarsity Press, 1981. By an outstanding evangelical scholar.

Harris, Murray J. *From Grave to Glory.* Grand Rapids, Mich.: Zondervan, 1990. A comprehensive exegetical, theological, and apologetic study of the Resurrection and its implications.

_____. *Jesus as God.* Grand Rapids, Mich.: Baker Book House, 1992. Demonstrates that the New Testament explicitly teaches the deity of Christ.

_____. *Three Crucial Questions about Jesus.* Grand Rapids, Mich.: Baker Book House, 1994. Deals with the historical existence, the Resurrection, and the deity of Jesus.

Hurtado, L. W. *One God, One Lord: Early Christian Devotion and Ancient Jewish Monotheism.* Philadelphia and London: Fortress Press and SCM Press, 1988. Shows that the early Christians really worshiped Jesus as they would worship God.

_____. "The Origins of the Worship of Christ." *Themelios* 19. No: 2 (January 1994): 4-8. Summarizes what is argued for in the above book.

The Jesus Seminar. *The Five Gospels: The Search for the Authentic Words of Jesus.* New York: Macmillan, 1994. Seventy-four New Testament scholars claim that 82 percent of what the Gospels give as the words of Jesus are inauthentic, and that the other 18 percent is only doubtfully authentic.

Jones, E. Stanley. *The Word Became Flesh.* Nashville: Abingdon Press, 1963. A daily devotional that demonstrates the supremacy of the Gospel over other ideologies.

Ladd, George Eldon. *I Believe in the Resurrection of Jesus.* London and Grand Rapids, Mich.: Hodder and Stoughton and Wm. B. Eerdmans, 1975. Discusses evidence for and the significance of the Resurrection.

_____. *A Theology of the New Testament.* Revised edition. Ed. Donald A. Hagner. Grand

Rapids, Mich.: Wm. B. Eerdmans, 1993. This updated version of Ladd's 1974 classic tackles many issues relevant to our discussion.

Lewis, C. S. *Mere Christianity.* New York: Macmillan, 1943-1952. A classic explanation of Christianity.

Lutzer, Erwin. W. *Christ Among Other Gods.* Chicago: Moody Press, 1994. The pastor of the Moody Church in Chicago demonstrates the supremacy of Christ.

Marshall, I. Howard. *The Origins of New Testament Christology.* Leicester and Downers Grove, Ill.: InterVarsity Press, 1976. An outstanding evangelical scholar discusses how the teaching of the New Testament about the person of Jesus has been handled by New Testament scholarship and does his own exposition of the teaching.

McDonald, H. D. *The Atonement of the Death of Christ.* Grand Rapids, Mich.: Baker Book House, 1985. Describes the different views that have appeared in the history of the church about what the death of Christ means and achieved.

McDowell, Josh. *Evidence That Demands a Verdict* and *More Evidence That Demands a Verdict.* Historical evidences for the Christian faith. Arrowhead Springs, San Bernardino, Calif.: Here's Life Publishers, 1979. Helpful apologetics handbooks.

Meier, John P. *A Marginal Jew: Rethinking the Historical Jesus.* Vols. 1 and 2. New York: Doubleday/Anchor Bible Reference Library, 1991, 1994. A massive project by a Roman Catholic scholar that emerges with moderately conservative conclusions about the historicity of the gospel records about Jesus.

Morris, Leon. *The Apostolic Preaching of the Cross.* Grand Rapids, Mich.: Wm. B. Eerdmans, 1955. The classic defense of the evangelical understanding of what the Cross achieved.

_____. *The Atonement.* Leicester and Downers Grove, Ill.: InterVarsity Press, 1983. The content of the above book (*Apostolic Preaching*) presented in a simpler form.

_____. *The Lord from Heaven: A Study of the New Testament Teaching on the Deity and the Humanity of Jesus Christ.* Leicester and Downers Grove, Ill.: InterVarsity Press, 1974. Very helpful summary.

Morison, Frank. *Who Moved the Stone?* Bromley: STL Books, 1983 reprint of 1930 edition. A classic presentation of the case for the Resurrection.

Neill, Stephen. *The Supremacy of Jesus.* London: Hodder and Stoughton, 1984. A brilliant reflection of the Gospel in contrast to other ideologies.

Orr, James. *The Christian View of God and the World.* Grand Rapids, Mich.: Kregel Publications, 1989 reprint of 1887 edition. A classic, brilliant apologetic study.

Ramm, Bernard. *An Evangelical Christology: Ecumenic and Historic.* Nashville: Thomas Nelson, 1985.

Sherwin-White, A. N. *Roman Society and Roman Law in the New Testament.* Grand Rapids, Mich.: Baker Book House, 1978 reprint of 1963 edition. A specialist in Roman public law and administration at Oxford University shows that what the New Testament gives about the historical, social, and political background of the time attests its basic historicity.

Smith, Wilbur M. *Therefore Stand.* New Canaan, Conn.: Keats Publishing, 1981 reprint. An apologetic study written in the 1940s but still helpful.

Spong, John Shelby. *Born of a Woman: A Bishop Rethinks the Birth of Jesus.* San Francisco:

Harper San Francisco, 1992). An American Episcopalian bishop denies the orthodox views.

Stott, John. *The Authentic Jesus*. Basingstoke, Hants: Marshalls, 1985. The reliability and implications of the gospel portrait of Jesus presented with Stott's usual clarity.

_____. *The Cross of Christ*. Leicester and Downers Grove, Ill.: InterVarsity Press, 1986. This masterpiece of biblical and theological erudition deals with many of the questions that arise about the "crux" of the gospel.

Thiering, Barbara. *Jesus and the Riddle of the Dead Sea Scrolls*. Garden City, N.Y.: Doubleday, 1992. British Edition: *Jesus the Man: A New Interpretation of the Dead Sea Scrolls*. London: Corgi Books, 1992. A bizarre reconstruction of the life of Christ by an Australian Dead Sea Scrolls "expert."

Thomas, M. M. *The Acknowledged Christ of the Indian Renaissance*. London: SCM Press, 1969. Describes how Hindu leaders like Gandhi viewed Christ.

Thomas, W. Griffith. *Christianity Is Christ*. New Canaan, Conn.: Keats Publishing, 1981 reprint of 1949 edition. A classic exposition of the biblical case for Christ's supremacy.

Weerasingha, Tissa. *The Cross and the Bo Tree*. Taichung, Taiwan: Asia Theological Association, 1989. Helpful discussions of some issues of the Gospel as they relate to Buddhists.

Wilson, A. N. *Jesus: A Life*. New York: Fawcett Columbine, 1992. Another of the bizarre 1992 reconstructions of the life of Christ; by a British novelist.

Wilson, Ian. *Jesus: The Evidence*. London: Weidenfield & Nicolson, 1984. Questions the historical validity of the portrait of Christ in the Gospels. Was made into a popular TV series in Britain.

Wright, N. T. *The New Testament and the People of God*. Minneapolis and London: Fortress Press and SPCK, 1992. First volume of a massive five-volume series by an eminent Oxford don called *Christian Origins and the Question of God*. Looks at the world of Judaism and argues for the historicity of the New Testament.

_____. "The New Unimproved Jesus." In *Christianity Today*, September 13, 1993. A description of and response to current skeptical views of Jesus.

_____. *Who was Jesus?* Grand Rapids, Mich. and London: Wm. B. Eerdmans and SPCK, 1992. Responds to A. N. Wilson, Thiering, and Spong.

BOOKS LOOKING AT QUESTIONS REGARDING THE WAY TO SALVATION

Abeysingha, Nihal. *A Theological Evaluation of Non-Christian Rites*. Bangalore: Theological Publications of India, 1979. Strongly inclusivist, Roman Catholic.

Anderson, Sir Norman. *Christianity and World Religions: The Challenge of Pluralism*. Leicester and Downers Grove, Ill.: InterVarsity Press, 1984. Mildly inclusivist, evangelical.

Ariarajah, Wesley. *The Bible and People of Other Faiths*. Geneva and Maryknoll, N.Y.: WCC, 1985 and Orbis Books, 1994. Thoroughgoing pluralism attractively and simply presented by a Sri Lankan Methodist WCC official.

_____. "Toward a Theology of Dialogue." *The Ecumenical Review of Theology* 19,

No. 1 (January 1977). An earlier writing of Ariarajah that shows his developing pluralistic theology.

Crockett, William and Sigountos, James, eds. *Through No Fault of their Own: The Fate of Those Who Have Never Heard.* Grand Rapids, Mich.: Baker Book House, 1991. A compendium giving a cross section of evangelical thought.

Dowsett, Dick. *God, That's not Fair!* Sevenoaks and Bromley: OMF Books and STL Books, 1982. Argues for the exclusivist position in the form of letters to a student.

Fernando, Ajith. *The Christian's Attitude Toward World Religions.* Wheaton, Ill.: Tyndale House, 1987. British edition: *Jesus and the World Religions.* Bromley: STL, 1988. Exclusivist.

Hillis, Dick. *Is There Really Only One Way?* Santa Ana, Calif.: Vision House, 1974. A popular exclusivist treatment.

Knitter, Paul. *No Other Name? A Critical Survey of Christian Attitudes Toward the World Religions.* Maryknoll. N.Y.: Orbis Books, 1985. Critiques the different views from a pluralistic perspective.

McQuilkin, Robertson. "The Narrow Way." In *Perspectives on the World Christian Movement.* Eds. Ralph D. Winter and Steven C. Hawthorn. Pasadena: William Carey Library, 1981, 129-34. Evangelical, exclusivist.

Neuner, Joseph, ed. *Christian Revelation and World Religions.* London: Burns and Oats, 1967. Contains the views of Hans Küng, among others.

Panikkar, Raimundo. *The Unknown Christ of Hinduism.* Maryknoll, N.Y.: Orbis Books, 1981. A Roman Catholic inclusivist who argues that Christ saves through the rituals of Hinduism.

Pinnock, Clark H. *A Wideness in God's Mercy: The Finality of Jesus Christ in a World of Religions.* Grand Rapids, Mich.: Zondervan, 1992. Strongly inclusivist, evangelical.

_____. "The Finality of Christ in a World of Religions." In *Christian Faith and Practice in a Modern World.* Eds. Mark A. Noll and David F. Wells. Grand Rapids, Mich.: Wm. B. Eerdmans, 1988, 152-68.

_____. "Toward an Evangelical Theology of Religions." In *Journal of the Evangelical Theological Society* (September 1990): 359-68.

Rahner, Karl. *Theological Investigations.* Volume 5. *Later Writings.* London: Darton, Longman and Todd, 1966, 115-34. This is where the esteemed Roman Catholic theologian presents his inclusivism.

Richard, Ramesh. *The Population of Heaven. A Biblical Response to the Inclusivist Position on Who Will Be Saved.* Chicago: Moody Press, 1994. A vigorous response to John Sanders and Pinnock by an outstanding young evangelical scholar. Exclusivist.

Sanders, J. Oswald. *How Lost Are the Heathen?* Chicago: Moody Press, 1972. British edition: *What of Those Who Have Never Heard.* UK: Highland Books, 1986. A sensitive and well-reasoned defense of the exclusivist position.

Sanders, John. *No Other Name: An Investigation into the Destiny of the Unevangelized.* Grand Rapids, Mich.: Wm. B. Eerdmans, 1992. Evangelical, inclusivist.

BOOKS CONSIDERING THE ISSUES OF CHRISTIANITY AND THE WORLD RELIGIONS AND OF PLURALISM

Anderson, Gerald H. and Stransky, Thomas, eds. *Christ's Lordship and Religious Pluralism.* Maryknoll. N.Y.: Orbis Books, 1981.

_____. *Mission Trends No. 5: Faith Meets Faith.* Grand Rapids, Mich. and New York: Wm. B. Eerdmans and Paulist Press, 1981. Presents different approaches.

Bavinck, J. H. *The Church Between Temple and Mosque. A Study of the Relationship Between the Christian Faith and Other Religions.* Grand Rapids, Mich.: Wm. B. Eerdmans, 1966. A former Professor of Missions at the Free University in Amsterdam arrives at evangelical conclusions.

Braaten, Carl E. *No Other Gospel!: Christianity Among the World's Religions.* Minneapolis: Fortress Press, 1992. Argues for the uniqueness of Christianity.

Carson, D. A. "Christian Witness in an Age of Pluralism." In *God and Culture,* eds. D. A. Carson and John D. Woodbridge. Grand Rapids, Mich. and Carlisle: Wm. B. Eerdmans and Paternoster Press, 1993, 31-66. A persuasive response to pluralistic thinking on witness.

Clark, A. D., and Winter, B, eds. *One God, One Lord.* Grand Rapids, Mich. and Carlisle: Baker Book House and Paternoster Press, 1993. Discusses different views and topics.

Cox, Harvey. *Many Mansions: A Christian's Encounter with Other Faiths.* Boston: Beacon Press, 1988.

Cragg, Kenneth. *The Christ and the Faiths.* Philadelphia: Westminster Press, 1986. A leading Islamics expert discusses inter-religious encounter.

D'Costa, Gavin. *Theology and Religious Pluralism.* Oxford: Basil Blackwell, 1986. An Indian Roman Catholic theologian who affirms the uniqueness of Christ.

Fernando, Ajith. *The Christian's Attitude Toward World Religions.* Wheaton, Ill.: Tyndale House, 1987. British edition: *Jesus and the World Religions.* Bromley: STL, 1988.

Gnanakan, Ken. *The Pluralist Predicament.* Bangalore: Theological Book Trust, 1992. A comprehensive survey by a leading Indian evangelical theologian.

Hesselgrave, David. *Communicating Christ Cross-Culturally.* Grand Rapids, Mich.: Zondervan, 1978. A standard on the topic that has helpful chapters on the different religions systems.

Hick, John. *God and the Universe of Faiths.* London: Macmillan, 1973. Probably the foremost pluralist of our time.

_____. *An Interpretation of Religion.* New Haven, Conn.: Yale University Press, 1988.

_____. "Jesus and the World Religions." In *The Myth of God Incarnate,* ed. John Hick. London and Philadelphia: SCM Press and Westminster Press, 1977, 167-85.

_____. *Problems of Religious Pluralism.* New York: St. Martin's Press, 1985.

Hick, John and Hebblethwaite, Brian, eds. *Christianity and Other Religions.* Glasgow and Minneapolis: Collins, Fount Paperbacks and Fortress Press, 1980. A compendium challenging the traditional view.

Hick, John and Knitter, Paul, eds. *The Myth of Christian Uniqueness.* Maryknoll, N.Y.: Orbis Books, 1987. A compendium. The title indicates the slant!

Kraemer, Hendrik. *The Christian Message in a Non-Christian World.* Grand Rapids, Mich.: Kregel, 1969 reprint of 1956 edition. Uniqueness, Barthian style.

Lyden, John, ed. *Enduring Issues in Religion*. San Diego: Greenhaven Press, 1995. A collection of articles with views from a cross section of religious positions on key religious issues.

Martinson, Paul. *A Theology of World Religions. Interpreting God, Self, and World in Semitic, Indian, and Chinese Thought*. Minneapolis: Augsburg, 1987. Looks at the approaches of the different religions to key issues.

Neill, Stephen. *Christian Faith and Other Faiths*. Downers Grove, Ill.: InterVarsity Press, 1984. British Edition: *Crises of Belief*. London: Hodder and Stoughton, 1983. A brilliant discussion about the different religious systems.

Netland, Harold. *Dissonant Voices: Religious Truth and the Question of Truth*. Grand Rapids and Leicester: Wm. B. Eerdmans and Apollos, 1991. A careful, comprehensive, and superior study from an evangelical perspective.

Newbigin, Lesslie. *The Finality of Christ*. Richmond and London: John Knox Press and SCM Press, 1969. An affirmation of the uniqueness of Christ written while Newbigin was bishop of Madras, India.

_____. *The Gospel in a Pluralist Society*. Geneva and Grand Rapids, Mich.: WCC Publications and Wm. B. Eerdmans Publishing, 1989. Vintage Newbigin.

_____. *Truth to Tell: The Gospel as Public Truth*. Geneva and Grand Rapids, Mich.: WCC Publications and Wm. B. Eerdmans, 1991. A brief, powerful statement about the implications of the Gospel being the truth.

Ratnasekera, Leopold. *Christianity and the World Religions: A Contribution to the Theology of Religions*. A privately published Paris dissertation by a Sri Lankan Roman Catholic inclusivist.

Seamands, John T. *Tell it Well: Communicating the Gospel Across Cultures*. Kansas City: Beacon Hill Press, 1981. Profound, non-technical, and eminently practical.

Smith, Wilfred Cantwell. *Religious Diversity: Essays by Wilfred Cantwell Smith*. Ed. Willard G. Oxtoby. New York: Harper & Row, 1976. Considered the Dean of Inter-religious Studies.

_____. *Towards a World Theology*. Philadelphia: Westminster Press, 1981.

Speer, Robert E. *The Finality of Jesus Christ*. Grand Rapids, Mich.: Zondervan Publishing House, 1968 reprint of 1933 edition. A classic statement of the supremacy of Christ by a lay U.S. Presbyterian missionary statesman.

Thomas, M. M. *Man and the Universe of Faiths*. Madras: CLS, 1975. By a leading Indian pluralist theologian.

Tillich, Paul. *Christianity and the Encounter of the World Religions*. New York: Columbia University Press, 1963.

Toynbee, Arnold. *Christianity Among the Religions of the World*. New York: Charles Scribner's Sons, 1957. A pioneering effort at pluralistic thinking.

Troeltsch, Ernst. *The Absoluteness of Christianity*. Atlanta: John Knox Press, 1971 and London: SCM Press, 1972. Reprints of the 1901 book, *The Absolute Validity of Christianity*, by an influential German theologian who later adopted a more pluralistic approach to the issue.

Wells, David F. *No Place for Truth: or Whatever Happened to Evangelical Theology?* Grand Rapids, Mich.: Wm. B. Eerdmans, 1993. An evangelical theologian shows how modernity has affected evangelicals and caused them to lose sight of the value of truth.

_____. *God in the Wasteland.* Grand Rapids, Mich.: Wm. B. Eerdmans, 1994.

Wright, Chris. *What's so Unique About Jesus?* Eastbourne: MARC, 1990. A leading British biblical scholar introduces the issues in simple language.

SCRIPTURE INDEX

James
1:2   217
1:2-4   214

1 Peter
1:8   237
1:20   164, 218
2:3   72
2:6   71
2:22   62
2:24   128
3:14-15   71
3:15   72
3:18   128, 245

2 Peter
1:1   72
3:18   71

1 John
1:7   132, 155, 183

1:9   129, 132, 155
2:1   135
2:2   132
3:1-10   136
3:5   62
3:6,9   180
4:4   240
4:10   132

Jude
5   70

Revelation
1:5   70
1:5-6   71
1:8   72
1:10   255
1:13-16   71
1:17   71
3:7   70
3:14   70

5:2   211
5:4-6   211
5:8-12   71
5:8-14   71
5:9   134, 211
5:11-12   211
5:13   71
7:13-17   211
11:15   70
13:8   164, 218
14:1   70
21-22   211
21:4   211
21:6   70, 72
21:22   70
22:1   70
22:3   70
22:13   70, 72

Name Index

GENERAL INDEX